Modern Fiction
and Human Time

Modern Fiction and Human Time

A Study in Narrative and Belief

Wesley A. Kort

University Presses of Florida

University of South Florida Press

Tampa

UNIVERSITY PRESSES OF FLORIDA is the central agency for scholarly publishing of the State of Florida's university system, producing books selected for publication by the faculty editorial committees of Florida's nine public universities: Florida A&M University (Tallahassee), Florida Atlantic University (Boca Raton), Florida International University (Miami), Florida State University (Tallahassee), University of Central Florida (Orlando), University of Florida (Gainesville), University of North Florida (Jacksonville), University of South Florida (Tampa), University of West Florida (Pensacola).

ORDERS for books published by all member presses of University Presses of Florida should be addressed to University Presses of Florida, 15 NW 15th Street, Gainesville, FL 32603.

Library of Congress Cataloging-in-Publication Data

Kort, Wesley A.
    Modern fiction and human time.

    Bibliography: p.
    Includes index.
    1. Fiction—20th century—History and criticism.
2. Time in literature.   3. Plots (Drama, novel, etc.)
I. Title.
PN3352.T5K67   1985   809.3'924   85–13547
ISBN 0–8130–0833–6 (alk. paper)

For Anne, Eva,
and Alexander

Contents

Melodic Time

Conclusion

Acknowledgments

Two chapters of this book, in somewhat different form, were published as journal articles: "Human Time in Hemingway's Fiction" appeared in *Modern Fiction Studies* (Winter 1980–81) and "Social Time in Faulkner's Fiction" in *The Arizona Quarterly* (Summer 1981). I am grateful to the editors of these journals, Professors William T. Stafford and Albert Gegenheimer, for their interest in my work and for permission to draw from this material for my book.

Because I began this project a decade ago, I have benefited from talking and corresponding with many people about it. They are too many to list here, and were I to try I would likely forget to include several. I do want to mention the names of a few people, however, who in varying ways have particularly helped and encouraged me as I was writing this book: David Rhoads, Samuel Chell, and Kris Rabe of Carthage College, Howard Harper and Townsend Ludington of the University of North Carolina at Chapel Hill, and my chairman here at Duke University, Kalman Bland.

Duke University also provided me the opportunity to pursue this study. A sabbatical semester in Freiburg, Germany, allowed me to begin work on it, and Duke's excellent libraries and their staff have made the long process pleasant and convenient. My graduate seminar allowed me to share my work with students, and I am grateful to several of them, particularly Amy-Jill Levine, for their interest in and contributions to it. Finally the secretarial staff in the department, ably directed by Wanda Camp, has treated this inveterate rewriter with extraordinary patience.

Finally, I want to thank the staff of University Presses of Florida for their intelligent and patient direction.

Introduction

ONE

Plot and the Image of Time

Two related questions are central to this work. The first concerns the image of time in modern fiction. How do the characteristics of plot determine the appearance of time? The second concerns the relation of time as determined by plot to time in human life. Do the characteristics of plot make fictional time like or unlike time as it is generally experienced?

Rather than from a definition developed in abstraction, the characteristics of plot have been drawn from the fiction and allowed to stand as defining. While the authors form a heterogeneous group and provide a wide range of narrative art, their work, taken together, reveals three defining characteristics quite clearly.

The first is that in this fiction the sequence of events is prominent, even dominant; plot, in other words, is more important for the force and meaning of the work than are the interests or intentions of characters, the attitudes of the narrators, or the conditions under which characters live or to which narrators react. The effect of this characteristic of plot —that it is dominant in the novels to be studied—is to grant time *primacy*.

A second characteristic of plot is that it provides coherence to the sequence of events so that the fiction becomes a whole,

3

a "concord," to use Frank Kermode's term.[1] Rather than minimized in this fiction, the potential of plot to grant coherence is emphasized. Because plot grants wholeness or meaningfulness, time appears as *trustworthy*.

Finally, this fiction, seen as a whole, reveals more than one kind of coherence. Three patterns appear, three ways of granting wholeness. While all three can be found in the work of each writer, it is possible to pair writers according to which pattern emerges as the most important in their work. The effect of this characteristic of plot is that time appears as *complex*.

These characteristics yield a definition: Plot refers to the events of a narrative meaningfully related to one another by three patterns of coherence. With this definition in mind, the question of plot's relation to the actual experience of time in human life can be raised: Does human time also have such characteristics? To help answer this question, three philosophers or theorists whose work concerns the human experience of, or response to, time are included. While their presence may not guarantee an answer to the question, it does provide sufficient basis to consider seriously a substantial relation or a remarkable similarity between time as determined by fictional plot and the human experience of time.

In making a connection between fictional time and time as it is analyzed by theorists, emphasis should not fall on the ideas of authors, as though we are treating writers of fiction as philosophers in disguise. Their work has not been chosen because they have given extended thought to the nature of time and the problems that time creates for modern consciousness, even though all of them had sophisticated interests in such matters.[2] Rather, they have been chosen because their work reveals something about time in and through narrative plot. This emphasis on form makes them recognizably modern; of the many qualities shared by modernist literature—cosmopolitanism, a break with the immediate literary past, a preoccupation with the vocation of the artist, and an interest in the reality or force of the subconscious and of death—attention to the formal properties of literature is paramount.[3] The narrative form becomes, then, "not simply an enabling means for handling content, but in some essential sense . . . the content."[4]

The question of plot's relation to human time, while it may at first appear extraliterary, is called for by the fiction. Incorporated in these works, along with the characteristics of time produced by their plots, are alternative understandings of time. These negative images highlight the kind of time produced by the plots and are discredited by them. In the contrary understanding, time, rather than primary, is assumed to be subjected to social conventions and personal intentions. Rather than as trustworthy, time in the contrary depiction is treated as inherently meaningless, as a threat that should be resisted or even denied. Rather than complex, time is taken to be uniform and simple. This situation of conflict between the characteristics of plot with their effects and the negative depictions of time or attitudes toward it in these novels creates alternatives requiring the reader to choose: Which is more faithful to human experience, time as determined by the characteristics of plot and advocated by this fiction or the implied or depicted understandings of time that are put under pressure by this fiction? What is provocative about these novels is not only that the potentials of plot are fully actualized and their consequences for time articulated but also that a polemic is carried on within these works against understandings of time that counter or contradict time as determined by plot. It can even be said that the understandings of time negatively depicted in this fiction are presented as typical of the society. Implied in the conflict, then, is an invitation issued to the reader to exchange notions of time typical of modern society for an understanding of or participation in time made available through the force and meaning of plot. The philosophers are needed, therefore, to help in determining whether that invitation can possibly be accepted.

Since the characteristics of plot will serve as foci for the analyses of the fiction, they should be discussed more fully. At the same time, it will be possible to indicate their negatively depicted equivalents and to suggest why they may be typical of the society. It will be only then that we can examine both the invitation implied by these plots and the possibility of accepting it.

Time as Primary

The first characteristic of plot revealed by these fictions is its ability to dominate the other elements of the narrative system: character, atmosphere, and tone. The result of this potential is to make the sequence of events in the narrative the principal locus of force and meaning. But plot is not unique among the elements in its ability to dominate; the others bear that potential as well. The narrative system, while constant because of the four elements that constitute it, is subject to varying dominants. The four elements of narrative are indispensable, interdependent, and equally capable of subjecting and deforming the others.[5]

The dominance of plot should not be confused with the obvious interest in time expressed by authors in and through their characters and narrators. The authors share with many of their contemporaries a preoccupation with time, with the changes in understandings of time brought on by new developments in technology, science, and philosophy, and with such traumatic moments in recent history as rapid urbanization and, even more, World War I. Rather than for their explicit interest in the problem of time, these authors take their places here because in their fiction plot reveals this first characteristic. Other writers who are equally interested in the topic of time are not included because their work is not formed in that way. James Joyce and Marcel Proust, the two examples that would come most quickly to mind, give us fiction less dominated by plot than by atmosphere and tone.

The ability of plot to dominate a narrative, because it is not generally recognized, causes confusion among literary critics and theorists. Many assume that plot is always subject to one of the other elements of narrative.

Most frequently tone is taken as the determiner of plot. For example, Günther Müller and Gérard Genette, in their widely influential studies of narrative time, assume that plot is always subject to tone, to the way the tale is told.[6] While in the work of Proust, the basis of Genette's study, tone is more important than plot, it need not be. The error lies in failing to recognize variability in the narrative system. Müller and Genette should be singled out because they make explicit for narrative time a distinction carried into contemporary criticism and theory from Russian formalism between *fabula* and *sjuzhet*.[7] The first term refers to the material of the story as it is assumed to stand prior to being narrated; the second refers to the way the material is presented. By means of this distinction, Jonathan Culler points out, "Action becomes something that exists independently of narrative presentation; in principle it exists prior to any narrative presentation and could be presented in other ways."[8] Due to the pervasive influence of this distinction, the topic of narrative time repeatedly appears as determined by interest in tone; the events of the story are subsumed under the ways they are handled by the narrator or implied author. One sees this occur in Seymour Chatman's discussion of "story" and "discourse," in Meir Sternberg's contrast between the actual, causal, or sequential relation of events and the way they appear in a narrative, and in David Higdon's analysis of the ways in which time is given "shape" in fiction.[9] To repeat, the error here lies not in the acknowledgment that tone may be more important than plot in a given narrative but in the assumption that it always is. One should not assume or conclude, as do Scholes and Kellogg, that "quality of mind . . . not plot, is the soul of narrative."[10] Neither plot nor tone is the soul of all narrative. Both are always present, and either may hold the principal position.[11]

Plot's potential for dominance is also slighted by those who take character as the principal locus of force and meaning in narrative. The most important instances are to be found in methods arising from structural analysis.[12] The tendency toward the favoring of character can be detected in Vladimir Propp's study of Russian folktales, a work that, since its translation into English in 1958, has become a primer for the structural analysis of narratives.[13]

Propp's principal move is to isolate from a large number of tales a set of thirty-one "functions." These functions appear in the tales constantly, and they form, he argues, the basic repertoire. While no tale contains the whole set of functions, all tales are dependent on it. These functions, such as lack, departure, test, magical agent, pursuit, return, and recognition, are more closely tied to character than to plot. Although the functions imply action, they are static units and define characters. Propp defines character by way of function because functions are less variable than other aspects of character, such as motivations, attitudes, and names. It appears, moreover, that Propp attends to function more directly than to character because in the traditional society from which the folktales arise functions are more unchanging than people. "Function," for Propp, becomes more a way of simplifying and fixing character than a way of talking about plot. Structural analysts make this tendency in Propp toward the dominance of character explicit in their work. Roland Barthes does so, for example, when he describes the analysis of narrative as a classification, first of all, of the attributes, functions, and actions of characters.[14] But none makes this turn toward character clearer than does A. J. Greimas.

Basic to the work of Greimas is his six-part *actantial* model.[15] An *actant* is a minimal, determining unit of meaning. The six are "sender" and "receiver," "subject" and "object," and "helper" and "opponent." These *actants*, because they operate at a deep structural level, maintain a high degree of steadiness. *Actants* and their relationships determine characters and their interactions. Narrative discourse, for Greimas, is the particular or surface manifestation of an underlying structure. The result of this structural method, as Tzvetan Todorov and Fredric Jameson have pointed out, is to suppress time.[16] Given the widespread importance of structural analysis for critical theory, the integrity of plot and its potential for dominance must be reaffirmed.

Subjection of plot to atmosphere, to the boundaries and conditions of the narrative world, can occur whenever narrative is treated as "spatial form." Plot may then be little more than the means by which the more important element, the conditions under which characters live, can be delineated. The novel's action is construed as a kind of guided tour through a basically static situation. While such domination of plot by atmosphere occurs, as in Camus' *The Plague* or Kafka's *The Trial*, this potential of atmosphere does not create a new kind of narrative or establish a new shape for all modernist or postmodernist fiction, as those attentive to "spatial form" suggest.[17]

While plot's potential for dominance is frequently denied in critical circles, a contrary error also appears. Some assume that plot is always the most important aspect of narrative art. Neo-Aristotelians, such as Elder Olson and R. S. Crane, share a methodological orientation to the *Poetics* of Aristotle in which plot is the soul of tragic drama.[18] The defining feature of dramatic art is its imitation of human action, and plot becomes the principal "reality in the novel," as one critic puts it. The art of narrative lies principally, then, in its "chronomorphic" quality.[19]

A recent, complex example of Aristotelian literary theory applied to the nature of the narrative form is Paul Ricoeur's *Time and Narrative*. This study is the latest venture in Ricoeur's larger hermeneutical project, which also includes studies of symbol and metaphor. He turns to narrative because in it human time can be understood, since, as St. Augustine points out, time when directly investigated leads only to insoluble problems, such as the division of past, present, and future from one another. Consequently, human time must be understood indirectly, by way of narrative plot.

Ricoeur's observations concerning plot in Aristotle's work are important, particularly his delineation of two aspects of plot, configurational and episodic. (This distinction will be discussed further in the next section of this chapter.) But Ricoeur's interest is primarily to understand human time, and, as he turns to narrative art or to Aristotle, he slights the complexity and variability of narrative by taking plot as its necessary dominant.

The potential of plot to dominate the form of a particular narrative should be neither denied nor elevated to a necessity. If that would occur, confusion and conflict in the critical forum concerning plot and its relation to the potentials of narrative's other elements would be greatly relieved. Plot is always present in a narrative, but it need not be, as it is in the fictions gathered for this study, its principal source of power and meaning.

When plot does dominate, its effect is to grant time primacy. For example, Ernest Hemingway's characters step into the narratives from some place where they have been deprived or injured, and they undergo processes that grant them some degree of wholeness and realignment. Both sets of events, negative and positive, determine their condition. In Thomas Mann's fiction, characters are radically affected by events, such as disease or war, that carry them along in ways they do not understand. They are often behind time, in the sense of trying to adjust to events that have already occurred and that they have not initiated. In Virginia Woolf's novels characters constantly must cope with occurrences that are unexpected, or they must anticipate events that they cannot control. Because the future is uncertain and unavoidable, her characters are preoccupied by it.

The primacy of time is manifested not only by the manner in which characters are carried along by events rather than in control of them; it also appears in the way those events are depicted. They are not presented as though from above or as already having happened but as they occur or from within the consciousness of a character. This strategy heightens the sense of "unpredictability, surprise, and discovery"[20] concerning events and gives them a primacy they would lack if they were presented as though known beforehand by the narrator. To display events from above is to transmute them into a static field, like a plot of land.[21] The readers of *The Sound and the Fury* or *Mrs. Dalloway*, for example, do not stand above the characters' own experience in some observation booth provided by the narrator; they participate in events, experiences, and thoughts as they occur. The point of these strategies is "to capture the sense of time as it actually operates in the human awareness of it."[22]

Time as primary counters negative images of time or of attitudes toward it in this fiction. These images imply both that people err in thinking that time is subject to human will and intention and that their error is widespread in modern society. The principal images of this error are urbanization and World War I. Both introduced a regimentation and control of human events on an unprecedented scale and with destructive results. Characters in this fiction are often refugees from the experience of large urban centers or of war who are in need of an alternative time, a time not subject to human designs. The images of cities, whether of London in D. H. Lawrence's work, of Memphis in Faulkner's, or of Zurich in Hesse's, are largely negative, and the war is destructive in its consequences for culture and traumatic in its effects on individuals. With these larger, negative images are more individual instances of characters who attempt to control events and come to ruinous ends or reach an impasse in the process, characters such as Gerald Crich in *Women in Love*, Veraguth in Hesse's *Rosshalde*, and Thomas Sutpen in *Absalom, Absalom!*

While it is certainly possible that the negative images of time in this fiction play less a role in revealing something about modern society than of highlighting the nature of time advocated in the texts, it is not too much to say that such negative images have a social pertinence. The assumption of human control over time is revealed by the language commonly used to refer to time. Time is generally treated in society as though it were a possession or a commodity; people use it, spend it, save it, waste it, make it, and seize it.[23] While Victorians increasingly revealed misgivings concerning the human assumption of control over time and destiny, the rise of human nature above its conditions, including time, is characteristic of the entire modern period; it culminates in the nineteenth century and is finally only fully challenged by urbanization and the war.[24] These two events seem not only to be out of reach of human control but to produce consequences both unplanned and unalterable. It is in this situation that these writers were working, and the primacy of time advocated by their fiction is an alternative or an antidote to the conditions that result from the putative ascendancy of human intention over time.

Time as Trustworthy

The second characteristic of plot revealed by this study of modern fiction is that it grants coherence to the sequence of events in a narrative. Events are so related to one another that temporal wholeness is produced. Plot allows time to appear as meaningful movement.

E. M. Forster points to this characteristic of plot when he distinguishes between events that have only a sequential relation and events that reveal a relation typical of a plot. "The king died and then the queen died" is a sequence; "the king died and then the queen died of grief" grants, by virtue of a causal relation between the events, a germinal plot.[25] While the relationships between events in a plot may not be solely causal, as Forster implies, causality is surely very important for the coherence that plot grants the events of a narrative.

Frank Kermode ties temporal coherence to the boundaries that plot grants narrative time by having both a beginning and an ending.[26] Coherence is unavoidable in narrative, even if one means by beginning and ending only the first and last words. In at least some minimal sense, every event in a narrative has a location granted by its relation to the alpha and omega of the fiction. A reader, therefore, can never be completely disoriented by an event in a narrative text because it always has a certain place in the whole. Beyond such a minimal sense of beginning and end, of course, there are the more complex relations that beginning and ending have to events. A beginning is a point from which events arise, and an ending is a point at which they culminate. For Kermode, ending is the more important of the two terminals, for ending, especially as culmination, grants consonance to all of the narrative's events.

In his study of narrative and time, Paul Ricoeur draws a similar point concerning plot from Aristotle's *Poetics*.[27] A plot has distinguishable events, but those events produce a whole. Ricoeur names these two the episodic and configurational aspects of plot. The configurational aspect grants narrative its "followability."[28] The reader is led from event to event by an unfolding significance. Ricoeur develops a corollary from this point; plot combines, in various proportions, the unexpectedness or contingency of events with their necessity, intelligibility, even predictability. Aristotle's stress on the *peripeteia* makes clear that events can occur in a narrative that counter the expectations of characters and readers. Yet, in the long run, even a sharp reversal of expectation, however unsettling at the time it may be, will, in retrospect, be seen as part of a larger whole. Ricoeur concludes that it is erroneous to think of narrative plots as defined primarily by concordance while human experience is marked by discordance. Narrative plot contains both.[29]

This second characteristic of plot has another consequence: the combination of particular events with a conventional or universal pattern. This consequence is fully developed by so-called myth critics, who are primarily attentive to the recurring patterns of events in narrative plots. Northrop Frye, for example, offers an analysis of plot that yields a complete scheme for events. This scheme allows all plots to find a place somewhere on a circle, the parts of which are named by the seasons; comedy falls on the spring arc of the circle, romance on the summer, tragedy on the fall, and ironic plots on the winter.[30] Joseph Campbell offers a similarly inclusive scheme. He contends that all plots lie somewhere on a complex journey pattern that leads from a familiar world, across thresholds, to an unfamiliar place that holds a boon, and back once more to the familiar world. While any one plot need not incorporate all of this journey, all plots can be identified with at least some portion of it.[31] These two formulations serve primarily to point out that the events of a story, although they also pertain to some particular conditions and may concern distinct individuals, have a more universal or conventional side. While myth critics may err by overly stressing the conventional or universal side of plot, they make clear that plots have an irrepressible relation to recurring and inclusive patterns of action and events.

However one construes it—causality as with Forster, beginning and termination as with Kermode, followability as with Ricoeur, or convention or universal pattern as with myth critics such as Frye and Campbell—a configurational or meaning aspect is revealed by plot. While in some narratives the stress may be more on individual events that appear as unrelated, no novel can so militate against the meaning pole of plot that it will completely be repressed. The coherence plot provides is inextinguishable.

The result of this characteristic of plot is that narrative time appears as trustworthy. Events, no matter how painful or unintelligible they may be at first, are part of some larger coherence. Since, in the fiction gathered for this study, the configurational or meaning aspect of plot, rather than suppressed, appears clearly, the trustworthiness of time is strongly affirmed by it. This affirmation appears despite the fact that many of the events depicted are disruptive, even violent and traumatic: the loss of continuity with traditional authorities and values, personal dislocation, social fragmentation, and the devastation produced by war. The trustworthiness of time is tested by but finally vindicated in the face of events negatively related to meaning. For example, the characters who gather at the summer home of the Ramsays in the last part of *To the Lighthouse* have suffered many personal losses and disappointments. Perhaps more important, there seems to be in their lives no line of continuity between the time of this gathering and the time ten years prior to it, since the war has intervened. The times seem unrelated, and the characters' lives appear to be divided against themselves. But in this third part, despite the distance and differences between the times, continuity is revealed between the two through the completion of tasks, psychological and artistic, that were held over from that former time. In the fiction of Thomas Mann, especially in *Doctor Faustus*, the violently disruptive consequences of two world wars both for individuals and for German culture are depicted, but in the face of these consequences a sense of continuity with the past and a breakthrough to new cultural and personal potentials in the future are revealed through the compositions of Adrian Leverkühn.

With such affirmative images as these there also appear in this fiction negative depictions of societies that distrust time. Foremost among them is Faulkner's Yoknapatawpha, whose people are so distrustful of time that they have established a society that will prevent change. They have done this by isolating from one another people who differ so that interaction between them, which might produce change, is avoided. In *The Holy Sinner* Thomas Mann presents a similar society, one that has become increasingly isolated and incestuous because its principal intention is to avoid change. In *The Glass Bead Game* Hermann Hesse describes a culture that isolates itself from history and turns entirely to its own internal, synchronic relationships. These major negative images combine with many individual characters in the fiction who distrust time to reveal that the alternative orientation is called into question by this fiction.

The point to be raised again, however, is whether these negative images of time are typical of modern societies, as the fiction suggests they are. Does the fictional affirmation of time's trustworthiness counter a pervasive notion that time is not trustworthy, that it is threatening or inherently meaningless, and that it should be fled, ignored, or repressed?

Evidence that a negative evaluation of time is widespread lies close at hand in the study of fictional time by Frank Kermode, which already has been mentioned. While Kermode emphasizes that fictional time has coherence, he is emphatic on the point that time actually lacks such an attribute, that it is inherently meaningless. In fact, Kermode fears that readers will forget, as they encounter coherent time, that time is not like that at all. Coherence derives exclusively from the human mind and imagination, and it is imputed to time from without. Plots are the offspring, then, of two parents with little in common, the human mind with its penchant for order and the experience of time in its unordered, purely successive nature.[32]

Kermode's acknowledged source for this formulation of the nature of human time is Hans Vaihinger, a German philosopher who, in the early decades of this century, attempted in his philosophy of "as if" to reconcile Hume and Kant on the question of time.[33] Vaihinger acquires the idea of time as a sequence of "now" points from Hume's view of sensations as atomistically distinct. From Kant, he takes the theory that mind, primarily by its categories of time and space, grants intelligibility. This idealist tradition is combined with empiricism in Vaihinger's understanding of time as the product of two elements. He describes their combination using an arresting biological metaphor: "Just as the physical organism breaks up the matter which it receives, mixes it with its own juices and so thus makes it suitable for assimilation, so the psyche envelops the thing perceived with categories which it has developed out of itself."[34] Vaihinger's combination of perceptions and conceptions under the metaphor of digested food is directly comparable to Kermode's understanding of fiction as a combination of meaningless sequence and the mind's penchant for stasis and order. Fictional time, for Kermode, is unlike either of its parents although it takes something from both sides. Unlike mind it has movement; unlike time it has coherence. Being a little like both, it is neither and should be broken down into the parts that it comprises. While people are always making fictions and encountering those of others, they should treat them as tentative and fragile products of two, contrary realities.

Rather than being eccentric, Kermode's position, as its use of Vaihinger makes clear, draws together two major, modern epistemologies. Kermode reveals assumptions typical of modern culture that contribute to an understanding of time as inherently meaningless and of meaning as projected by human minds. Indeed, not only can it be said that the instances of distrust of time that are to be found in the fiction are characteristic of modern societies; it can also be said that the affirmation of this fiction that time is trustworthy goes against a central current of modern thought.

As with the first consequence of plot for narrative, the primacy of time, so also with this one, its trustworthiness, a choice must be made. Clearly, Kermode has chosen against the fiction and for the cultural assumption that time lacks coherence and meaning. For this reason, it seems wise to call on philosophers who allow us to take seriously the proposal of the fiction that human time, like the time produced by narrative plot, is meaningful movement.

Time as Complex

The fiction treated in this study reveals a third characteristic of plot. Events are related to one another by means of three fully distinguishable but also related patterns.[35] The three, which will be identified by the musical metaphors of rhythm, polyphony, and melody, constitute a system of narrative time.[36] While all three patterns may be present in a single narrative, one of them will subject the others to itself. Consequently, the type of narrative time in a work can be designated by identifying the principal pattern. The fiction gathered for this study has been selected not only because plot is its dominant element and because the potential of plot to grant meaning and coherence to events has been actualized but also because it reveals the distinctiveness and the interrelationships of the three patterns.

In a rhythmic plot, events are related by patterns of repetition. Here, time is often associated with circadian or seasonal cycles of nature. The common relation of this pattern to natural rhythms does not imply, however, that human experience is subjected, in such a plot, to natural time; the other patterns, by not being so closely oriented to nature, prevent this. Furthermore, rather than limited to diurnal or biological cycles, rhythmic patterns are suggestive of aesthetic and spiritual life as well, as human rituals and festivals suggest. The alternation of darkness and light, while most immediately related to the rudimentary acts of sleeping and awakening, also indicate the spiritual alternation of torpor and awakening. A rhythmic plot, in other words, cannot be identified with naturalism despite its common association with nature. Finally, rhythmic patterns tend to favor the past; the repetitions of rhythmic time carry the strong suggestion of return. Time is not extended on a line; nor does it look to completion in the future. Distance from the past increases the need to return to the beginning for renewal, so that the cycle can start again.

The narratives of Ernest Hemingway and D. H. Lawrence are patterned by rhythmic plots. Hemingway's fictions are shaped by a cycle of confrontation, challenge, retreat, and reflection. His short stories as well as the chapters of his novels often begin at the outset of this pattern, with the character entering a situation or awakening to a new day. Although events in his fiction are often tied to natural contexts, they also suggest aesthetic and spiritual repetitions, such as the relation of Robert Jordan to his grandfather, the recurrence of ideals and memories during Santiago's ordeal, and the ritual acts of *Across the River and into the Trees*. The plots of D. H. Lawrence's novels are shaped by departure and return, death and rebirth, depletion and revival. These rhythms produce individual development, the uniting of a man and a woman, and the emergence of cultural leaders. For Lawrence as well as Hemingway, rhythmic time, while also taxing and conveying loss, is in the long run renewing and the source of unexpected benefits.

A polyphonic pattern emerges when events arise from the interaction of contraries: varying aspects of life, differing groups, or contrasting individuals. Movement in fiction with this form reveals a pattern of conflicts and resolutions. The movement may be a progression that leads to accord or it may be marked by dissonance. While the degree of difference between parties or interests can vary greatly, there must be sufficient separation to produce tension yet not so much that interaction is prevented.

As a rhythmic pattern favors the past, a polyphonic pattern stresses the present. Interaction among varying people and their interests primarily occurs among contemporaries. People who differ from one another lack a common past, and the future, rather than shared by competing interests, threatens to exclude at least some of them. In the absence of a shared past and an inclusive future, emphasis falls on the interactions, conflicts, and resolutions among comtemporaries in present time.

As natural settings and metaphors are most congenial to rhythmic time, so social depictions of human life are most appropriate to polyphonic time. Rather than in the natural context or extensions of their lives, people in fictions shaped by this pattern are primarily in states of tension or interaction with one another. Persons or groups pursue their individual interests, but these pursuits affect their contraries. The resulting tensions require resolution, and the coherence of the plot and the social process depicted through it are tested by the severity of the conflict and the accessibility of reconciliation.

The novels of Thomas Mann and William Faulkner provide examples of such plots. In *The Magic Mountain* and *Doctor Faustus*, for example, time is produced by the interactions both of contrary moments of life—aesthetic and political, intellectual and emotional, active and passive—and of people who differ in nationality, physical attributes, tastes, and convictions. The fiction of William Faulkner reveals sharp distinctions between kinds of people—men and women, blacks and whites, children and parents, those at the center of society and those on the fringe—and between aspects of experience—past and present, nature and culture, and art and reality. The unfortunate condition of the society depicted is caused by its success in preventing differing people and aspects of life from interacting. The purpose and consequence of such prevention is to avoid movement or change. Because of these conditions, the plots of Faulkner's novels have an ambiguous relation to the image of social time. The positive point of how time really is or ought to be must be derived from the negative images primarily revealed as well as from the few, scattered moments in his fiction in which contraries do interact, moments which, because they are rare, stand out.

Plots reveal melodic patterns when they depict events as durations or lines of development. Process is the emergence of an individual, the actualizing of potentials internal to and inherent in a character, group, or culture. The process clarifies the individuality, even the uniqueness, of the entity. Melodic plots are most easily identified with narratives of self-development, such as the *Bildungsroman*, but the emerging individual can also be collective.

While rhythmic patterns place emphasis on the past and polyphonic on the present, melodic patterns are oriented principally to the future. The movement is directed toward completion. Carried with the movement is a strong sense of ending, to use Frank Kermode's phrase. Only at completion does the line of development stand out, like a melody, as a recognizable whole. Coherence is achieved in such a plot by the completion of a line of development and not so much in the reuniting with some real but neglected external resource, as in a rhythmic plot, or in the resolution of conflicts, as in plots that are polyphonic.

Since melodic plots find their most congenial associations in the developing internal life of an individual person or group, metaphors and settings of a psychological or internal nature are most congenial to it. Movement is caused neither by attraction to nor conflict with something outside the individual, as with the other patterns, but by an actualization of internal potentials. The process originates from within, and its end grants identity to the individual.

Virginia Woolf's plots reveal melodic patterns. The achievement of personal development and wholeness occurs in her novels for characters who must cope against heavy odds, such as threats to their personal integrity posed by authorities or disruptions and confusions in their lives caused by war and the complexities of urban life. Individual developments in the face of such threats are not only to be found in characters; they also

occur for a culture, as her novel *Orlando* makes particularly
clear. Such cultural development is also stressed in the novels
of Hermann Hesse, particularly in his *The Journey to the East*
and *The Glass Bead Game*, but the principal locus of internal
development is for him, as well, the individual person. His
novels reveal the movement of characters toward maturity, the
emergence of their individuality through a recognized continuity between their distant origins and their personal destinies.

These three patterns of coherence reveal narrative time to be
complex and variable rather than uniform and simple. This
third characteristic of time differs somewhat from the other
two in that negatively depicted images in the fiction of an
understanding of time contrary to it are not so readily available. The reason is that one pattern dominates in each of the
writers. The complexity and variability of time appear when
the works of the six are brought together, even though all three
patterns are often to be found in a single novel. True, images of
the uniformity of time, such as symbolized by the striking of
Big Ben in *Mrs. Dalloway* or by the Compson watch in *The
Sound and the Fury*, are alien to the complex processes in
which the characters are involved, but these images and others
like them lack the prominence of the negative depictions of
temporal attitudes that counter the previous two points.

Yet this third characteristic of plot, variation among the patterns of coherence, and its consequences for presenting narrative time as a complex system, is potentially as hostile to notions of time in modern society as are the other two. As Stephen
Kern makes clear, the establishment of uniform or standard
time at the end of the nineteenth century was a major, even
defining accomplishment of modern Western culture.[37] The
need and the possibilities for synchronicity and exactitude in
the measurement of time reveal the increasing authority of
science and technology first in the West and subsequently
throughout the world. While standard time is merely a convention which, for little more than a century now, has allowed separated people to say "now" simultaneously, such
time emerges as a great unifying, even homogenizing, force
within and between cultures. One adheres to uniform, simple
time as requisite for participation in a culture held together by

modes of communication and transportation. The polemic implications in this third characteristic of plot for prevalent understandings and orientations to time are major and extend beyond those depicted in the fiction. Narrative time, by being complex and variable, counters yet another assumption concerning time central to the culture.

Narrative and Human Time

Since these writers, through negatively rendered figures, counter understandings of time that differ from the images of time produced by plot, the reader is placed in a position of choice. Is primary, trustworthy, and complex time to be found only in narratives, or do such characteristics mark time in human experience as well? Is narrative time like human time?

In order to pursue these questions, three theorists have been included in the study. Their role is to provide a basis for taking seriously the kind of time proffered by the fiction, to grant a basis for a closer relation than might otherwise be allowed between narrative and human time. In spite of their diverse interests and methods, these scholars agree that time is or ought to be recognized as primary, trustworthy, and complex. After their work has been viewed in relation to the fictions, the qualities of human time will be taken up more fully in the conclusion to the book.

Rhythmic Time

TWO

Ernest Hemingway

Three tendencies in Hemingway criticism divert attention from the importance of human time in his fiction: subjecting the texts to the context of his life; allowing character and tone to be the dominant elements of his narratives; and interpreting his novels as advocating a philosophical skepticism or an existentialism that situates the person in a contrary relation to the world. These tendencies minimize the value, even distort the nature, of human time in his work.

The subjection of the texts to the biographical context occurs so often, of course, because of the visibility and controversial character of the author. Whether this subjection takes the archaeological direction of Philip Young's psychological approach or the teleological direction of Carlos Baker's desire to establish the writer as artist, whether it deals with Hemingway's increasing involvement with a hostile world, as Jackson Benson stresses, or with Hemingway's interests in erecting a public image of himself, as in Scott Donaldson's study, the narrative texts are used to illustrate a point or make a case about the man.[1] It is our contention, however, that Hemingway's fictions ask the reader to prefer the text to the context, to take the text as primary.

The tendency in Hemingway criticism to recognize character and tone as dominant narrative elements in his fiction is closely associated with the preference for context; his principal characters often resemble Hemingway himself or duplicate moments in his life, and the influence of his style of writing is enormous. Indeed, the Hemingway hero and the Hemingway style, the code and the economy, are very likely the two keys to his fiction that any student enrolled in a course on Hemingway can be expected to have in hand. Yet it can be argued that time in his fiction dominates character and style. Characters are carried along by events, changed by them as they are not able to change themselves, and tone subjects itself to a rendering of what actually occurred.

Certainly some critics have stated that time is an important element in Hemingway's work. Carlos Baker asserts, for example, that "the symbolic underpainting which gives so remarkable a sense of depth and vitality to what otherwise might seem flat and two-dimensional," this *Dichtung*, can be construed as the relationship between "the temporal and the eternal."[2] By "the eternal" Baker means those constants that underlie the changing surface of life, "seedtime and harvest, bread and wine, heat and cold, the rising-up and the going-down of the sun, and the slow turn of the seasons."[3] Furthermore, Baker emphasizes, especially in his discussion of *The Old Man and the Sea*, the rhythmic patterns in Hemingway's work, the alternation, especially, of pressure and relaxation, "as in the systolic-diastolic movement of the human heart."[4] This insight has prompted another critic to see a rhythmic pattern as the basic structural design of all of Hemingway's fiction.[5] Sheldon Grebstein advances this point by observing that Hemingway's stories as well as the episodes of his novels often begin with movement across a threshold, toward or away from a locale of action, a movement which creates a pattern in which characters are "impelled into conflict" and retreat from it.[6] Analyses of this kind, however, while indicating the importance of time in Hemingway's fiction, do not overcome the tendency to classify character and tone as the more important components of his works.

The third assumption, that a generally negative or even specifically hostile relation between the individual and the world is central to Hemingway's fiction, is supported by the other two tendencies—the interest in Hemingway's conflict-ridden life and the subjection of time to character and tone. Earl Rovit, for example, posits a basically contrary relation between the characters and the natural time in which they or the narrator exist. Memorable moments of individual time, he says, are plucked out of "the meaningless ticking of sequential time," and this "seized time" becomes for the individual "the immortality of *always* time."[7] For Rovit, the so-called Hemingway code is the way in which the author and his characters impute "*meaning* and *value*" to time, "to the seeming futility of man's headlong rush toward death."[8] Rovit's treatment projects onto Hemingway's fiction a radical skepticism concerning time.

These tendencies reduce the importance or distort the nature of narrative time in Hemingway's fiction. Rather than submit to them, we contend that textual time is preferred to the time of the context in Hemingway's work, that time often becomes the dominant element in his fiction, and that the "meaning and value" of time are more inherent within than imputed to it.

I

The relation of text to context is a major issue for modernist literature. Generally, images of the context are negatively depicted by the texts which, at the same time, advocate their own form as offering a preferred world. Hemingway's fiction likewise both rejects the context and prefers the time of the text. *In Our Time* and *A Farewell to Arms* provide good occasions for testing this claim.

The first query concerning the relation of text to context arises, for *In Our Time*, from the contrasts between the stories and the sketches. This problem is not easily addressed since the reasons for and the results of the juxtaposition are not completely clear. Although the two cannot simply be contrasted since there is substantial overlap in their relation, the sketches tend to deal with more public and the stories with more private issues and situations. The sketches also concentrate on external events while the stories turn toward the inward matters of personal experience. More to the point, the sketches tend to be static while the stories have more temporal movement; without the sketches, therefore, the temporal movements of the stories would be less noticeable. If we combine these characteristics of the sketches—their predominant orientation to the public and external, their likeness to reports and to reports of reports, and their static quality—they comprise a part of the text that not only is separable from the text of the stories but also is closer to the context. The sketches provide, in other words, a kind of vestibule text standing between the texts of the stories and the context.

A common trait of the stories is that characters enter them from some other place. Primarily what have been left behind are the city and the war. The war is clearly the context in "Soldier's Home," but something like war has also been forsaken as one enters the world of "Big Two-Hearted River." The Nick Adams stories imply the city which Nick and his family have left behind for the sake of a natural world in which they are sojourners.

This crossing of thresholds in Hemingway's fiction, moreover, is the first step of a larger, cyclical movement. The circle can be broken down into its components: entering, confronting, withdrawing, and reflecting. "The Battler," for example, opens at the end of one cycle; Nick reflects on the encounter he has just experienced and draws its lesson: "They would never suck him in that way again."[9] A new cycle then begins: Nick enters the camp, confronts the two men, and withdraws. The story ends before reflection begins, thereby formally tying the conclusion to the reflection with which the tale began. This pattern of cyclical movement also determines "Indian Camp," "Soldier's Home," and "Big Two-Hearted River." Other stories, such as "The Three Day Blow" and "Cross Country Snow," concentrate on only one moment of the pattern, especially reflection.

The third attribute of time in these stories is its ability to produce positive results. Processes entered into by characters grant wisdom, a more reliable understanding of the world, or they heal the negative effects of cities and the war. The result of movement is to free the character from illusion, distortion, and miscalculation. The teaching process is often painful, and it is made more difficult by the characters' tendency to underestimate the complexities of the situations they enter. While achieved in highly individual ways, lessons learned from life are not simply private. Hemingway's characters derive a "natural knowledge" from their experiences which is "available under the surface of their lives to all responsive human beings."[10]

The time of these stories involves both reader and character in an initial or repeated entrance into a world apprehended as more valuable than the one left behind. Implicit in the time to which the stories grant access is the affirmation that in every occurrence apart from the context of cities and war and in every human relationship there is an underlying directive that suggests how things are and how one should act. The value and meaning are not imputed to the time; rather, they arise from the juxtapositions of a particular situation and a responsive character. Nor do the value and meaning arise from some a priori rule; how one should act is taught by the encounter and is consequently a function of alignment and appropriation.

Contrast between context and text is also an important aspect of the structure of *A Farewell to Arms*. Of the two stories, one of war and one of love, the war story stands closer to the context. The two stories in the text contrast with one another, but they are joined by sharing a common housing that the natural time of days and seasons provides. The opening chapters render the passing of two years primarily by noting seasonal changes. The remainder of the book presents the full cycle of a year in the life of Frederic Henry, beginning in the spring of 1917. Natural time, by which the other times of the work are enfolded, exerts a determining force on the events recounted; weather dictates the process of the war, and the relationship between Frederic Henry and Catherine Barkley is affected by the pregnancy and terminated by the deaths the pregnancy causes. The characters have no control over natural time; it changes their lives and relationships,and it is responsible for growth and loss, life and death. Natural time is encompassing, determining, and double-faced. It establishes but also complicates the already complex relation between the stories of war and love.

Although the two stories are sharply distinguished, they overlap in two important respects. First, Frederic is changed in his attitudes toward both war and love. A drifter, a student, and an alien, Frederic at the outset is not a person whose intentions in relation to the war are clear; nor is he capable of a responsible commitment to another person. Reflections on his leave make clear his dissatisfaction with his state (chapter 3). But despite dissatisfaction and attraction to the idea of a different kind of life, such as that represented by Abruzzi, Frederic Henry is not able to produce needed changes in his behavior. Consequently, the two stories resemble one another in that in both Frederic Henry is changed as he would not have been able to change himself.

The initial transformation occurs in Frederic through his experiences with war. Both he and Catherine—she in an almost grotesquely romantic way—have underestimated and mistaken its nature. Henry, after a series of shocks—his wound, the chaos of the retreat, the death of his friend Aymo, and the executions at the bridge—recognizes the meaninglessness of war, severs himself from it, and enters the time of the love relationship. The war thus becomes the context for the second story.

The change that occurs during the love story, while always connected to the painful experiences of war, is productive. When he begins his relationship with Catherine, Frederic is self-centered, a facile liar, and a person incapable of commitment. He associates with Catherine because her companionship is preferable to that of prostitutes, of whom he seems to have tired. Gradually an ability to commit himself to Catherine and to care for her grows. Although Catherine is preoccupied with his interests and protects him, thereby creating a situation that favors his well-being, their relationship is a process through which new human capacities are created in Frederic.

The question remains as to the relation of these events to the inclusive natural time of seasons and years, of life and death. Crucial to this question is the passage toward the end of the novel in which Frederic speaks about the "they" who "killed you gratuitously like Aymo. Or gave you the syphilis like Rinaldi."[11] Three factors can contribute to an understanding of this passage. First, until the end, Frederic has protected himself and has been protected by Catherine from a full knowledge not only of the risks of pregnancy but also of the pain and loss that love makes possible; now he has confronted these aspects of life fully and unexpectedly. Furthermore, as Scott Donaldson points out,[12] Frederic Henry's indictment of the cosmos projects a burden of responsibility which he is unwilling to accept himself, even in part. Finally, his anger brings on a state of regression during which he recalls an experience from his earlier life of observing ants on a burning log. What occurs at this moment, then, is Henry's projection of his former self, a person coldly detached and indifferent to the fate of the ants, onto the "they" of the cosmic powers. His anger rends the fabric of the narrative and invokes a time that precedes his experiences of war and love.[13]

These observations indicate that in *A Farewell to Arms* four kinds of time are depicted. There is the time of Frederic Henry before the war and the love, the time of detachment and drifting. There are the contrasting times of war and of love, which we have been considering. And finally, there is natural or cosmic time, large, complex, enfolding, which Henry does not adequately appreciate. Rather than one story within another, we have in this work a series of context-text relations, a stepping-stone sequence leading to, but not fully entering, the story of a person's relation to natural time.

The series of context-text relations, which constitutes the structure of the work, makes interpretation difficult. The presence in the narrative of an image of the context, especially the war, reduces the discontinuity between text and context. Such compromise is lacking in other texts. In *The Sun Also Rises*, for example, Jake Barnes leaves the context behind and enters the story with the war wound. In *Across the River and into the Trees*, Colonel Cantwell comes to Venice as a refugee from the half century of warfare he has known. True, in *For Whom the Bell Tolls* the times of war and of love are combined, but here a distance is created between the warfare in the mountains and warfare of the more general scene. Those works that leave the context behind maximize the potential meaning that lies in the contrast between context and text. The time of the context is alienating or injurious; the texts grant access to another time, one of growth as well as loss, of insight as well as shock, of a new footing in the natural world.

II

We turn now to the question of the rhythmic pattern of time within Hemingway's narratives. To do so we shall examine *For Whom the Bell Tolls* and *The Old Man and the Sea*.

The time of *For Whom the Bell Tolls* at first seems linear since it is determined by Robert Jordan's orders to destroy the bridge and because it leads to his death. As the story progresses, this arrowlike quality is stressed by the increasing risk: the fascist preparations indicated by the passing airplanes; Pablo's resistance to the plan; the loss of El Sordo and his men; the snow; and Pablo's theft of some of the demolition tools. The fatal end is prefigured by conversations about death, especially those involving Pilar: her reading of Jordan's palm, her scent for death, her story of Pablo's execution of the fascists, and the demolition of the train. Yet this linear movement of events is modified in a number of ways.

First, the slow pace relieves the pressure on the ending. This pace results from the close attention to details, especially to physical movements and expressions, the many conversations, some of them extended, and the departures from the main narrative, either through stories told by characters or through embedded stories, such as Andrés's journey with Jordan's message.

More important than the pace for relieving pressure on the end is the cyclical movement of time. The largest cycle, of course, is marked by the presence of Jordan near the bridge at both the beginning and the ending of the work. Within that circle are the smaller rounds of the three days and three nights. For these internal cycles, the center is not the bridge but the cave. Movement is to and from, within and without it.

The primary consequence of the cyclical pattern is to alter Jordan's attitude toward dying. As he himself recognizes, he has been changed by his contacts, especially with Anselmo, Pilar, and Maria. One lesson he learned from these encounters is that cyclical time can change the status and meaning of past events.

For several characters the past constitutes a burden from which they need to be redeemed. Pablo's present loss of nerve and his unreliability result from the violence he has caused and witnessed, especially the execution of the fascists by the drunken, angry mob. If he could, Pablo would undo the past, he "'would bring them all back to life,' . . . 'Everyone.'"[14] Because he is unable to do so, he cannot be free from the burden of a past that reduces his stature. Anselmo, however, is less burdened and diminished by the past than Pablo because he believes in rituals that overcome the consequences of past actions, particularly guilt. The burden of the past is created for Maria not because of what she has done but because of what has been done to her. Maria believes Pilar's instruction—that sexual relations with Jordan, because of their love, will help remove the scars of rape: "'She [Pilar] said that nothing is done to oneself that one does not accept and that if I loved some one it would take it all away.'"[15] Although her scars remain, Maria's repeated acts of love with Jordan ameliorate the status of past events.

It is with Robert Jordan, however, that we have the most important instance of cyclical time's effect on the past. Troubled by the flaws of character revealed in his father's behavior, he concentrates on doing things right. His attention to detail grants his action a ritual quality.[16] For example, his father exhibited an unsightly sentimentality when Jordan left home for college. More important, his father committed suicide. When Jordan parts from Maria and especially when he prepares for his own dying, he acts in a way that will compensate for his father's inadequacies and faults. As with Anselmo and Maria, Jordan's actions in the present alter the status of the past.

In addition, Jordan's three days in the mountains, marked by the rhythm of departing from and returning to the cave, produce changes in his character. At the outset his work is of first importance and is consequently separated from personal feelings, but at the end this division in his life is healed:

> He had never thought that you could know that there was a woman if there was a battle; nor that any part of you could know it, or respond to it; nor that if there was a woman that

she should have breasts small, round, and tight against you
through a shirt; nor that they, the breasts, could know about
the two of them in battle. But it was true and he thought,
good. That's good. I would not have believed that.[17]

A unification of his life, an overcoming of the separation between love and work, war and peace, acting and resting, giving
and receiving is not something Jordan does for himself; it is
produced by the processes in which he is involved.

The time also fuses Jordan and Maria, and the marriage their
ecstasy seals is permanent. When Jordan tells Maria, as they
part, that he goes with her, he is not simply trying to make the
break less difficult for her; the words express his belief: "Stay
with what you believe now. Don't get cynical."[18] The fusion of
their lives, the unification of Jordan's private worlds, and the
alteration of the events of the past are results of time and not
the products of intentions; they are the boons of a kind of temporal grace, and these boons transform the linear movement
toward Jordan's death in a way that political commitments,
duty, or individual resourcefulness could not have done.[19]

In *The Old Man and the Sea*, linear or sequential time is
demonstrated by Santiago's advanced age and his eighty-four
days without success in fishing, but the time of the narrative is
principally cyclic: Santiago's going out to sea and returning.
This structural cycle is supported by the days and nights at sea,
the rhythms of the waves, and the repetitions, both mental and
physical, of Santiago's tightening and relaxing after the marlin
has been hooked.

As in *For Whom the Bell Tolls*, rhythmic time relates the
present to the past. In this work, however, the past is a resource
and not a burden; Santiago has adequate models, while Nick
Adams and Robert Jordan do not. Moreover, the importance of
models in the work is extended by the relation of the admiring
apprentice Manolin to his master. Implied in this layering of
time, then, is the belief that the past can be a resource, that
acts are guided and enlarged by their relation to an ideal. Santiago wants to "be worthy of the great DiMaggio who does all
things perfectly even with the pain of the bone spur in his
heel."[20] By virtue of their common vocation, Santiago also

feels related to St. Peter. Finally, almost instinctively, Santiago acts in ways that relate him to the trials of Jesus. Working under ideals is not simple duplication, however; Santiago goes out further than other fishermen. Thus in each experience unprecedented challenges appear, the new as well as the repeated.

The events of the story are also affected by natural phenomena. The marlin, for which Santiago has great respect, plays its indispensable role, as do also the sharks. Santiago acts in response to other aspects of the natural world as well: the sea, the sky, the birds, and the wind. Rhythmic human time, consequently, participates in both the ideal and the natural while being absorbed wholly into neither.

III

Ideals or paradigms, as we can see from *The Old Man and the Sea*, help to articulate the meaning of the rhythmic time. This aspect of Hemingway's work receives less attention than it deserves. We shall look at the way paradigms reveal the meaning of time in both an early and a later novel.

The paradigm present in *The Sun Also Rises* is immediately available through the tripartite structure of the work. The three parts order the plot according to a Dantesque pattern of Inferno, Purgatorio, and Paradiso. This structure undergirds the overall meaning of the time rendered by the work—its capacity to produce a sense of new individuality and peace despite irrevocable loss. This development is not caused by the character-narrator; it is not the product of individual intention or force of will. It is the result of a process that merits trust.

In the first part of the book, set in Paris, the narrator presents himself in a state of decline; time, with a few exceptions (primarily the moment at the opening of chapter 5), has been frustrating and disorienting. The problem brought into the narrative from the context is, of course, the injury Jake Barnes suffered in the war, the exact nature of which is only implied.[21] What accounts for the decline and pain in this part of the narrative is that Jake has not yet fully faced the consequences of the loss of his sexual organ. He picks up a prostitute, Georgette, only to admit to the difficulty when she makes, as could

be expected, a sexual advance. Jake has also not completely
recognized the effect the loss poses for his relation to Brett; he
is angered and frustrated by her associations with other men,
especially with Cohn, and he attempts desperately to salvage
or to negotiate some kind of sexual relationship with her.
In chapter 7, for example, after Brett has sent Count Mippipopolous away and they are in Jake's bedroom, she attempts to
comfort Jake in his distress and apparently succeeds in granting him some measure of physical gratification. Jake pleads for
a continuation of their relationship. Thus, during this first
part, Jake must descend to the hell of recognizing fully the consequences of his loss.

The Dantesque paradigm is suggested at two other moments
in this section. The first is Cohn's remark that he and Jake are
midway through life, an allusion to Dante's age at the opening
of the *Divine Comedy*. Cohn asks Jake:

> "Don't you ever get the feeling that all your life is going by
> and you're not taking advantage of it? Do you realize you've
> lived nearly half the time you have to live already?"
> "Yes, every once in a while."
> "Do you know that in about thirty-five years more we'll be
> dead?"
> "What the hell, Robert," I said. "What the hell."[22]

The other allusion to the *Divine Comedy* is the figure of Mippipopolous, whose arrow wounds and wide experience give
him a heroic stature. His strength offers Jake a respite analogous to Dante's moments with Mippipopolous' Greek ancestors in the Inferno.

In the second part of the narrative the upward movement of
Jake Barnes from the point of a full recognition of his situation
begins. The process is helped by the arrival of Bill Gorton, a
healthy, natural, even innocent person. Bill plays a role similar
to that of Dante's Virgil; he guides his friend, but only part of
the way, toward the needed wholeness and sense of peace. The
section begins with Jake, like Dante at the outset of the Purgatorio, in the company of pilgrims, in this case a trainload of

them from Dayton, Ohio. Like the Purgatorio, too, this part of the narrative is highly ritualistic and at times liturgical.

The fishing trip reveals the major consequence of rituals: rootedness. Bill lectures Jake on the importance of rootedness, a topic that addresses accurately Jake's physical loss and spiritual disorientation. The line in the water is a figure for the hidden connection of which Bill speaks, a tie with what is natural, hidden, and mysterious. But the inadequacy of Bill's contribution to Jake's healing is indicated by his comment, "'We should not question. Our stay on earth is not for long. Let us rejoice and believe and give thanks.'"[23] Admirable as it may be, Bill's childlike attitude toward life is not available to his companion. Jake has lost his first innocence and, if he is to have peace, must find a second one, a new beginning on the other side of his loss.

Churchgoing, also indicative of ritual, plays a minor but repeated role in this part. Jake enters churches deliberately, and he even tries to engage in pious acts: "'I'm pretty religious,'" he later tells Brett.[24] Churches and Roman Catholicism offer spiritually what nature offers in its way, something inclusive and mysterious to which the person can be related. These specifically religious matters constitute one of several ways by which Jake comes into contact with realities, both natural and spiritual, that are larger than himself.

Among those moments in the second part that contribute to its ritualistic quality, the bullfighting is, of course, the most important. It motivates the trip to Pamplona, and the other actions—the natural characteristics of the fishing, the ecclesiastical and Catholic exercises, and the rounds of celebrating—all culminate in the ring. Further, because of its associations with fertility, its tragic and comic aspects, its risks and style, and the certainty of death it involves, bullfighting is the most comprehensive and resonant of the inclusive activities in which Jake participates. It is a worthy object of his interest and an occasion for the dissolving of his personal condition in a larger, even universal whole.

The rounds of celebrations involve Jake in the antics of his companions, but they also cause conflict and, ultimately, a break with Montoya, Jake's friend, host, and principal connection with the world of bullfighting. At first Montoya tolerates Jake's friends; later he visits Jake's room to make explicit those values that are tacit in the community of aficionados. But, at the beginning of the third part, Montoya does not appear when Jake and Bill are having lunch. While each group of friends relates to needs and interests Jake possesses, the conflicts between them deprive him of both. At the end of Book II Jake is alone; he appears no longer to need the support of other people.

Conflict, pain, and loss appear in the second part of the narrative, but Jake emerges as a more complete person. The festival is over, and Brett is gone. Yet, he seems at peace. We read early in the third part, "It was pleasant to be drinking slowly and to be tasting the wine and to be drinking alone."[25] Jake, through participation in rituals, has overcome his dependence upon his friends.

It is fitting for the Dantesque parallel that early in the third part Bill Gorton leaves. Like Virgil for Dante, Bill is too uncomplicated a person to accompany Jake to the end. In addition, this part, like the Paradiso for Dante, is the most personal. Its center lies in Jake's two swims. The first begins with a reminder of his injured state; a couple sits on the raft, the girl with her bathing straps undone. But Jake dives deeply, staying down a long time. During the second swim he floats on the water, rising and falling with the swells: "The water was buoyant and cold. It felt as though you could never sink."[26] That the water is both deep and supportive suggests the kind of benefit Jake receives from swimming. When Brett summons him, he goes to help her, moving in his new strength to address her pain and loss.

The paradigm of the work immediately suggested by its structure parallels Dante's *Divine Comedy* and articulates the meaning inherent in the narrative's movement. It reveals that new wholeness and tranquility can be obtained on the other side of traumatic loss and pain if the individual recognizes the full weight of that loss, relates to realities that have primacy and magnitude, and allows a new sense of internal peace to be born. Meaning is not imposed on narrative time by the Dantesque pattern; rather, the pattern can be extracted from the work as an expression of the meaning inherent in the movement of events.

Hemingway's use of Dante is more noticeable in *Across the River and into the Trees*, primarily because Dante is so often mentioned.[27] It is this later novel in Hemingway's corpus that is most attentive to the trustworthiness of human time.

Colonel Cantwell brings more of the context into the text than does Jake Barnes in *The Sun Also Rises*. Cantwell rehearses his military experiences; his vocation corresponds to the century's principal occupation, war. Moreover, his age coincides with the age of the century.

The time of the text is complicated by the combination of two stories, the duck hunting with which the book begins, and which is continued again near the end, and the intervening story of Cantwell's visit to Venice. The duck hunting takes place on Sunday, the framed story during the few days preceding, especially the Saturday. The hunting provides a frame because the principal action, the relation of Cantwell to the surly boatman, is not resolved until the story is taken up again. A critical question, to which we shall return, concerns the relation of these two stories to one another.

As in *For Whom the Bell Tolls*, linear time in the center story, the chronology of a half century of wars and Cantwell's movement toward his death, is transformed by rhythmic and ritualistic time. Such time also eases the tension between the two stories, making the return to duck hunting a part of the cyclical pattern. Further, chapters usually begin with a movement over a threshold, the characters leaving or entering a building or room. The cyclical movement of time is also suggested by Cantwell's return to Venice after many other visits; he knows the city, its history, and its inhabitants well.

Since Cantwell understands this visit to be his last, he relieves himself of matters that have been burdensome. He alters the past by performing a ritual at the place near Fossalta where he had been wounded. He also performs a ritual of confession to Renata and then to her portrait in order to divest himself of the burden of his past, especially his failures as a leader.

The processes of divestment have their counterpart in the increasingly free rounds of activity in which Cantwell and Renata engage. They do not make firm plans for their weekend together, one they seem to recognize as their last. They are playful, spontaneous, celebrative. There is a good bit of gift giving and receiving, the positive correlate to Cantwell's need for divestment.

To determine the meaning of the rhythmic and ritualistic time, we must begin with the contrast between Cantwell and his surroundings. While he admires Venice and knows about its history and art, and while he loves the radiantly beautiful and personally gracious Renata, Cantwell is not himself a refined man. Bearing the scars of the context as well as sharing some of its violent characteristics, Cantwell is received by the city of art and by Renata. Contact with them changes Cantwell. During the days before Sunday he is still somewhat short-tempered, as Jackson his driver or as the elevator boy whom he reprimands would testify. But during the duck hunt Cantwell tolerates the unpleasantness of the surly boatman and, moreover, forgives the breach of hunting etiquette of which the man is guilty. The juxtaposition of these two stories makes clear the meaning of the time in Venice: the world of beauty and grace has evoked from the bitter, scarred man his latent capacity for honesty, generosity, and gentleness.

In this redemption of Cantwell, the allusions to Dante are particularly striking. Here, as in the *Divine Comedy*, we move from one world to another, from the perplexing world of the context to a serene realm of beauty and grace. Venice, the city of art and truth, is more durable than the world of the context; it is able to receive Cantwell and, through generosity and confessions, allow him to change. Second, the figure of Renata assumes some of the qualities that Beatrice and the Virgin have for Dante. Associations are made between Renata and the Virgin, the perpetually young woman who receives the broken body of the dying man. Renata, full of beauty and grace, is the giver of gifts, the fully accepting and renewing woman. Her role is shared by the city and by others who live there, especially the Maestro.

All of this, however, is preliminary to the central matter of the work, the dying of Colonel Cantwell. Here, too, the *Divine Comedy* holds a position similar to its importance in *The Sun Also Rises*. Dying is hellish, purgatorial, and paradisiacal. It is first of all the threatening, enervating, and final undoing of the person. Cantwell is aware of its hellish qualities, and he bears on his body and in his memory the marks of its sudden and gradual assaults. But death is also an antagonist with which one can struggle. The fight against death makes dying itself a human event, ritualizes it, allows it to draw resources out of the self. Finally, death is also a benefit. The use of Stonewall Jackson's words for the title, the need of Renata's mother to leave Venice periodically for a place where there are trees, and the references to American trees during Renata's and Cantwell's reverie suggest that death is a place of desirable rest. It offers an attractive peace beyond the truthful, beautiful, and gracious world which the Maestro, Venice, Renata, and perhaps the novel itself, represent.

The meaning or paradigmatic pole of human time is especially important to *Across the River and into the Trees*. While the movement of time in Hemingway's fiction seems easily related to natural rhythms, its meaning is articulated most fully by paradigms of an aesthetic and spiritual nature. Human time is, in his fiction, neither only natural nor only spiritual; as meaningful movement, it is both. It is a time contrasted with that of the context. Its power and meaning are not projected on it by the will of the characters or interests of narrators. And it is productive of those changes that are urgently needed but are beyond the reach of characters to provide for themselves.

THREE

D. H. Lawrence

Although not always at the same pace, events in a D. H. Lawrence novel move forward with strong, relentless insistence. Characters, while aware of this movement and, with help from the narrator's descriptions, often understanding its meaning and direction, do not control it. Rather they are carried along by the inexorable advance of time. As Lawrence explained, "In every great novel, who is the hero all the time? Not any of the characters, but some unnamed and nameless flame behind them all. Just as God is the pivotal interest in the books of the Old Testament."[1] This "flame," as we shall see, is a life-giving force, and it is temporal.[2] Time in Lawrence's fiction, consequently, lies ultimately beyond human comprehension and control.

This temporal force is primarily rhythmic. Its effect both for the characters' experience and for Lawrence's style is the generation of power and significance through repetition.[3] Finally, time in Lawrence's fiction is trustworthy. Since human life is so thoroughly temporal, the attitudes of characters toward time have radical consequences for their self-understanding, relations to others, and orientation to their world. Characters who distrust time must undergo a change of attitude, but, because this change involves uncertainty and risks, some who need a fundamental shift in their orientation to time are unwilling to change or even fail to recognize their plight. The willingness to trust temporal process constitutes an act of faith,[4] and it provides a basis for referring to Lawrence as a "religious writer."[5] The fruits of time are the birth of individual freedom or wholeness, unity between a man and a woman, and social or cultural leadership.

These general characteristics of time should be related to four recurring interests or strategies in Lawrence's fiction. The first is an interdependence between the narratives within a single novel, an outer and an inner, related to one another as husk to kernel. A second feature is a pattern of departure and return that is complicated by points of transition that are difficult for characters to negotiate. Third, Lawrence's novels, with all their stress on repetition and cycles, are also oriented to the future and to continuity. Their endings are remarkably open; indeed, in some instances the narrative of the text is preliminary to a story projected into the future beyond the text. Finally, Lawrence uses music and dance to suggest the nature of time and its consequences for personal fulfillment, a sense of unity between people, and a new relation of people to their environment.

I

Several of Lawrence's novels present a contrast between an outer and an inner text. The shell narrative, which depicts a social context, often frames a more personal, core narrative. In *The Trespasser*, for example, this device is found in the sharp break established between the core account of Siegmund's vacation with Helena on the Isle of Wight and the shell formed by the beginning of the novel, set six months after the time of the vacation, and the ending, which takes place one year after it. The five days of the core narrative are set apart from the rest of the characters' lives. As in other instances of contrast between core and shell narratives, the world of the outer narrative is alien to, even antagonistic toward, the interests and needs of the characters.

The standing of the outer world is not, in some of Lawrence's other novels, however, so negative as it is in *The Trespasser*. Maturing young people, the principal figures in several novels, expect this outer world to provide them a larger, more challenging life. Both Paul Morel in *Sons and Lovers* and Ursula Brangwen in *The Rainbow* turn toward this external shell to provide release from a confining home environment. This ambiguous standing of the outer, larger world in relation to the more personal, domestic one constitutes a deep ambivalence in Lawrence's fiction.

Primarily, however, the outer narratives present an alien context. Urban settings are particularly forbidding. Of London it is said, for example, "How had helpless savages, running with their spears on the riverside, after fish, how had they come to rear up this great London, the ponderous, massive ugly superstructure of a world of man upon a world of nature!"[6] Structures within urban society, such as the educational systems that Ursula enters, produce nonhuman collectivities opposed to personal growth and exert power arbitrarily. Intellectual life in the wider society depends upon repressive abstractions and generalities. Lawrence relates the destructive attitudes typical of the outer narrative to its culture's distrust of time: "But now, after almost three thousand years, now that we are almost abstracted entirely from the rhythmic life of the seasons, birth and death and fruition, now we realize that such abstraction is neither bliss nor liberation, but nullity."[7]

The principal characteristic of the context is imperviousness to the movement of human temporality. The town of Wiggiston in *The Rainbow*, for example, is "fixed and rigid."[8] Lawrence judges this fear of time, "this desire for constancy, for fixity in the temporal world," to be evil.[9] The outer world, the context, denies time's creative ability to undergird and carry forward human intentions and actions. In the core text, not in the outer shell, life is pulsing, vital, and productive.

The action depicted by several of the novels, then, is the rejection of the social world of the context and the corresponding search for a more authentic, personal world. In *Women in Love, Aaron's Rod,* and *The Lost Girl*, English society is depicted as inhospitable to personal development, relationships, and new cultural forms. Other locales are preferred; for example, Italy promises "mystery" and "magic"[10] because it retains a sense of the past.[11] Even here, however, the potential for life has been violated by war.[12] Indeed all of Europe becomes, as in *Kangaroo* and *The Plumed Serpent*, the rejected context; Harriet and Richard Somers and Kate Leslie are forced to seek a more supportive cultural life in distant places, Kate Leslie in Mexico and Harriet and Richard less successfully in Australia.

Contrast between the inner and outer texts is also striking in *Lady Chatterley's Lover*. The context is the wider world of her marriage and friendships, which Connie rejects. She enters the inner narrative of her new love relationship, although she continues to move back and forth between the two worlds throughout the novel. Clifford remains identified with the context because of what Lawrence in one of his essays calls "the static ego, with its will-to-persist, [which] neutralizes both life and death, and utterly defies the Holy Ghost. The unpardonable sin."[13] The context lacks faith in the temporal nature of life. Mellors has rejected that world in order to begin a new life in the midst of the woods. Connie, by entering the core narrative, risks changes that produce new vitality.

In many of Lawrence's novels then, the time of the inner narratives gains importance and meaning from contrast with the context. Trusted in the core narratives, temporality creates new possibilities; repressed in the context, its potentials are negated by the deadly stasis that mind, will, and habit produce. As we saw, *The Trespasser* presents an early, clear instance of this divided structure. Lawrence's use of this device cannot, therefore, be attributed primarily to his growing disillusionment with English and even European culture.[14] Indeed, his ideas about culture may also have been influenced by his artistic interests, his narrative technique of juxtaposing two stories or two settings. In any event, it is the core narrative that grants access to "the true heart of the world," what Lawrence understands as temporality.[15]

II

The contrast between an inner and an outer narrative, between core and context, is complicated by a second narrative feature, a pattern of departure and return. This pattern, in fact, frames the entire corpus. Departure is the principal form of movement in *The White Peacock*, Lawrence's first novel, while return shapes *Lady Chatterley's Lover*, his last.

Natural cycles support the pattern of departure and return in *The White Peacock*. Many of the chapters, especially those in the first two parts of the novel, concern a single day, and the position of the sun is often noted. Characters, correspondingly, do what is appropriate for the particular hour; leave home or return, work, eat, unite into groups or disperse. Just as significant as the daily round are the lunar cycles, the change of seasons, and the recurrence of annual holidays, particularly Christmas and the New Year. This pattern is enlarged by the action of the novel: the departure of a group of people from the place of their childhood, a setting adorned by the narrator with Edenic and maternal imagery.[16] The stress is on departure and scattering, although the magnetic pull of Nethermere is strong.

The direction of *Lady Chatterley's Lover* is contrary to that of *The White Peacock*; rather than outward, movement is toward the center.[17] The setting can be construed as a set of concentric circles: the external world from which both Clifford Chatterley and Mellors have returned after the war and with which Clifford attempts to maintain contact through his writing and his radio; England, depicted as largely industrialized and as economically unified; the midlands, where mining is the principal focus; Wragby, the Chatterley home; the woods on the estate, to which Connie goes with increasing frequency and urgency after chapter VI; and the cottage where she and Mellors meet. The pattern of departure and return also shapes Connie's relationship with Mellors; she comes to him and leaves his side, and, at the end of the novel, the two await their reunion in the spring, a year from the time during which their relationship began.

In both *The White Peacock* and *Lady Chatterley's Lover*, time near the center moves more slowly than does the time of the outer world. Chapters in the first part of *The White Peacock* encompass short periods of time, usually a day or part of a day; later chapters comprise seasons and years. In *Lady Chatterley's Lover*, the same effects occur, although in contrary sequence. Time at the outset, the time of the exterior circles, moves rapidly from before the war to the years following it. Once the story of Connie's relation to Mellors begins, time moves more slowly.

These directions away from or toward the center are not smooth. When characters pass from one circle of relationship to another they encounter hazards or experience loss. Yet the course of life for Lawrence's characters requires these difficult transitions. In *The White Peacock* Lettie, forced out of her youth by her twenty-first birthday, awakens with "cries of dismay," with a sense of deprivation and foreboding.[18] In the same novel, marriage and births propel characters into larger circles which, while offering new possibilities, threaten pain along with the gain. Conversely, in *Lady Chatterly's Lover*, risk and loss are experienced, especially by Connie, in the movement toward the center. While the outward movement of life is supported by social rituals, return to the center seems to lack social approval, to move against the current of social interests. Connie and Mellors must improvise their own way toward renewal.

A pattern of departure determines other novels. Although at times with great uncertainty, Paul Morel moves out to increasingly wide circles of interest and contacts in *Sons and Lovers*. Ursula's experiences in *The Rainbow* also form a series of outward movements, as the chapter title "The Widening Circle" suggests; and the transitions are hazardous. Alvina Houghton, in *The Lost Girl*, leaves the security of her home when she begins nurse's training and later risks association with a group of antinomian artists and travels to Italy.

Characters submit to the uncertainties and risks of outward or inward movement primarily because their lives in the immediate circle are unsatisfying. In *Aaron's Rod*, for example, the principal character feels compelled to depart from the home he experiences as increasingly confining. The word often used by the narrator or a character to describe the static life of a circle that must be abandoned is "unreal"; transition and its uncertainties accompany the search for reality.

Lawrence's novels would be far simpler—and probably less interesting—were the tension between this structural feature and the first lacking. If they presented an unambiguous contrast between an inner narrative rendered positively and an outer narrative representing a world to be rejected, choices would be clearer. Or, if his novels simply traced the movements of characters from centers to peripheries and back again, the meanings behind each departure and return would be considerably less ambiguous. But the inner world, often a place of birth and renewal, can become a confinement that one must escape, while the outer world, indicated by cities and distant places, is both deadly or dreary and a locus promising a more abundant and freer existence. This persistent contrast between the inner core and the outer shell, combined with the crossing of thresholds from one circle of life to another, creates constant movement in the novels. While the inner world enjoys a privileged position more often than does the outer, neither is final, for there is no rest from the need either to depart or to return.

III

A third feature of Lawrence's novels, one that cuts across the pattern of departure and return and that has important temporal consequences, is the persistent future orientation of the action. Lines of organic connection leading from the past into the future appear in three ways: The emergence of an authentic self, the creation of unity between two individuals, and the appearance of new cultural or political leaders. These goals and products of temporal movement, while never permanent, grant wholeness to the novels and account for their open endings.

Sons and Lovers depicts fully the first form of continuity. The rhythmic enterings and exits, crestings and fallings, encounters and retreats are the pulsations that produce the birth of an authentic self. Gertrude Morel, a predominant force in this process, gives birth to Paul in more than a biological manner; she also delivers him from the confining life of the colliers to the larger and more promising outer world. However, the warmth and support that she provides threaten Paul's freedom because he becomes, after the death of his brother, William, the principal object of her devotion. Miriam helps in the birth process by fostering Paul's aesthetic development. But, as an inspiring virgin who denies the sexual dimensions of their relationship, she also impedes the process of his maturation. Clara's function is to nurture Paul's sexual growth, but inherent in the nurture is the threat of sexual absorption.[19] Paul's emergence from the womb as well as from the limitations of his origins is the birth of a whole individual. The rhythmic process, at times painful as well as exhilarating, produces a line of development across widening circles to the point of release. The "quickly" at the end of *Sons and Lovers* signifies the confirmation of his individuality, as he turns from the ground of his origins toward his future. The novel's ending releases him into life.

We find a similar form of continuity in *The Rainbow*. The background from which Ursula Brangwen emerges pulses with vitality.[20] The Brangwen men of the earlier century lived close to the land and to the animals; they could feel "the pulse and body of the soil," and "the pulse of the blood of the teats of the cows beat into the pulse of the hands of the men."[21] Rather than to this repetition the women look to extension and the future.[22] The tensions and complements between the cyclical orientation of the men and linear temporality stressed by the women produce complex relationships.

Moments of union are marked by the rainbow, the symbol of a continuing order, the guarantee that life has duration as well as rhythm, continuity as well as change. Like the river that supports the barge-dwellers Ursula and Anton visit, the flow of temporality directs and uplifts human life. Even the colliers of Wiggiston carry a future within them, "the heaving contour of the new germination."[23]

The process by which interpersonal, and especially marital, relationships are created grants a second form of continuity in Lawrence's work and is most fully rendered by *Women in Love*. With the "frictional to-and-fro" of their lives can be found a line of developing commitment between Birkin and Ursula.[24]

This line finds its negative counterpart in the lack of growth between Gudren and Gerald. Initially, Ursula and Gudren are much alike; they sense the power of their beauty and intelligence, and they despise marriage and ordinary people. Rupert Birkin and Gerald Crich also share attitudes: they are misanthropic, and Rupert, although he stresses spontaneity and individuality, largely agrees with Gerald on the issues of race and nationality. But Rupert's life moves in a new direction. For years the lover of Hermione Roddice, he has begun to resist the absorption of everything into mind which she represents. He turns toward darkness, breaks with Hermione, and rejects the society of sanity for what appears to be the madness of his own sensuous feelings. Gudren and Gerald, unlike Ursula and Rupert, do not overcome or respond to inadequacy by undergoing change. Rather, they seek compensatory experiences and relationships.

In the second part of the plot, Rupert and Ursula discuss their developing relationship. While they both confess to a faith in the durability provided by a deeper reality,[25] they also feel threats to their independence. Ursula believes Rupert wants to master her, while he fears her role as the absorbing woman or Great Mother. The couple is also cautious regarding sex because they sense its capacity to foster an unhealthy dependence. It is commitment that finally creates or expresses continuity in the relationship, and this linear dimension points toward the future. Lawrence stresses this mixture of sexual attraction and commitment in relationships when he wrote later, "Mankind has got to get back to the rhythm of the cosmos, and the permanence of marriage."[26] As F. R. Leavis comments, "What, in fact, strikes us as religious is the intensity with which his men and women, harkening to their deepest needs and promptings as they seek 'fulfillment' in marriage, know that they 'do not belong to themselves,' but are responsible to something that, in transcending the individual, transcends love and sex too."[27]

In the third section the sexual intimacy of Rupert and Ursula is increasingly experienced as ritual. The union of two individuals depends upon the yielding of the ego's supremacy to a larger reality by which both are enfolded. Consequently, "the quest for self-realization becomes involved in self-abnegation. . . . They surrender their stable egos in order to gain an ultimate unity which cannot itself be stable."[28] This Lawrentian ritual, basic to his depiction of sexual activity and often related to the presence of the moon, is similar to the ritual of the *heiros gamos* or heavenly marriage, in which complete sexual surrender is required.[29] At the end of this section a future has been secured for their relationship.

The fourth stage, beginning with the voyage to the continent, emphasizes rejection of the social context. Furthermore, the contrast between the two couples is amplified; while Gerald and Gudren continue their destructive pattern of control and submission, Ursula and Rupert grow together by being rooted in "something infinitely more than love."[30]

The importance of continuity is even more explicit in *Lady Chatterley's Lover*. One major instance of it is Clifford's desire for an heir and his inability, due to war injuries, to father one. But the injury does not lessen his high evaluation of continuity: "'One is only a link in a chain,'" he affirms.[31] Clifford elaborates on the importance of continuity: "'It's what endures through one's life that matters; my own life matters to me, in its long continuance and development. . . . It's the living together from day to day, not the sleeping together once or twice. You and I are married, no matter what happens to us. We have the habit of each other.'"[32] But "habit" is not creative and oriented toward the future; it is not, as another character describes it, "organic."[33] Clifford's continuity suggests conformity to the past and imprisonment. Hilda, Connie's sister, also comments on continuity in a lecture to Mellors, but he replies, "'What continuity 'ave yer got i' *your* life? I thought you was gettin' divorced. What continuity's that? Continuity o' yer own stubbornness.'"[34] Mellors, because of disappointments and dislocations in the wider social world, fears the future and does not want to entrust children to it.[35] Only with Connie's help, particularly her belief that his tenderness guarantees a future for the child, Mellors changes. At the end of the novel he is able to express in his letter a faith in the continuity provided by "'the little forked flame between me and you.'"[36] The book ends with an openness to the future.

With the development of the complete individual and of the union between two people the emergence of a cultural leader represents a third form of continuity or future direction in Lawrence's novels. While, as critics have noted, Lawrence abandoned interest in this process, its role must be noted despite his discouragement with it as a foreseeable possibility.[37] It is particularly important for *Kangaroo* and *The Plumed Serpent*.

Richard Somers, in *Kangaroo*, attributes the lack, in Europe generally and in England particularly, of a cultural future after World War I to the pervasive rejection of the distant past. The long chapter entitled "Nightmare" articulates his sense of the disjunction between English society and its historical context. The rocks of Cornwall, for example, "the mystery of the powerful, pre-human earth, showing its might," have no impact on the culture.[38] Because he believes in the importance of culture for the reconstitution of life, Richard suffers in England "one of his serious deaths in belief."[39]

Australia offers no viable alternative; here the gap between the society and the history of the continent is greater and more rigorously maintained. Because Richard's search for a more promising culture cannot, therefore, be fulfilled,[40] he responds by securing provisions for social resources in nature and in his home. His proximity to the sea allows its rhythmic language to enter his soul, there to establish, "a pledge of unbroken faith, between the universe and the innermost"[41] and to give him a social message, "to make that strange translation of the low, dark throbbing into open act and speech."[42] He views his home, on the other hand, as a place of nurture for personal life.

The need for a new European cultural future is more fully depicted in *The Plumed Serpent*. Although the emergence of cultural and political leaders takes place in Mexico, the process is experienced by Kate Leslie, who links it to Irish history and, by extension, to European possibilities. The conflict in Mexico is between the present society and the movement, led by Don Ramón Carrasco, a scholar, and Don Cipriano, a military leader, to revive religious practices and ethnic forms that antedate the arrival of European culture and religion. The new or reemerging culture is strongly associated with rhythmic and natural time and is characterized by the rituals of the ancient religion, especially by the drumbeats and by dancing. It is not controlled by human consciousness or intellectual underpinnings but is, rather, a time which people of faith can reenter.

A cultural future does not seem to be a possibility for the Europe depicted by Lawrence's novels, however. The "man's world" that Ursula Brangwen encounters in *The Rainbow*, the England she and Birkin leave behind in *Women in Love*, the "ash-grey coffin" of England which Alvina Houghton rejects in *The Lost Girl*, the Egypt of England from which Aaron departs in *Aaron's Rod*, the Europe that Richard and Harriet Somers flee in *Kangaroo*, and the wider circles that Mellors and Connie abandon for the sanctuary of the center reveal that no new culture will follow the catastrophe of the war. European culture lacks a viable future because it is under the domination of will and mind and because it represses organic connection with its remote past.

IV

Music and dance provide a final way in which the characteristics of time are secured in Lawrence's novels. The role of music is clear in *The Trespasser* not only because the principal character is a musician but also because music provides both incidental and programmatic ways of interpreting experience. The metaphoric relation of music and experience is often merely allusory: "What music do you think holds the best interpretation of sunset?"[43] On other occasions it undergirds the narrative as a whole; the action is associated with operatic literature in general and with *Tristan and Isolde* in particular.

Such parallel relation of experience to music, each component distinct yet an interpreter of the other, at times yields to merging. For example, Siegmund recalls playing his violin the previous evening: "he played the rhythm with all his blood."[44] Unity between blood and music marks Siegmund as a finer musician than Helena, who, when she plays the piano, moves her body artificially: "Her white dress, high waisted, swung as she forced the rhythm, determinedly swaying to the time as if her body were the white stroke of a metronome."[45] This relation of the physical to the musical is extended in Siegmund's experience; the rhythms of his body are continuous with the rhythms of the cosmos; as Helena lies with her head on his chest, the throb of his heartbeat seems to resonate with a larger sound: "Was there also deep in the world a great God thudding out waves of life, like a great heart, unconscious?"[46]

The connection between music and experience, however, is not limited to rhythm. Experience is also interpreted polyphonically. Helena perceives her relation to her world as "discordant,"[47] and she views time as a process by which unharmonious elements in life are resolved: "All along Fate has been resolving, from the very beginning, resolving obvious discords, gradually, by unfamiliar progression; and out of original combinations weaving wondrous harmonies with our lives."[48] She is not alone in suggesting a relation of music to experience in polyphonic terms; Siegmund at one point tells her, "'You seem to have knit all things in a piece for me. Things are not separate; they are all in a symphony.'"[49] Lawrence's turn toward this element of music finds its larger counterparts in the many tensions and conflicts within his work between aspects of life: male and female, darkness and light, nature and culture, and passion and mind. Some critics, in fact, refer to Lawrence's work as "dialectical" because of these tensions and discordant impulses.[50]

Siegmund most often relates experience to music by means of melody rather than rhythm or polyphony. This accords with his role as violinist; his life is a melodic line directed toward its conclusion: "I have come so far. Now I must get clarity and courage to follow out the theme."[51] Melody, therefore, is important for the structure of the novel, since Siegmund's strong individuality leads to disharmonious relations with both his wife, Beatrice, and his mistress, Helena: "The discord of his immediate situation overcame every harmony."[52]

Although all three musical elements—rhythm, polyphony, and melody—are present in The Trespasser, and although melody is most important for the depiction of Siegmund's self-awareness, rhythm is primary in the novel, as it is in all of Lawrence's work. While rhythm can occur without the other two elements, full or satisfying experiences cannot be melodic and harmonious without a rhythmic basis.

A similar situation can be found in Lawrence's other musical novel, *Aaron's Rod*. Melody is the most important musical element for the principal character, Aaron Sisson, because his flute provides not only his livelihood but also the means of access to self-actualization in the wider world. When life in his home becomes confining, he finds release in music. His music transforms his life and his relationships with others; it grants him seductive power, a "male godliness."[53] As a flutist, Aaron strongly favors melody: "'I wish,'" he says, "'we could go back to melody pure and simple,'"[54] and, although he plays in orchestras, his sense of the instrument's potential for solo performances is strong. Despite the strong tie between his personal well-being and melody, however, music and experience are rooted primarily by means of rhythm in this novel. This is achieved in several ways. One is the rhythmic pattern of the plot, the several experiences of loss and gain, isolation and association, and death and rebirth.[55] Another is through the negative depiction, especially of artists in England, of precious and unrooted art. The flute, melody, and Aaron's male self-actualization carry the dangerous tendencies of abstraction and self-containment. Art, no less than biological life, must be rooted if it is not to die. Music, no less than the treelike flowers of Florence, must have deep origins and connections. This tie between musical melody and organic, rooted life is secured by the novel not only through Aaron's search for the kind of sexual fulfillment that the Marchesa provides but also by the interweaving of the image of the flute with the more feminine image of trees. The two images are combined in the figure of the biblical Aaron whose rod, unlike those of the other heads of families, sprouted.

Music plays such a fundamental role in relation to human time in this and others of Lawrence's novels because music indicates a kind or a level of meaning which is non- or pre-verbal. For example, music evokes a level of meaning in Aaron's life which runs below that of language: "The inaudible music of his conscious soul conveyed his meaning quite as clearly as I convey it in words; probably much more clearly. But in his own mode only; and it was in his own mode only he realized what I must put into words. These words are my own affair.

His mind was music."[56] Music indicates a form of meaningful movement that runs more closely to experience than language can. As Frank Kermode puts it, "He is one of the great crowd of thinkers who have held to the notion that there is a consciousness other than the mental, and that modern civilization has repressed it."[57]

Since meaning lies below language, physical motion, especially dancing, also becomes a significant form of expression. The young people engage in a moonlight dance in *The White Peacock*, thereby setting the stage for similar moments in Lawrence's other novels. Because dance unifies people both with one another and with their setting while also allowing the individual to stand out, it is often expressive of human life at its fullest. Dance emerges in many situations. At the end of this novel, George and Cyril watch two men who are gathering wheat move "in an exquisite, subtle rhythm, their white sleeves and their dark heads gleaming, moving against the mild sky and the corn." Cyril turns to George and says, "'You ought to be like that.'"[58] Dancing expresses or creates the interrelations among life's natural, cultural, and individual elements.

Physical movement depends on and releases the rhythms of life. In *The Rainbow*, Anna and Will, gathering corn, are drawn to one another by "a rhythm, which carried their feet and their bodies in tune,"[59] and sexual desire is created in Ursula by the dancing at her Uncle Fred's wedding. A central scene in *Lady Chatterley's Lover* depicts Connie's dance in the rain; her movements express and invoke sexual desire and fertility. Here Connie reflects on the programmatic importance of rhythm both for her own experience and, more generally, for the narrative form:

> It is the way our sympathy flows and recoils that really determines our lives. And here lies the vast importance of the novel, properly handled. It can inform and lead into new places the flow of our sympathetic consciousness, and it can lead our sympathy away in recoil from things gone dead. Therefore, the novel, properly handled, can reveal the most secret places of life: for it is in the *passionate* secret places of

life, above all, that the tide of sensitive awareness needs to
ebb and flow, cleansing and freshening.[60]

Rhythm, associated with the elemental life of passion and pro-
creation, also inspires awareness and sympathy, compassion, as
well as desire. Music and dance, especially the latter because of
its relation to rhythm, connote the level of meaningful temporal movement in human life both for individual consciousness and for relationships.

The characteristics of narrative time in Lawrence, then, are
articulated in these four kinds of figures. The juxtaposition of
inner and outer, texts and contexts, creates a constant evaluation of different kinds of time. Furthermore, life is rendered as
unending transitions from one circle of relationship to another. Third, along with the cyclical patterns of departure and
return, there is a strong orientation toward the future, a sense
of continuity which creates the open endings of his novels. Finally, consciousness, human relationships, and rapport between
people and their environment are grounded in a level of meaning that is too elusive or complex to articulate in words but
that can be evoked or expressed in music and dance. The result
of these features of Lawrence's novels is to render time as primary, rhythmic, and trustworthy.

FOUR

Mircea Eliade

Despite the many ways in which they differ, the fictions of Hemingway and D. H. Lawrence are alike in this respect: time, even though complicated by many factors, is rhythmic. Because a rhythmic pattern suggests repetition or return, time in this work is primarily cyclical. Human experiences that accord with this pattern of rhythm and cycle easily become ritualistic.

In Hemingway's fiction, as we saw, action often follows a cyclical pattern: the character enters a situation, confronts something unexpected, withdraws from the confrontation, and reflects on what has occurred. Or events conform to a diurnal, cyclic pattern, as they do for Robert Jordan during his three-day sojourn at the cave or for Santiago in his days and nights alone at sea. Seasonal changes create this pattern on a broader scale in *A Farewell to Arms*, since the progress of the war depends on the weather. This rhythmic and cyclical time imparts to human acts a ritual quality, such as the pilgrimage of Jake Barnes to Pamplona for the festival of San Fermin or the repeated pilgrimages of Colonel Cantwell to Venice. These characters often participate consciously in rituals, Jake in church-going, eating and drinking, and bullfights and Cantwell in the

58

ritual of relieving himself at Fossalta and through confession
to Renata. Such rituals affect and are affected by the meaning
of past events; in *For Whom the Bell Tolls* the pains and inadequacies of the past are removed by action that has ritual
quality, while in *The Old Man and The Sea* the actions of Santiago are given meaning by incorporation in the paradigms that
heroes and images from the past provide.

Rhythm, repetition, and ritual are no less important for
Lawrence's work. A pattern of departure and return not only relates his first to his last novels; it also shapes the action of individual books. This movement is constant, since both the
center and the periphery, the personal and the social worlds,
have beneficial as well as limiting qualities. Not only does
rhythm shape the movements of characters from one locale to
another, but it also infuses this experience with pulsation: for
example, the rhythms of the waves have a life-giving effect
on the vacationing couple in *The Trespasser* and on Richard
Somers in *Kangaroo*; Ursula Brangwen's ancestors lived close
both to the rhythms of the soil and seasons and the pulse of
animal life on the farm. Such rhythms and cycles easily allow
human action to become ritualistic, as in the revival of the
pulsations of ancient religion in *The Plumed Serpent*. All
meaningful movement, including work, can become dancelike,
as we see in *The White Peacock* and *The Rainbow*; and dance
becomes ritual, as with Anna's dance in *The Rainbow* and
Connie's in *Lady Chatterley's Lover*. The relation of the moon
to such rituals is common in Lawrence's fiction; lunar cycles
or the presence of the moon in his novels grants human actions
a powerful background of natural, cyclical time.

It should not be surprising that rhythmic patterns appear in
the narratives as detectable ways in which human actions and
behavior reveal a shape. Rhythm is a constant formal aspect of
human experience. "Not only does man experience rhythmic
patterns in the surrounding world, he carries within himself
the continuous up and down of rhythmic waves: heartbeat and
respiration." Indeed, it can be said that from this rhythmic
base other human actions acquire a pattern—"walking, running, marching, and . . . manual labor."[1]

Not only does rhythm present itself as an immediately recognizable pattern of human temporal behavior, it also grants narrative a basic organizational principle which, as we have seen, can run from specific gestures to larger cycles of entering and leaving or departing and returning. In this way a common structure unifies scenes, novels, and, in the case of Lawrence, the whole corpus of a writer. Rhythmic patterns help answer the need for narrative coherence by providing significant events an undulating orderliness.

Finally, rhythm, in addition to being easily recognizable and to granting order, suggests an orientation to natural, even cosmic forces and structures. Writers such as Hemingway and Lawrence, for whom integration with natural and bodily potentials has an important theoretic place, will most likely rely on the tie that rhythmic time creates between human awareness or action and its vital natural context. As one scientist puts it, "rhythms are apparent at all levels of biological organization. They can be seen in the lashing cilia of unicellular organisms, in the division of cells and nuclei, in locomotion, feeding and excretion. Groups of cells, tissues and organs are no less rhythmic, their periodicities being harmoniously synchronized within the living organism."[2] In fact, scientists are becoming increasingly convinced that plant and animal processes are determined as much, if not more, by internal rhythms, such as circadian patterns, as by external, environmental conditions. Rhythm, therefore, offers narratives the opportunity to reveal, without need for apology, two characteristics of time as we experience it: temporality as fundamental to and determining of our behavior and temporality relating us to a natural context, signaling our embodiment in processes patterned by rhythm.

Polemical issues regarding time often appear in this fiction, particularly decrying the loss of an organic connection between human and natural time. An emphasis on speed, temporal homogeneity, and abstraction, in an often violent though unnoticed way, divorce human time from natural cycles, and this fiction offers a temporality that is an alternative to that which it negatively depicts as pervasive in the culture. Cyclical time is tied to ancient cultures and rituals, primarily by bullfighting in Hemingway or by the Aztec rituals in *The Plumed Serpent* and the ancient monuments of Cornwall in *Kangaroo*. In other words, the polemic points themselves take on a pattern of return, the call to revive a form of human time more characteristic of ancient life than of modern. Participation in these fictions results in a deeper appreciation for the connection that ancient and traditional societies observed between their own lives and their natural contexts.

Rhythmic human time, with this bundle of relationships with natural cycles, ritual actions, and return to the past, has been fully and clearly delineated by Mircea Eliade in his many books on religious symbols, rituals, and myths in ancient societies. Furthermore, Eliade fully agrees with the polemic, in the work of Hemingway and Lawrence, against the abstraction of modern consciousness from its ties with ancient cultures. He, along with them, advocates rhythmic time as an antidote to inadequacies and faults in the notions about time characteristic of the modern West.

Mircea Eliade distinguishes himself among recent thinkers not only by his interpretation of time in traditional societies as grounded in rhythm but also by commending this form of temporality to his contemporary audience as a valuable alternative to the linear and abstracted notions we have about time. For these reasons, along with the fact that he is himself a novelist and a person interested in modern art generally and in modern literature particularly, his work stands out as an appropriate resource for articulating what is involved in appropriating, as we read this fiction, the kind of time that Hemingway and Lawrence make available. Furthermore, he is able to reveal how and why human time leads to or arises from belief even now; he indicates how temporality in traditional societies is itself a mode of belief. As we turn to his work we shall be concerned with three main points to which he is attentive: the relation of human time to natural rhythms; the relation between rhythmic time and myth, ritual, and symbol; and the importance of ritual time for human lives.

I

Human time in traditional societies is grounded in and patterned by natural rhythms. The principal characteristic of archaic people is that they feel "indissolubly connected with the Cosmos and the cosmic rhythms."[3] There is not for them, consequently, a basic separation between human time and the natural processes that they observe around them. Experience, events, actions, a sense of what it means to exist, and influences of natural phenomena on their existence are construed together as constituting a whole. People in traditional societies live within a cosmos that houses existents to which they are related as fellow particulars within a shared whole. Some of these natural existents become particularly potent ciphers or symbols of the processes that all particulars have in common. For Eliade, chief among these, as far as time is concerned, is the moon.

While the sun seems more often to suggest continuity and constancy, thereby holding a position in relation to the moon that is analogous to the relation of rocks to trees in ancient symbolism, the moon, because of its ever recurring cycle of departure and return, of waning and waxing, is "*the* heavenly body above all others concerned with the rhythms of life."[4] The moon's rhythmic patterns are extended to cover other aspects of life—bodies of water, rainfall, plant life, and fertility. Eliade notes that the lunar calendar is ubiquitous; it is a commonly shared temporal point of reference.[5]

The cycles of the moon are central to an understanding of rhythmically patterned processes not only because the moon is believed to control and to affect so much of life but also because the moon provides an interpretative point by which much of the remainder of life is understood. All of life is taken as inherently marked by a pattern of decline and reconstruction. Consequently, not only are all things related to one another by their common cosmic housing; they are also unified by their participation in a shared pattern. Rhythm becomes the lowest common denominator for all forms of existence, and all of life is subject to one law or pattern. "The rhythms of the moon weave together harmonies, symmetries, analogies and participations which make up an endless 'fabric,' a 'net' of invisible threads, which 'binds' together at once mankind, rain, vegetation, fertility, health, animals, death, regeneration, afterlife, and more."[6] Human time, therefore, conforms to this pattern and is integrated with its natural context.

The constantly changing moon grants the pattern of rhythmic time great and unavoidable standing. Change can even be sudden, since the moon, by completely disappearing, seems to account for catastrophes such as flood and infertility. Disasters reveal the moon's dark side, its participation in, if not control over, the periodic destruction of created forms. But, while change in relation to the moon includes destruction, it equally reveals reconstitution or returning. Change, then, while it is disconcerting and threatening, replaces loss with restoration. The pattern is basically a reassuring one, since the moon is never finally overcome by darkness. "Such is the law of the whole sublunary universe."[7]

While the moon is ubiquitous as a focal point for interpreting time and events rhythmically and for understanding human life as grounded in its natural context, other phenomena also become powerful expressions of this law or pattern of time. Water, especially for people subjected to periodic flooding, destroys while it also fertilizes or creates anew. Forms indefinitely separated from water lose their vitality and must again go through the flood in order to experience both dissolution and re-creation.[8]

Another common and powerful sign of this shared, cosmic process is the tree: "The tree comes to express the cosmos fully in itself, by embodying, in apparently static form, its 'force,' its life and its quality of periodic regeneration."[9] The tree has an inexhaustible life, and its capacity for continual regeneration allows it to be a clue to the whole of a people's ontological situation.

Consequently, time, for archaic peoples, is not homogeneous or inherently neutral. Time is always a process, always an expression of decaying and being reborn. For this reason, as well, there are suitable times for certain actions and suitable times for all events. There are lucky times and unlucky ones. "Time as such appears under different forms, varying in intensity and purpose."[10] Time is not empty, waiting for people to give it meaning and content. Time has import, and that import varies according to a pattern that is more or less known and predictable.

II

While it is important to emphasize this relation of archaic people to natural rhythms in Eliade's work, it would be an unfortunate mistake to conclude that for him human life in such societies is subordinated to nature. This is far from the situation, as he understands it. For mankind distinguishes itself from its natural context by incorporating rhythmic patterns in myths and rituals, thereby cooperating with the natural rhythms but also affecting them. Moreover, by means of myths and rituals, traditional people distinguish themselves from the natural round by coming into relation with an extranatural world of gods and the sacred. The "Cosmos reveals itself in a cipher; it 'speaks,' it transmits its message by its formation, its states of being, its rhythms. Man 'hears'—or 'reads'—these messages and consequently behaves towards the Cosmos as towards a coherent system of significance."[11] The principal message is that the people have a special place in the cosmos and that the cosmos was created by gods. In other words, rather than draining their distinctiveness as human beings or as a human society into the larger pattern of natural process, the role of ritual, of natural rhythms ritualistically incorporated and observed, allows the whole of the cosmos to receive significance from the central position that the society holds within that cosmos because of their relation to the gods who created it.

Eliade makes this point very clearly in his discussion of rites of initiation. Boys in those practices are not introduced simply to knowledge of natural phenomena and the patterns that mark change within them; they are introduced primarily to a world of spirit and culture. They learn the meaning of the people's origins, place in the cosmos, and relation to the gods. They are taken out of their natural relation to their mothers and brought, by means of a rebirth, into another, higher form of life.[12] The young man is thereby oriented to what is more than natural, to something which is *"powerful,* something utterly *other* than himself."[13] The natural rhythms, in other words, must be deciphered, their real meaning exposed. "'Deciphered' in the light of religious symbols, human life itself reveals a hidden side: it comes from 'elsewhere,' from very far away; it is 'divine' in the sense that it is the work of Gods or supernatural Beings."[14] This orientation to the world of spirit and the sacred that initiation provides is true, for Eliade, of all myths and rituals. While they refer to and are affected by the natural and the visible, they reveal the derivative nature of all forms of life and all rhythms in nature; indeed, they finally expose "the ontological unreality of the Universe."[15] Myths and symbols draw a people away from identification with the natural world and create a relation with that time and power that stand behind or prior to it. Basic to all myth and ritual is the overcoming of time as experienced and a going back to the point of beginnings.

New Year festivals grant a ready access to this process. The orgy, which often marks the close of the year, is crucial to the restoration of order at the outset of the new year: "The orgy is a symbolic re-entry into chaos, into the primordial and undifferentiated state. It re-enacts the 'confusion,' the 'totality' before the Creation, the cosmic Night, the cosmogonic egg. . . . It is to recover the original wholeness out of which sprang differentiated Life, and from which the Cosmos emerged."[16] Withdrawal from what is less real or what is profane in order to reach what is real, original, and sacred, rather than limited to one set of rituals, is the pattern and intention that binds them all. Even in individual disciplines, such as undertaken by a yogin, a withdrawal from ordinary time allows participation in a deeper, truer time:

Proceeding backward against the stream, one must necessarily come to the point of departure, which, in the last analysis, coincides with the cosmogony, with the first cosmic manifestation. One arrives at the beginning of time and one finds nontime, the eternal present that preceded the temporal experience begun by the first fallen human life. In other words, one "touches" the nonconditioned state that preceded man's fall into time and the wheel of existence.[17]

This is possible because the time of beginnings, the time of cosmogony and of the gods, is not back there, locked at some point at the beginning of a sequence of time, but is eternally present and available. Rites have efficacy because they participate in that primordial time, and a rite "reactualizes, shows it as happening, *here and now*."[18] This is not rehearsal in a sense of remembrance or faint imitation; it is rehearsal in the sense of participating in and unleashing force.

Another way of putting it is to say that for Eliade traditional societies consider each form of life, even though it exists in relative independence, both to derive from some sacred source and to require return to it for reconstitution and revitalization. Prolonged separation from the source depletes and eventually exhausts the life originally given to it. "Any form whatever, by the mere fact that it exists as such and endures, necessarily loses vigor and becomes worn; to recover vigor, it must be re-absorbed into the formless if only for an instant; it must be restored to the primordial unity from which it issued."[19] While it is obvious, from observing lunar or vegetation cycles, that this is true of nature, it is, for traditional societies, also true of cultural forms. The entire fabric of the society, along with its particular forms, must return to a time prior to its origin, in order to be re-created and to receive power to continue for another period of time.

However, it is not merely specifically religious acts and disciplines, such as initiation rites or New Year festivals, that follow this pattern. In a traditional or archaic society, every deliberate human action is or can be creative by involving a return. This is true because every human act has its archetype or paradigm in the time of beginnings. A person acts under the influence of large, reinforcing counterparts to his own actions which have their place in the time of the gods, heroes, and ancestors. Planting, building a house, having sex, eating—all involve or require going back to and invoking the paradigmatic act of its kind. This understanding of act as repetition may sound confining, but, Eliade points out, it is not because the paradigms have such scope and profundity that they allow for human innovations; "the possibilities for applying the mythical model are endless."[20] The archetypal acts anticipate all pos-

sible variations on a comprehensive set of basic human gestures. Every meaningful act is ritualistic, therefore, and like
ritual involves a rejection of profane time, the time in which
things waste away, and a recovery of or an alignment with real
time, what Eliade calls *illud tempus,* the time of beginnings or
creation. The result is a creative human act which produces a
form; that form degenerates in time and needs periodically to
be replaced or renewed.

Myths are important for these processes because the actions
and accomplishments of the gods and heroes cannot be simply
described; they must be narrated so that the hearers can relive
them. The realm of the gods has its own time, a "history of
acts freely undertaken, of unforeseeable decisions, of fabulous
transformations, and the like."[21] By rehearsing the myth, "one
reactualizes, in some sort, the sacred time in which the events
narrated took place,"[22] or one transcends profane time and enters "mythical Great Time," a time that cannot be approached
apart from the myths.[23]

In addition, myths are crucial in this process because they
are stories that have been passed down from the gods or the
ancestors. They structure the memory and condition a people's
experience of reality. The telling of stories, in this situation,
suggests a going back, a "retracing one's footsteps in the sands
of memory right back to the *illud tempus*—which implies the
abolition of profane time."[24] They relate and make available
the time of the cosmogenesis. Consequently, they lead to and
convey the sacred. Rather than being conjectural or even ex-
planatory, myths of creation grant access to the world of gods
and heroes, and by participating in that world the hearer is
brought into relation with them and revitalized or realigned by
that contact.

III

As I indicated at the outset, Eliade does not delineate the
temporality of archaic societies, its natural grounding and its
transformation by means of symbols, myths, and rituals, for
the sake of scholarship or curiosity alone. He does so in order
to commend this form of temporality to his modern readers.

For there is, he believes, something very wrong with our temporality and understanding of time because they are dissociated from our natural context and are not incorporated in ritual.

People err gravely not when they participate in a time that is profane and fragmenting—indeed, such a time is part of the cycle and is unavoidable—but in believing that such time is primary or exhaustive of time's possibilities. For example, the Hindu conception of Maya "does not necessarily lead to asceticism and the abandonment of all social and historical existence. This state of consciousness generally finds expression in quite another attitude . . . that of remaining in the world and participating in History, but taking good care not to attribute to History any absolute value."[25] When sacred or real time is forgotten, people are seduced into mistaking history as exclusively real. Linear time is unable to bear this imputation of reality and primacy.

Such seduction is virtually complete in the modern West, according to Eliade. The time that we take as real, namely historical time, has the effect of leading us further and further away from beginnings, wholeness, and creative newness. Moderns identify themselves in relation to a time that has actually become a "terror" rather than a boon or blessing.[26] The error is mistaking history or linear time as real and valuing novelty, uniqueness, and individuality too highly. The intellectual consequence is historicism, the depicting of human life as a sequence of occurrences and the identification of the meaning and value of events with the simple fact that they occurred at a certain time. Entities break off relations with their sources, lose their common ground, and become meaningless.

Modern people are, as a consequence, alienated from their natural context and from other people; they are even estranged from themselves. "But the nostalgia for a lost mystical solidarity with nature still haunts Western man."[27] A modern person is still made aware of the powers of rhythmic time and the significance of beginnings as ways in which the unity and meaning of life are restored. "He has only to listen to good music, to fall in love, or to pray, and he is out of the historical present, he re-enters the eternal present of love and of religion. Even to open a novel, to attend a dramatic performance, may be enough to transport a man into another rhythm of time—what one might call 'condensed time'—which is anyhow not historical time."[28] Every time a person steps out of history, by entering an aesthetically constructed world or participating in a game or a party, even in sleep, that person is able to sense something of the rhythms that unify and grant meaning to life, and this sense grants existence a more complete "destiny and significance."[29]

Art is particularly important in this regard. The reason lies in the fact that the artist attempts, in order to complete something new, to sever ties with existing forms and products in order to come at the task of creation freshly. This means that the artist is removed from ordinary time, from human time manifested by ordinary behavior, and takes up a position from which to render human life in a fresh way. This movement feels like going upstream, like withdrawing from a present state of affairs that is perceived as inadequate, as requiring a new, creative act. Consequently, even though artists may not be in any way consciously or explicitly religious, the sacred may be recognizable in their work.[30]

This situation, according to Eliade, is pronounced in the dynamic and the self-understanding of creativity in modernist art. "The two specific characteristics of Modern art, namely the destruction of traditional forms and the fascination for the formless, for the elementary modes of matter, are susceptible to religious interpretation." "In effect we might say that for the past three generations we have been witnessing a series of 'destructions' of the world (that is to say, of the traditional artistic universe) undertaken courageously and at times savagely for the purpose of recreating or recovering another, new, and 'pure' universe, uncorrupted by time and history."[31] Eliade here reveals his intense interest in modern art as a manifestation of the human need to overcome a time that has become unreal in order to recover or make available a time that is fresh, whole, and meaningful.

It is also clear that within the spectrum of modern art Eliade has particular interest in narrative and the novel. This interest can be anticipated in his high evaluation of myths or narratives that grant access to a time different from the time of waste and fragmentation. "It is not surprising," he says, "that critics are increasingly attracted by the religious implications, and especially by the initiatory symbolism, of modern literary works . . . it is only natural that modern man should seek to satisfy his suppressed or inadequately satisfied religious needs by reading certain books that, though apparently 'secular,' in fact contain mythological figures camouflaged as contemporary characters and offering initiation scenarios in the guise of everyday happenings."[32] Modern fictions, therefore, perform significant ontological, even religious functions for Eliade because they make available to the reader "other temporal rhythms than that in which we are condemned to live and work."[33] The time of narrative is more like real time because it is further upstream, so to speak, than the time that we normally take as real.

Eliade could have cited Hemingway and Lawrence in his discussion of modern literature's potential to awaken in the reader a latent awareness of the relation of "biocosmic rhythms" to a "system of periodic purification" and to the "regeneration of life."[34] The force and shape of their fiction match well the temporal orientation that Eliade describes. Their explicit interest in ritual, in the symbolism of rite and of such natural phenomena as water (Hemingway) and the moon (Lawrence), and the temporal patterning of events and human actions lend themselves to elaboration of the sort Eliade provides. Eliade's orientation to aesthetic and religious phenomena in contemporary life, as well as his advocacy of the relevance of traditional temporality to contemporary needs, makes him an appropriate explicator of the kind of time that we encounter in the fiction of these two moderns.

Polyphonic Time

FIVE

Thomas Mann

T ime in the novels of Thomas Mann in several respects resembles that of Ernest Hemingway and D. H. Lawrence. We shall find time in his work to be no less primary than in theirs; characters are affected, even determined, by events and forces over which they exercise little control. And faith in the trustworthiness of time is as fundamental to the narratives of Mann as it is to those of Hemingway and Lawrence.

With these similarities, however, an important difference arises between Mann's work and the fiction that we have examined thus far. Rather than a rhythmic, cyclical, or repetitious pattern, events in his novels reveal patterns of interaction and conflict between differing kinds of people and contrary human interests and forces. In this respect his narratives resemble those of William Faulkner. Mann and Faulkner, consequently, depict time more as a social than as a natural phenomenon. In their fiction interdependencies and tensions appear within human communities and produce changes; temporal movement is the result of the conflict between the influence upon one another of diverse people and human needs or interests. The attention is on interactions in present time, while the direction of the movement is toward the resolution of conflicts and a larger, enriched community. In Mann's fiction, in contrast to

Faulkner's, this movement is rendered in primarily a positive way: "Out of this discord, however, and echoing the artist's comprehensive sympathy, the unity of mankind emerges as a symphonic whole of many voices."[1] Whether a society accepts and is changed by such a process or denies or distrusts it, the nature of time in the two instances is the same. An appropriate name for it is "polyphonic."[2]

The social quality of time is noticeable in the intense interest the characters and narrators of Mann's novels take in events that affect the status and meaning of German life. This is especially clear in novels concerned with either or both of the world wars. Characters realize that the continuity, and therefore the viability, of their society is threatened by these wars. The import of German life and its relation to its European context is called into question. Due to its geographical centrality and achievements, Germany holds potential promise as a unifier of European culture. But in the twentieth century it has played, instead, a disrupting role in the course of European life, and the result is a loss of cultural continuity and identity.

The central issue in *The Magic Mountain*, for example, is the conflict and possible relation between the culture prior to World War I and that of postwar Europe.[3] This question is incorporated into the structure of the work because the story, which precedes the war, is narrated after it is over. But this basic contrast is camouflaged under a far more obvious one, the relation of the Berghof to the flatland. The pre- and postwar periods stand to one another as do the flatland and the Berghof, with sharp contrasts and with some connections.

Both the flatland and the prewar societies, for example, tend to be unreflective. Hans Castorp realizes that his home environment did not encourage him to question goals and ends. Work was deemed good in itself, and one's social and vocational positions were accepted as natural. In the mountain sanitarium, however, innocence is lost, uncertainty and dislocation alter familiar patterns, and radical questions of identity and purpose easily arise. These are characteristics as well of the postwar society.[4]

Furthermore, Hans encounters at the sanitarium a far greater variety of behavior, ideas, and kinds of people than he had known in the flatland. His responses to this diversity range from fascination to repulsion, and, in the process of encountering pluralism of this magnitude, his own humanity is challenged and enlarged. Here again, then, a connection may be drawn to the postwar world—its greater mobility, complexity, and behavioral variety.

Finally, people in the Berghof in contrast to the people of Hans's earlier life, constantly confront illness and death. The reality of death, while also repelling, creates a situation that allows people in the Berghof to appear more aware of life's ambiguities and of the common human plight than the more complacent people Hans had left behind on the flatland.[5] Recognition of misfortune and mortality allows people in the sanitarium and in postwar Europe to be more tolerant of and interested in one another than are the citizens of the protected world down below and prior to the war.

After the differences have been felt and evaluated, Hans remains aware of continuities between his present and former existences. He recognizes, for example, that his experiences on the mountain had antecedents in his early years. At the Berghof he is referred to as the Engineer, and the interests in technological and scientific matters that underlay his vocational identity below continue during residency on the mountain. Furthermore, he realizes that his illness, diagnosed at the Berghof, began while he was living on the flatland.

The Berghof, in other words, has many characteristics of postwar European society: shifting moral standards, familiarity with suffering and death, international mobility, sharp ideological differences, antibourgeois attitudes (embodied by Naphta and Settembrini), the increasing influence of Russian life (from the obscenely boisterous activities of one pair of lovers to the iconographic beauty of Clavdia) and, finally, the pervasive sense of dislocation and isolation. This prophetic setting has prepared Hans to become a citizen of postwar Germany. Associated with both the flatland and Berghof, being both German and international in his orientation, and having both practical and speculative aesthetic interests, he is capable, as are few others, of adjusting to the postwar period.

The narrator and principal character of *Doctor Faustus* also reveal a sophisticated awareness of the conflicts that mark the times in which they are living. Both Serenus Zeitblom and the subject of his biography, Adrian Leverkühn, recognize that World War I ends an epoch begun in the late Middle Ages. This ending constitutes a crisis not only for German history but also for the individual artist. Simple continuation would ignore the cultural hiatus, and the music that Adrian composes cannot merely extend the tradition of musical forms. A breakthrough, something radically new, is required, and Adrian's artistic destiny is to respond adequately to the crisis.

Zeitblom is also aware of cultural threats posed by World War II. He is writing his biography of Adrian in Germany while the war is in its final, most destructive period.[6] He comprehends the destruction that his people have unleashed, and he anticipates its cultural consequences. The task of discovering or salvaging lines of continuity is even more difficult during this period than during and after World War I.

The relation of Mann's narrators and characters to the social and historical significance of events indicates that the artist as well stands in unavoidable interaction with the social context. In fact, the artist may be more deeply affected by and involved with social movements than other people. Consequently, art does not simply record the interactions, conflicts, and resolutions of various social interests; art is a party in that process. This mutual influence is nicely illustrated in *Royal Highness*. Klaus Heinrich, the king, holds a position like that of the artist because he represents the identity of a people. Furthermore, whenever he involves himself in their lives they are affected.[7] His cultural role is aggravated by critics and reporters who comment on his activities, magnifying and distorting whatever he does in order to make their accounts more interesting. Because events and their meaning are altered by his interest in them and by the public's interpretation of his relation to them, Klaus must develop elaborate strategies of distance and indirection. Correspondingly, fiction affects the events it depicts. This means, for example, that the fractures in German history created by the war are not only described by the fiction but are both suffered and mended by it.

The attention of Mann's fiction to events that are critical to twentieth-century culture differs from that of a historian, not only because fiction affects those events but also because the events are not unilinearly and objectively presented. The teller is aware of his own temporal position and experience of time while the narration occurs. Castorp, in *The Magic Mountain*, notes the uneven pace of his account; increasingly longer periods of time, he realizes, are being recounted in briefer narrative spans. He is also aware of the tension between the time it takes to read the account and the time depicted in it. Furthermore, he is concerned with the discrepancy between one's awareness of the passing of time and the amount of time that actually elapses.[8] Finally, interacting individuals and groups often differ so markedly from one another that social time appears like an assemblage of varying, individual processes unified in some unspecifiable way. Serenus Zeitblom, in *Doctor Faustus*, repeatedly notes differences between the content of his biography and the actual life and times of its subject. He even refers to the time of the reader, thereby providing another source of complication and tension. Mann further complicates the situation with an additional time, that of his own life during which he was writing this novel, and he makes it the basis of a separate narrative.[9]

Mann's novels, then, are attentive to and participants in the multiformity of time. This characteristic is central to Mann's art because it allows the novel to be a unique form for the depiction of the nature of human temporality. Public events and narrative time are placed in a mutually dependent and revealing relation to one another.

I

Time in the novels of Thomas Mann is, first of all, primary. His characters are carried along by events in which they find themselves implicated. They are often quite passive, and they spend considerable time reflecting on what has happened to them. Mann is resourceful in his deployment of devices that expose this situation.

Depiction of a family or family history is one such technique. *Buddenbrooks*, the work that secured Mann's reputation at the turn of the century, is a genealogical tale or saga, a major example of the subgenre of family chronicle.[10] The stress on descent and family heritage also plays a major role in *Royal Highness, The Magic Mountain*, and *Doctor Faustus*, while the last great family chronicle in the Mann corpus is, of course, the Joseph cycle. In all of these works characters find their lives determined or at least deeply affected by inherited traits, problems, and traditions. In general it can be said that we know the characters in Mann's novels in part because we know something about their parents. The time in which characters find themselves, therefore, is not of their own choosing; they have as little control over the content and direction of the times into which they are born as they have choice of parentage.

A second way in which the primacy of time is rendered is through prophecy and prediction. Certain characters are fated to live out some kind of previously decreed destiny.[11] For example, because he was born with a physical deformity, Klaus Heinrich appears to be the fulfillment of a prophecy made a century earlier by a gypsy woman. Consequently, his every action assumes an almost messianic meaning. And in the Joseph novels prophecy not only determines subsequent events and their meaning; many of the events in the narrative, especially Joseph's dreams, have a determining force. The novels depict an elaborate temporal interplay, therefore, between events and prediction. The characters are involved in a script that they did not write; their actions have a meaning that goes beyond both their intention and control.

A third evidence of time's primacy is that characters are carried along by processes—war, disease, and aging—they neither initiate nor understand. We have already suggested the importance of war for *The Magic Mountain* and *Doctor Faustus*. Like war, disease has the power to control and disrupt. For example, the residents of *The Magic Mountain* are, like corks on a sea, affected by the uncontrollable fluctuations of their disease, and they register this fact daily by the rise and fall of their temperatures. The life they share, the interest they take in one another, and their individual situations are determined to a large degree by disease. This external control is especially strong for Hans Castorp, who at first planned only a short visit but stays on when he is found to be infected. Similarly, in *Doctor Faustus* the advance of Adrian Leverkühn's syphilis is a constant, determining factor for his creative career; his musical compositions depend on the heightening effects the disease contributes to his mental capacities.

Aging, a third determining process, is particularly powerful because it is connected to the prospect of dying. This association is clearly depicted in Mann's well-known "Death in Venice" and in *The Black Swan*. In the latter, the principal character, at the time of her fiftieth birthday, feels like a fruitless husk cast off by nature. Deceived into thinking that she can reverse or counter aging, she merely demonstrates by her error how incontrovertible a process it is.

Moods and affects, neither understood nor controlled by characters, also influence behavior. The power of sexual desire, for example, frequently determines the actions and thoughts of characters. Hans Castorp is possessed by his attraction toward Clavdia, as is Potiphar's wife by her desire for Joseph. The behavior of Aschenbach in "Death in Venice," like that of the aging widow in *The Black Swan*, is radically altered by erotic interest. Almost the entire plot of *The Transposed Heads* concerns the attraction of two male characters for one another and of a young woman for both.

Erotic fascination is often aggravated by the lure of the contrary. Mann's characters are attracted to people who differ from them; light or blue-eyed males are drawn, as is Klaus Heinrich, to women who are dark and non-German. The young American, Ken Keaton, is attractive to the widow in *The Black Swan* because he is both much younger and non-European. Hans Castorp's love for Clavdia, Aschenbach's for Tadzio, Potiphar's wife for Joseph, Adrian Leverkühn's deadly fascination for the prostitute Esmeralda, and Moses' desire for the Ethiopian woman in *The Tables of the Law*: the allure of the alien and the different is ubiquitous in Mann's novels.[12]

II

The description of this lure of the contrary leads us to the second major characteristic of time in Mann's fiction. Temporal movement is created by the interaction between differing aspects of human life or between contrary kinds of people. Opposites, seeming to require or presuppose one another, are engaged in mutual attraction and repulsion.[13] Mann's novels expose several major antinomies of life that antagonize and influence one another, thereby creating movement and change.

The first and perhaps most important of these contraries is the need to produce and fortify structures for the enhancement of life and the impulse to subvert or dismantle them. Both society and art share this dialectic, the tendency to build up and to tear down.[14] *Buddenbrooks* reveals this complicated process very well.

A tension exists between members of the family who try to establish its wealth and social standing and those members who subvert the family's position. Early in the novel we are made aware that this house, divided against itself, will fall. The conflict, appearing between the Consul Buddenbrook and his half-brother Gotthold, is in fact described as "a hidden crack in the building we have erected."[15] Less clear, however, is the implication that all human constructions house the tendency both to be reinforced and to be dismantled. The tension continues in the relationship between the Consul's two sons. Tom, sensible and dependable, is destined to perpetuate the family business, while Christian, a poet, resents his brother and is oriented to possibilities that threaten the family's security.[16] The subversive role of art is augmented by a local leader of the Revolution of 1848 who, ironically, is a lover of poetry and a translator of Lope de Vega's collected dramas. As much as Christian, the political revolutionaries believe art has the power to dissociate the interests of people from existing social structures. In contrast, art for Tom is socially decorative and reinforcing. *Buddenbrooks*, then, does not simply describe a particular family and segment of German social and economic history; it depicts a constant interaction between the establishment and fortification of social structures and their subversion and replacement. Those contrary impulses determine the internal developments of both society and art while also complicating the relation of the two to one another.

Contraries and the tensions created by them cause constant movement and uncertainty in Mann's novels. In *The Magic Mountain*, for example, the education of Hans Castorp consists largely of adjusting to contrary forces: health and illness, flatness and elevation, activity and reflection, personal concerns and national or international interests. Castorp is able to find within these conflicts an emerging personal ground: life and death are not mutually exclusive but interpenetrating; love and disease or intellect and feeling are both opposed and bound to one another. He neither treats phenomena in isolation nor minimizes differences between contraries. Yet his life, while housing many contraries, also reveals a developing wholeness.

The Joseph novels are no less insistent on the importance of contraries and their interaction. The setting establishes a sharp contrast between the religion of the patriarchs and the polytheism of the cultural context. This conflict characterizes the relation between Jacob and Laban, as well as Jacob's companionship with Tamar, a former worshiper of Baal. Cultural conflict becomes increasingly great as the patriarchs encounter Egyptian society. Joseph can mediate these cultural differences because his strong attraction to motherhood, darkness, and death predisposes him toward Egyptian culture, and the delight he takes in his own appearance, especially in relation to his special coat, makes him more Egyptian than his brothers. Furthermore, Joseph's youthful dreams of a nondemocratic future conform to the hierarchical collectivism of Egyptian society. Finally, his interests in reading and writing tie him more to the culture of Egypt than to the traditions of his fathers. Joseph's success in the new environment is anticipated by tastes that set him apart from his family. Yet, when he moves into that new environment, Joseph does not reject his former life for the sake of the new. Cross-cultural movement and identity, such as Joseph demonstrates, are possible for people whose personal interests extend beyond and therefore unify characteristics of single cultures.

Another source of conflict in Mann's novels is the relation of experience to text. This tension often complicates one already mentioned, that between art and society. For example, in *Lotte in Weimar* Charlotte Kestner is both the youthful character in Goethe's *The Sorrows of Werther* and the aging woman who returns to Weimar in Mann's story. The conflict, based on differences between the fictional character and the real woman, is so fruitful because it reveals the perennial mixture in time of change and constancy. Charlotte is both like and unlike the character in the text and like and unlike her real youthful self. These opposites form the background for the figure of Goethe who, in personal style and interests, combines many contraries: he can be both discreet or punctilious and extreme or daring; his interests encompass both natural phenomena and the world of art and culture. This capacity to combine contraries allows his secretary Reimer to conclude that even God and the Devil are two sides of a single force.[17] This complex of contraries in *Lotte in Weimar* is further aggravated by the inclusion of political elements, especially the differences between Prussian interests in nationalism and military discipline and the pan-European culture which Goethe favors. Such fundamental rifts within human life, as well as between individuals and the causes they promote, do not escape Goethe. He struggles with this situation; he reflects on the conflict between change and duration in time; and he attempts to unite conflicting forces in his work. Rather than being daunted by the tensions that contraries create, he affirms their role in human life as giving rise to both uncertainty and growth.[18]

The principle of dynamic contraries is embodied in the two male characters of *The Transposed Heads*. Nanda and Shridaman both differ from and complement one another. Nanda, son of a cowherd and smith, is strong and physically confident, while his friend, the son of a merchant, is interested in intellectual pursuits; "on account of their very differences they intrigued each other."[19] Sita, the young woman who first attracts Shridaman, desires both men because of their differing strengths. The combinations in this triangle are, of course, further complicated when the two men decapitate themselves and their heads are interchanged. Subsequently, it no longer

matters with whom Sita sleeps, since she always sleeps with
both. When Kali receives the sacrifice of all three characters,
she reveals the nature of time: to desire resolution rather than
the tensions created by separated parts is really to yearn for
death. Temporality arises from movement produced by the
interaction of contraries; completion, the cessation of tension,
is the abolition of time.

The many contraries in *Doctor Faustus* are housed between
the differences that distinguish the narrator from the subject of
his biography. Although friends, Serenus Zeitblom and Adrian
Leverkühn are opposite in many ways. The one is restrained by
reason; the other is compelled by impulse and fate. The one is
temperate; the other fluctuates from hot to cold, height to
depth. Healthy and sick, Roman Catholic and Protestant, married and unmarried: the contrasts are sharp.[20] And as suggested
by the way their names span the alphabet—of the names Mann
considered for Adrian, all began with "A"—they include the
world between them.[21] Moreover, the contraries possess a complementary function. For example, both disruptive and con-
serving behavior can counter the environment. While Adrian's
nonconformity as an artist was subversive in his own time,
Zeitblom's writing the biography—an attempt to conserve
continuities despite the Nazi regime—is also a subversive act
which, if detected, would bring punishment.

In *Doctor Faustus* the interplay between contraries within
a person's life and between individual and group interests is
elaborated by the image of musical polyphony. So important is
this image that the musical theory in the novel can be read as
narrative theory, and Mann's novel can be called polyphonic.[22]

Adrian's interest in polyphony is almost lifelong. He is introduced to it as a youth by the stable girl Hanna, and its possibilities are inexhaustible.[23] He believes that it is an ancient
form, antedating harmony, and he learned from his teacher,
Kretchmar, that only some cultures are destined to actualize
its potential.

One of the principal characteristics of polyphony is its stress
on a complex of individually developing musical lines. Chords,
rather than primary, are occasional moments of simultaneity
derived from individual notes. In polyphony one is less aware

of the pause and resolution than of multiple forward movement. Polyphony allows for dissonance, and dissonance makes
one aware of both the individuality of lines and the movement
of tones toward new combinations.

Musical theory in *Doctor Faustus* suggests narrative theory
because the many components of this narrative are both contemporary and in movement.[24] Diverse and often contrary elements are inextricably connected: sublimity and horror, destruction as ending and as beginning, despair and hope. Yet the
individuality of moments, of persons, and of dimensions of life
is not compromised when each is related to other, often conflicting particulars. Furthermore, this musical sense of time is
important for the understanding of society in the modern period that the novel espouses. Both Leverkühn and Zeitblom
move to new forms by reappropriating neglected moments of
the tradition; as early music is important for Adrian, so the
German culture of Faust and Luther is important for Zeitblom.[25] In *Doctor Faustus* polyphony is related not only to narrative theory and to culture but also to ontology.[26] This relationship is explored by Leverkühn's *Apocalypsis cum figuris*,
in which the cosmos and the world of music are connected and
in which music becomes "an organization of time."[27]

Unlike these characters, however, others attempt to avoid
the conflicts that are produced by time as polyphonic movement. For example, the tension between contrary desires for
individuation and for inclusion in some larger whole can break
down into a one-sided emphasis.[28] Aschenbach's behavior in
"Death in Venice" reveals an unbalanced desire for absorption,
a complete corrosion of his distinctiveness. At the other extreme are characters in danger of securing their individuality
by avoiding contact with others. Tom Buddenbrook is aware
that his exclusive attention to business and financial security
isolates him; "all better, gentler, and kindlier sentiments creep
away and hid[e] themselves before the one raw, naked, dominating instinct of self-preservation."[29] The Germany depicted
in *Royal Highness* is isolated from its neighbors and, consequently, in a state of stagnancy. And the marriage of Klaus
Heinrich to Imma Spoelmann, the American heiress, is con-
tracted to break that isolation. As royalty, Klaus and his wife

recognize the danger of isolation from their subjects, and they struggle to resist it by continually interacting with them. Through these positive attempts to counter isolation, the new comes into contact with the old, the alien with the instituted, the outside with the inside, and the arresting of movement is avoided.

In addition, insistence on the exclusive validity of a particular position or an attempt to destroy the positions of others can damage the temporal process. Naphta and, especially, Settembrini are practitioners of this error in *The Magic Mountain*. The Joseph of Mann's tetralogy, in contrast, reveals a capacity to recognize that differences between people call for patience, understanding, and interpretation. His counterpart is Dudu, who aggravates such differences and exploits them for his own benefit.

A contrary danger is to move, in the face of differences, to an overly hasty resolution. This can occur whenever people are sexually attracted despite great differences between them. Thoughtless union can be as unproductive as exclusion or rejection of others. This problem is exemplified by the desire of Potiphar's wife for Joseph and by Aschenbach's self-abasement in pursuit of Tadzio.

Desire for the culturally different can lead, as well, to a denial of one's own culture. Mann's fiction contains much self-conscious scrutiny of modern Western culture as well as extensive interest in cultures separated from it by space and history: the ancient Near East, India, the Europe of the Middle Ages and the Reformation, and the world of Goethe. These interests are not ends in themselves; rather, they are ways in which differing cultures can be seen as expressions of various potentials within human nature. For example, both Adrian Leverkühn and Serenus Zeitblom are concerned with the past, but their interests are juxtaposed to those of other characters in the novel, such as Baron Riedesel and Dr. Chaim Breisacher, who are oriented to the past because they reject the present and think of history as a process of decline. Leverkühn seeks contact with forgotten musical possibilities in order to appropriate them for the present, to combine them with contemporary interests, and to produce movement into the future. Thus the past and other cultures are explored not for escape but for contact with the alien and for the fruit that contact will produce.

Several of these strategies for avoiding or arresting the movement of polyphonic time are found in exaggerated form in *The Holy Sinner*. Chief among them are the society's habit of banning dissidents and the royal family's tendency toward incest. Desire for greater homogeneity results in self-reproduction. The contrary move is toward factionalism and strife. This tendency is epitomized in Rome by the two popes, each of whom claims legitimacy and condemns the other. Grigorius provides a strongly compassionate antidote to this situation. He represents a moral and spiritual expansiveness large enough to transcend the contrary distortions of homogeneity and fragmentation and to restore the movement of time by bringing unlike components of society into contact.

The final error is comprised of incorrect notions concerning the relation of human time to natural processes. Particularly poignant examples of this are the mistaken attitudes toward nature held by Rosalie von Tümmler and her daughter Anna in *The Black Swan*. Rosalie is deceived by nature because of her sentimental affection for it. Yearning for the youth she has lost, she mistakes her flow of blood, a symptom of cancer, as a sign of returned youthfulness. Anna, on the other hand, tries to practice her highly abstract, cubist art in isolation from nature. She seems to defy the natural because of her physical deformity. Neither attitude is acceptable. In contrast, several of Mann's major characters—Hans Castorp, Joseph, Goethe, and Adrian Leverkühn—achieve size and importance in part because they are able to comprehend the unavoidable involvement of human time in nature without simply identifying it with natural processes.[30]

III

Along with its primacy and its polyphonic nature, time in Mann's novels also reveals a unity and forward direction that merit human trust. His narratives reveal that time moves within limits and banks and that it provides a forward flow to the torrent of human interests, impulses, and actions. Because his novels expose the social complexity and conflicts of this century, the issue of unity, direction, and trustworthiness becomes urgent.

In his fiction several receptacles contain the widely divergent events and interactions. One of them is the family or tribe. This is notable, of course, in *Buddenbrooks*, in which siblings display diverse orientations and temperaments. In the Joseph novels, brothers and half-brothers, despite their major differences, are required to communicate, and even Joseph, no matter how much his experiences in Egypt have changed him, continually acknowledges familial ties. The family becomes a microcosm of society, and societies in Mann's fiction, even such a diverse and bizarre group as the inhabitants of the Berghof, resemble extended families.

Discussion of *The Magic Mountain* leads us to a second device for creating unity amidst diversity and the tumult of temporal movement: common plight. While it is partial in its interests and is, therefore, by no means a perfect society, the Berghof unites a large number of people who differ markedly from one another in age, sex, nationality, vocation, and personal style. Their common illness creates a unity that counteracts the diversity. A similar situation exists among the servants in the house of Potiphar and among the prisoners in *Joseph in Egypt*; shared conditions create common responsibilities and hardships.

Temporal unity amidst diversity can best be expressed by social metaphors. Hans Castorp, reflecting on the social quality of time, concludes that even the life of simple organisms, of cells, is social. Life, at both simple and complex extremes, is constituted of societies and of societies of societies: "The city, the state, the social community regulated according to the principle of division of labour, not only might be compared to organic life, it actually reproduced its conditions."[31] Although Hans tends to resolve disputes into harmless compromises, his stature is established by his ability to take diverse interests seriously. For example, he discounts neither Settembrini nor Naphta but associates with both.

Like Hans, Joseph embodies a society of contrary interests and forces. No other character he encounters is as expansive and inclusive as he. Adrian Leverkühn, too, houses a wide range of contrary, even conflicting values: height and depth, old and new, beauty and ugliness, natural and cultural, cosmic and individual. His very uniqueness and value reside in this capacity. He can utter a new musical statement by first taking so deep a breath that he draws in a whole spectrum of human accomplishments and needs. These characters are more inclusive than their social contexts.

Yet family, common plight, society, and expansive individuals must yield to art, particularly to narrative, as a potential housing for widely divergent aspects of life. In addition to their concern for the individual, *The Magic Mountain*, the Joseph novels, and *Doctor Faustus* are cultural narratives. As one critic put it, "Synthesis is the principle that governs the pattern of the 'Zauberberg' from first to last. All other themes . . . are grouped, as it were, in so many pairs of answering melodies that ultimately interwine and blend their voices in patterns of a higher order."[32] In the famous snow scene of *The Magic Mountain*, "Castorp concludes that all the warring opposites, all the antagonistic values which have been so much part of his 'Berghof' experience hitherto, do not prove the fragmentariness and dislocation of man; rather, all these opposites are the function of—and hence are encompassed by—what is ultimately a coherent human wholeness."[33] In fact, the musical compositions of Leverkühn and the biographical work of Zeitblom establish this surprising paradox: the more complex and inclusive life (or *a* life) becomes, the more its unity can be sensed. Constriction produces fracture, while inclusiveness reveals unity. Mann's fictions, even those rather confined in settings and characters, open to wide, even vast implications. The narrative itself is the real "Magic Mountain," the consequence of an alchemy that reveals communality amidst diversity and constancy within change.[34] Much has been said about various techniques of unity in Mann's work: motifs that provide a constant pattern in the face of change, irony that prevents stasis, and the crisscrossing of experiences from past and present with resulting patterns of repetition. But beyond these particular strategies, Mann unleashes the potential within the narrative plot for wholeness and coherence, as does Adrian Leverkühn's music. The art unifies and moves forward much that is scattered and stagnant while not denying the individuality of its many diverse components.

An even more provocative aspect of the narrative theory that is an implied, although constant, interest of Mann's novels is the interdependence revealed between narrative and human experience. Individuals and societies can include so much diversity because individual life and social life have a narrative quality, and narrative time can be so complex because it reflects human life.

The ancient world recognized, more than do moderns, this interdependence between narrative and life. The characters of the Joseph novels are often preoccupied with telling stories. Furthermore, they view their own lives as stories or continuations of stories. They do not make a sharp distinction between history and myth, life and narrative, fact and story. In their stress on the continuity and interdependence between human temporality and narrative, the Joseph novels present assumptions contrary to those typical of the modern period.[35] In the world of Joseph no clear distinction is maintained between what actually happened and what could or should have occurred. Further, characters continually relate themselves to figures recalled from the past, and, in turn, they anticipate that they themselves will be characters in stories told to later generations. Third, Joseph lives as though in a story. He never loses his belief that his life has, despite its many extreme turns and dips, a single, forward, meaningful direction. Finally, because the narrative begins in the middle of things and takes a new direction at its ending, it represents human temporality as an ongoing reality.

This refusal to treat narrative and human experience as separate phenomena produces an important analogy: narrative always includes a teller, a voice or vision. In the Joseph novels the teller is identified as God; it is in God's story that Joseph lives. But this God is not a transcendent controller and manipulator. Implicit in events, God is that spirit in human time which grants it a forward movement and unity. Mann, in his Library of Congress Address, takes this notion and applies it to all human events. God is involved in temporal process: "For

God, too, is subject to development, He, too, changes and advances: from the desert-like and demoniacal to the spiritual and holy; and He can do so without the help of the human spirit as little as the human spirit can without Him."[36]

An aesthetic participation in narrative is like an attitude toward time that rests on faith, on a sense of participation in the grand polyphony of human life.[37] Movement with meaning, diversity with unity are marks of both narrative plot and human time. In both, "'the best is still to come'; he [and the maker of tales] always gives us something to look forward to."[38] As Mann says "what I, personally, mean by religiousness, I should say: it is *attentiveness* and *obedience*; attentiveness to the inner changes of the world, the mutation in the aspect of trust and right; obedience which loses no time in adjusting life and reality to these changes, this mutation, and thus in doing justice to the spirit."[39]

The most severe test to the faith in time implied by narrative plot and required by human temporality is, for Mann, World War II. For this, along with so many other reasons, *Doctor Faustus* is crucial. The novel implictly addresses the question whether the inclusive, forward-moving qualities of human time can survive the demonic and destructive forces represented and unleashed by Nazi Germany. Mann's response is appropriately given in his most German novel, a narrative ostensibly written in Germany and depicting German characters, German music, German culture and history. He also brings his art close to history by writing a novel that claims to be a biography and that includes actual people, settings, and events as well as credible reproductions of cultural crises and musical possibilities native to the time it narrates.

The most provocative point of the book is the relation of Adrian's demonic behavior to that of Nazi Germany. Important for this relation are emphases in the novel on breakthrough. The need to break through is created by the cultural impasse that Germans and, by implication, the Western world face. The creation of a new form, a new, more inclusive order of things, has destructive potential, but that aspect can be checked by an overriding sensitivity and humility. Human innovation can coincide with the discovery rather than the imposition of new forms. While attentive to the destruction of Adrian's attitudes and work, Zeitblom seems to believe that his music can overcome the cultural impasse and even move beyond the present German madness. The question finally concerns the relation of destruction, ending, and the demonic to creation, beginning, and God. Adrian's destructive behavior—his elaborate plot to rid himself in one act of both a woman he loves and the friend who courts her for him and his intentional contraction of syphilis—serves his goal of producing works of unparalleled inclusiveness and of providing a future not only for German music but for German culture. While also offensive, neurotic, and arrogant, his actions create or discover a thread of fulfillment that binds Germany's new future to aspects of its neglected past. Here, as in Goethe's *Faust*, divine and demonic, creative and destructive, obedient and sinful are included in one great movement, a dialectic elaborated in the novel by the lectures of Eberhard Schleppfuss.[40]

The evil unleashed by the Nazis, however, their pact with the devil, is exclusive and only destructive. Furthermore, unlike Adrian, who confesses his evil consorts before a cross section of German society invited for an introduction to his new work, the Nazis make no confessions and ultimately have nothing to show for their destructive behavior.

Yet, Zeitblom's biography, however negatively, is stimulated by the Nazi horror around him. Their evil has a place in the narrative and stands in implicit dialectic with it. This inclusion means that even the Nazi offense can, however negatively, be taken into the forward movement of narrative and human time.

This final characteristic of Mann's novels, faith that narrative and the time in which we live are undefeated by the impasses, crises, and horrors of the century, leads back to the first point, the continuous involvement of his fiction in actuality. His novels, even when placed in distant settings, awaken in us an appreciation of narrative time and its relation to human temporality. Primary, polyphonic, and trustworthy, narrative and human time require and reveal one another.

SIX

William Faulkner

The fiction of William Faulkner, although native in its pre-occupations and dominantly regional in its settings, received earlier and more serious attention from European readers than from North American. One French critic justifiably asserted, "He had been one of ours long before his own country had deigned to pay attention to him."[1] While there were additional reasons for their interest—less impatience with literary experimentation and sexual deviance, for example—French critics were engaged by the central role Faulkner gave to time in his work.

Two aspects of Faulkner's fiction became especially important in this respect, the depiction of his characters' consciousness, particularly in *The Sound and the Fury*, and his fictional societies' orientation to past events and their corresponding neglect of the future. These aspects conform well to two philosophical interests of French critics: Bergsonian theories concerning time and consciousness, and existentialist analyses of anxiety and orientation to the future. Categories from Bergson can appropriately be related to the first three sections of *The Sound and the Fury*, for example, because time is rendered not as external, general, or chronological but as inseparable from the flow of consciousness itself. Existentialist interests, on the other hand, are well suited to the social attitudes toward time in Faulkner's novels because the destructive consequences of his characters' orientation to the past at the expense of the future are obvious. Existentialist critics can advocate the morality of a contrary temporality: freedom from the past, responsibility in the present, and openness toward the future. Jean Pouillon's essay, "Time and Destiny in Faulkner," is a clear example of analysis based on Bergsonian theory. He says that Faulkner "places one moment into another and shuffles all habitual order because, according to him, lives are not lived chronologically. . . . Chronology . . . belongs to the domain of knowledge."[2] The Bergsonian distinction between human awareness of time and the ordering of time by reason is effectively made. Jean-Paul Sartre provides an example of the existentialist emphasis. Faulkner's characters "are explicable only in terms of what has been," even though, as Sartre goes on to say, we understand a thing in terms of its future, "through what it will be."[3]

While analyses of this kind were important for recognizing the role of time in Faulkner's work, their ties to specific philosophical interests tended, as well, to restrict discussion of the topic. Consequently, Robert Penn Warren and Cleanth Brooks have called for both a more comprehensive and a less specifically motivated study of time in Faulkner's fiction. They argue that the discussion should not be limited to specific aspects of the novels, such as the narration of consciousness or the preoccupation of characters with the past, and that time in Faulkner's work cannot be fully appreciated when directed to or by philosophical issues.[4] They ask for a more capacious and complex understanding of this topic in Faulkner criticism.

We can begin a response to their request by noting that all three of the kinds of time we are considering here are important in Faulkner's fiction. Personal or melodic time—the move of characters and narrators toward resolution of some internal uncertainty—is often found. One thinks, for example, of the importance such a process has for Quentin Compson in *Absalom, Absalom!* Natural or rhythmic time is even more a major force. The passing of days and of seasons, the processes of growth and decay, and the association of people with natural cycles and animal life pervade Faulkner's novels. Of greatest importance, however, is social time—the relation, often hostile, between differing kinds of people and diverse human interests within a society. As Melvin Backman says, the novels are "polyphonic."[5]

A second complicating factor in the time of Faulkner's fiction is the separation between temporal meaning and movement. The *movement*, extending roughly from the second quarter of the nineteenth century to the second quarter of the twentieth, is marked by traumatic and even violent changes. Furthermore, it is complex because the violence not only has been suffered by the people of Yoknapatawpha County but also has been perpetrated by them on others. The *meaning* of time, however, is provided by the social structure, which attempts to be static. Society resists change by separating, even isolating from one another, people who differ. The divorce between the movement and meaning of social time keeps change from bearing meaning and meaning from undergoing change.

Faulkner's novels do contain instances of meaningful movement, however, times in which the separation of social movement from social meaning is overcome. While these moments have little effect on the general situation and, in relation to it, appear tentative and infrequent, they are normative. From the insights into the nature of temporality that they provide, the pervasive split in social time can be judged as a disease. As we shall see, such normative moments, when movement and meaning are unseparated, arise from and depend upon trust. In other words, the depiction of a social time that is diseased is also the depiction of a society that lacks faith in human temporality.

I

Sartoris (*Flags in the Dust*) is an appropriate starting point not only because it is the earliest of the Yoknapatawpha works but also because it depicts various attitudes toward social change. The opening scenes of young Bayard and Caspey returning from the war reveal the major problem. The inability of the two, white and black, to reenter easily a society that has remained "silent, sickly desolate of motion or any sound"[6] illuminates the pervasive separation of social change from social structure. This disjunction between society and the effects of World War I constitutes an initiating problem both for this novel and the entire corpus since it is also central to Faulkner's first novel, *Soldiers' Pay*. Those who did not participate in the war are incapable of comprehending or adjusting to it; this failure reveals a continuing problem in American social temporality.

The young men try to effect some contact between their war experience and the static society. Caspey insists that black people, because they participated in the war along with whites, should hold a new social position. But his expectations are frustrated by an impervious social structure, and his protests degenerate into posturing and surly disobedience. Young Bayard, traumatized both by the war and by the death of his brother in it—a death for which he feels responsible—tries to share his experiences with Narcissa and Buddy. He is unable, however, to articulate the horrors of the war in comprehensible narratives. Restless and distressed in the static atmosphere, he spends most of his time alone, venting his inner torment by driving his new car at high speeds.

Bayard's new car represents a second social change. Not only more egalitarian than the buggy, horse, and driver, the automobile also threatens the isolation of the static society, opening it to outside influences. Consequently, the attempts of Colonel Sartoris, despite his precarious health, to resist and control its use are understandable. Further change is signaled by the failure of the society to recognize or to respond adequately to the behavior and goals of the Snopes people. While this family represents the infusion of a mercantile class into a culture determined by inherited wealth, the problem of their arrival is not simply an economic shift. The Snopeses insinuate themselves into the society without sharing the tacit conventional proprieties that characterize the attitudes of the established families. The practice of medicine too is changing; the movement from the Indian recipes of Old Man Falls, to Doc Peabody, to the young Doctor Alford, and finally to the Memphis specialist indicates a heightened impersonality in the profession, which the Sartoris household resents.

These twentieth-century events should be seen as part of a long history of traumatic social changes. The disruptions that marked the nineteenth century, especially the Civil War, emancipation, and Reconstruction, were also severe. Events of the past, however, have been modified by domestication in stories told in the Sartoris household. The newer changes are too recent to have undergone that process and may even resist it by being too violent, pervasive, and subtle. The war, the Snopes people, the automobile, and developments in commercial and professional life hold the social structure under a siege it largely does not recognize.

Not only does the society resist changes brought about by forces from without it; it also represses the changes it itself produced through a violent treatment of both people and the land. This situation can be seen in *Absalom, Absalom!*, especially in the complex character of Thomas Sutpen and in Quentin Compson's depiction of him as both violent and ingenuous, offensive and attractive. Sutpen's traits are shared by the male citizens of Yoknapatawpha whom he entertained at his baronial estate. White people in the antebellum period extracted land from the Indians, imposed on the natural setting an aristocratic social ideal, and enslaved black people to accomplish their designs. This exploitation went on largely concealed under the convivial nature of its perpetrators and, even decades later, remains hidden beneath a Calvinist piety and a Puritan code which grant white people the facade of an elite spiritual and moral status.[7] Telling the story implicates the larger citizenry as well as Sutpen, revealing the culpability of all.

Social change constitutes a threat, then, both because events of the nineteenth century, especially the Civil War, have been traumatic and because white society itself has effected violent changes on the land and in the lives of other people. Rather than by interpreting events, appropriating the changes, and acknowledging guilt, the people of Yoknapatawpha County locate meaning in a social structure disassociated from the history of change.

II

The society remains static primarily by isolating differing kinds of people and contrary aspects of life, thereby preventing processes of interaction, conflict, and resolution. Of special importance for Faulkner's work is the separation between men and women. Some critics have concluded that Faulkner favors the women in his work and condemns the men,[8] but the problem is a mutual one. Men and women are isolated from and even disdainful toward one another, and both help to create and preserve this unfruitful situation. However, because in this diseased social structure men have greater power, it is likely that women will more often be exceptions to the problematic conditions.

This division can be detected already in Faulkner's early works. *Soldiers' Pay* juxtaposes male comradeship to a female realm; men and women fight, have different values, and cannot interact successfully. In *Mosquitoes*, Mrs. Maurier wants the men and women to be together, but the men leave the women and congregate by themselves. In *Sartoris* the two realms are sharply contrasted. The female world of the garden and sitting room is presided over by Aunt Jenny, while Narcissa contrasts the "uncomplaining steadfastness of those unsung (ay, unwept too) women" and "the fustian and useless glamour of the men that obscured it."[9] Corresponding to this exclusively female world are the places where only men gather, the back rooms of banks and stores, the MacCallum cabin, and the Beard Hotel.

Perhaps it is *The Hamlet* that most fully presents the separation and tension between male and female. Jody Varner, "the apotheosis of the Masculine Singular,"[10] Labove, and Flem Snopes, all in quite different ways, live apart from women while Mrs. Littlejohn and Eula are removed from men. Along with these states of separation are enmities between men and women: the antagonisms between Will and Mrs. Varner and Ab Snopes and his wife over the dominant role in their relationships. An epitome of the incompatibility between men and women is the marriage of Flem and Eula. Although Ratliff acts as a bridge between these two worlds, he loses his role when drawn into the avarice that marks the male realm. Frenchman's Bend is governed by separation between the female and the male populations. Stasis results.

The separation between male and female worlds is often aggravated by anger and rejection. For example, the Sutpen story is made more difficult for Quentin to tell because he receives it from two conflicting sources, one of which is Rosa Coldfield, a woman angry with men, especially with Sutpen. Moving outside the Yoknapatawpha material we encounter, in *The Wild Palms*, a woman who is angry *"not at the race of mankind but at the race of man, the masculine,"* while in "The Old Man" the male character turns "his back on her forever, on all pregnant and female life forever and return[s] to that monastic existence of shotguns and shackles where he would be secure from it."[11] Narcissa's outcry in *Flags in the Dust*, "I hate all men," seems to articulate a pervasive feeling of Faulkner's characters for members of the opposite sex.[12]

A second manifestation of social division is the separation of people at the center of society from those at the fringe. The text that depicts this situation most fully is *Light in August*. All of its major characters live on the edge of a society from which they have been excluded and by which they are observed, discussed, and harassed.[13] Lena, the unwed mother, Joanna Burden, a vestige of Northern intrusion, Gail Hightower, the outcast in the midst, Lucas Burch, drifter, Joe Christmas, the illegitimate and raceless son, and Byron Bunch, the quiet bachelor, obtain their identity largely by their peculiar and particular relations to the center. While only implied, the center of society is strongly present in the novel and requires the fringe for its own definition as those it excludes require it. In addition, the fringe provides the center excitement, as does the fire at the Burden house, and offers it victims that satisfy its need to exclude and condemn. At the same time, the center provides individuals on the fringe both with a security that their positions lack and with something to reject; the latter dependence we see particularly in the attitudes of Joe Christmas. However much they need one another, the center and the fringe live in a state not of creative tension and interaction but of mutual rejection or, at best, limited tolerance. Their need and value for one another go unacknowledged by both.

A third instance of social separation is provided by the relationship of whites to blacks. This situation can be found, of course, wherever blacks appear as servants of whites, such as in the Sartoris and Compson households. It is evident in the frantic attempts of Thomas Sutpen to extricate himself from his relations to black people. The attitude of the Gouries in *Intruder in the Dust*—that blacks want to kill whites and should be lynched—is an extreme version of a general hostility which those with social power want to maintain.

The richest text for exploring racial separation in the Faulkner corpus is *Go Down, Moses*. Among the many vivid examples in the work, "Pantaloon in Black" is unmatched. The juxtaposition of the young black man's grief and anger at the death of his wife to the subsequent interpretation of him given by the white sheriff reveals how incomprehensible the black man's actions and deep emotions are to the white. Separation between the races is exacerbated by the eagerness of the white sheriff to misinterpret the situation in a self-serving manner. This story presents a sharply focused instance not only of social separation but also of the denial of the black man's humanity. The role of Ike McCaslin in *Go Down, Moses* must be seen in the context of this violent situation. Ike repudiates his heritage because his view of the relation of white to black people does not conform to that of the social structure. He establishes his alternative response through his association with Sam Fathers and, through Sam, with the wilderness. An argument is thereby created: if white people ought not and cannot subject the land to their own purposes, they should not exploit the lives of blacks. What is more, they should not do so to people to whom they are often related as parent and child, brothers, or cousins. While Ike, in his room in Jefferson, has adopted a morally sensitive position in response to the heritage of curse and crime, his solution is too private to match the measure of evil inherent in the social structure.

The society restricts movement by preventing interaction

between people: male and female, insiders and outsiders, whites and blacks. Without interaction there is no change, and social meaning consequently remains static. A similar problem exists in the relation of various aspects or interests of human life, such as nature and culture or past and present. In *As I Lay Dying* and *The Sound and the Fury* these two kinds of divorce are clearly seen.

Although we may sentimentally expect that people exposed to nature will live in rapport with it, this is not the case in *As I Lay Dying*. Culture and nature are both boldly depicted in this text, but they stand at odds. Culture is epitomized in the human act of burying the dead; nature is presented in all its elements: water by the flood, fire in a burning barn, earth through the long distance, and air in the odor of the decaying body and the buzzards it attracts. While the Bundrens may appear to have a close contact with nature, they live separated from it. Addie's attitude toward language, Anse's interest in the cosmetic effects of false teeth, Cash's vulnerability to accidents, and Dewey Dell's rejection of her pregnancy all reveal life not in rapport with but distant from and opposed to nature. Darl, who is sensitive to natural change, is in turn threatening to others. Finally, the journey to bury Addie in Jefferson rather than in the countryside is a fulfillment of her longstanding rejection of rural life. The Bundrens, like all others in the work—the Tulls, Armstids, MacGowen, and the storekeepers of Jefferson—live in a society that stands in opposition to nature.

The separation of the past from the present, which we find in *The Sound and the Fury*, results from a general design, however unconscious, to avoid movement within the structure of social values. The design appears primarily through the way the sons treat the present as though it were the past. For Benjy, present moments are stimuli that catapult him into the past, especially to a set of traumatic losses and separations. Quentin continues to live out a role taken from the past, however inapplicable that role may be for his present circumstances. And Jason attacks the present and future enraged by the unfair treatment he has, he thinks, received in the past. Disjunction between past and present also appears in the relation of the children both to one another and to their parents. Lack of adequate parents, a problem that many children in Faulkner's novels suffer,[14] often leads to a break between children and their heritage because the parents fail adequately to mediate or interpret the past. Furthermore, children, because they lack adequate parents, damage their sibling relationships by becoming parents to one another. In *The Sound and the Fury* Quentin plays the fatherly role of protecting his sister's virginity, Caddy mothers Benjy, and Jason provides for the household. Parents even can become their offspring's children, as demonstrated by Mrs. Compson's dependence upon Jason. This unfortunate relation of children to parents is one way in which the present and the past are set at odds. The most important result of this separation is that temporal continuity is lost. No meaningful change can occur.

The separation of culture from nature and of present from past is characteristic of a society that also divides men from women, central from peripheral, and white from black. Consequently, the movement that would take place if contraries in life or if differing kinds of people were in a state of interaction is prevented. The structure of social meaning has been erected to frustrate movement, and the social changes that do occur lack acceptable meaning. Movement and meaning are divorced. The rift between actions that produce change and those that are determined by the meaning and value of the established society is a defining characteristic of Yoknapatawpha time.

III

The third component of social time in Faulkner's fiction is the set of paradigmatic moments that reveal the diseased situation of the society. In these instances, the movement and the meaning of human time are unified. While tentative and rare in comparison with the pervasive form that time takes in the fiction, paradigmatic moments occur whenever differing kinds of people or contrary aspects of human life interact positively. Such moments are potent and unexpected, instances of generally unacknowledged temporal possibilities.

One example is the Christmas dinner which Bayard Sartoris shares with the black family just before his departure from Yoknapatawpha County. The rapprochement at Christmas of these very different people, the guilt-ridden, restless, wealthy white man and the poor, rural black family, is an extraordinary event: "two opposed concepts antipathetic by race, blood, nature and environment, touching for a moment and fused within an illusion—humankind forgetting its lust and coward-ice and greed for a day. 'Chris'mus,' the woman murmured shyly."[15] For an instant, the separation between man and woman, central and peripheral, black and white is overcome. It is a moment of reality in which the general situation can be judged as "an illusion."

A second, often-noted instance is the Easter morning sec-tion of *The Sound and the Fury*. The experience of Dilsey can do nothing to alleviate the conditions depicted by the rest of the work, but her spiritual participation in the wholeness of time stands as an alternative to the disjunction of time in the sons' experiences.[16] The occurrence is similar to the worship service near the end of *Soldiers' Pay*. Like these moments, too, is the role of Nancy in *Requiem for a Nun*, although the mur-der she has committed seems, as Michael Millgate points out, to block the reader's access to her faith and self-sacrificial act.[17] Such instances reveal that the burden of broken time and the loneliness it produces can be alleviated when "all the longing of mankind for a Oneness with Something, somewhere,"[18] is at least temporarily satisfied.

The promising relation between a man and a woman, such as the coming together of Lena Grove and Byron Bunch toward the end of *Light in August*, can also provide a normative mo-ment. True, this relationship is not consummated, and it is de-picted indirectly through the report of the furniture dealer to his wife. Yet it is a tentative union of "two opposed concepts antipathetic by . . . nature and environment."[19] Lena is very much female, even an earth goddess. While her nature is gener-ous and her trust is charming, her carefree attitude is rather irresponsible, and she is overly dependent on other people. By-ron, by contrast not self-indulgent, is studiously responsible. He brings to Lena the kind of social legitimacy she lacks and undervalues. Byron and Lena need one another. Their coming together is a rare event in the Faulkner corpus, sacred, as Ike McCaslin describes such moments in *Go Down, Moses*: "I think that every man and woman, at the instant when it dont even matter whether they marry or not, I think that whether they marry then or afterward or dont never, at that instant the two of them together were God."[20] Because separation and antagonism between man and woman are so common in Faulkner's fiction, infrequent moments of union carry great weight.

Another way in which the separation between movement and meaning can be overcome is by the narrative imagination. This is found in Quentin Compson's achievement of telling the Sutpen story. The story emerges from antipathetic female and male perspectives. It concerns the violence perpetrated on the land and on black people by whites desiring an aristocratic society. It involves incestuous attraction, to which Quentin himself is vulnerable, and it requires interpreting a history that was not mediated, as it should have been, by Quentin's father. It transpires in the presence of an outsider, the Canadian Shreve. Despite these difficulties, whole cloth is woven from many strands. Here, or at other moments in the Faulkner corpus, such as those associated with that "damned unique" Chick Mallison,[21] the antinomies of cultural conflict and the separation of social movement from meaning can be transcended by interpretation and imagination.

Although paradigmatic moments are scattered throughout Faulkner's fiction, *The Reivers* has a disproportionate number of them. For example, Lucius Priest, because he benefitted from such a relationship himself, does a good job of mediating the past to his grandson. In addition, Jefferson does not hold an isolated and defensive position. Some virtues of Jefferson have a creative effect in Memphis, as indicated by the redemption of Everbe as a result of Lucius's fight with Otis. The story also depicts an increasing respect from white people toward black, seen in the relation between Lucius and Uncle Parsham and Ned. The uniting of a man and woman is portrayed in Boon Hogganbeck's change from one who visits prostitutes to one who is a good husband and father and Everbe's change from being a prostitute to being a wife and mother. Furthermore, throughout the story there is commentary on the moral consequence of temporal change and on the need to accept movement or "Motion" as meaningful.[22] *The Reivers* gives us, more than any other text, positive examples of what Michael Millgate points to as "perhaps Faulkner's single most fundamental belief . . . that life was motion."[23] Human life is, or ought to be recognized as, motion, and motion, as we have seen, is meaningful movement.[24]

The paradigmatic moments in the Faulkner corpus are not sufficiently inclusive or forceful to match the problems in the established society. The rift in its temporality between a change that lacks acceptable meaning and a social structure that resists change is too great. More particularly, these rare occurrences are not able to bring differing kinds of people and contrary aspects of life into continuing, productive, but also unpredictable, interaction. Yet they do provide points from which the social time characteristic of Yoknapatawpha can be judged as unfortunate. Although these moments do not provide clear directives for solving the many problems created by the system of temporality without a fundamental change in that structure itself, they do grant relief from the impasse created by the pervasive social time. Moreover, they adumbrate an alternative future.

The fundamental change that would be required is an attitude of faith. Trust undergirds meaningful interaction. Acceptance of life as "Motion" affirms that a society should be unafraid of open relationships between contraries. Required is a belief that meaning can change and that change can be meaningful. As Frederick Hoffman asserts, "Above all the reader must understand that Faulkner sees time in a complex of human tensions."[25] Fearing these tensions because they lack faith in the processes and results of interaction, characters restrict their options; they resist the meaning in movement and avoid in the social structure an interaction that would produce change.

Human temporality that is not diseased, then, requires faith, vulnerability to "Motion," and trust that out of interaction between dissimilar people and between contrary aspects of life meaning will arise. This faith releases the fullness of human life, a fullness which, as Olga Vickery states, "consists of submitting to time and change while preserving . . . identity and . . . continuity."[26]

SEVEN

Alfred North Whitehead

Distant though they are from one another in so many important respects, Thomas Mann and William Faulkner can be placed together in this section because temporality in their fiction is polyphonic. By this I mean that time is fundamentally a process resulting from the interaction, dissonance, and resolution between individuals, groups of people, and diverse social, political, or cultural interests. While sharing this common form, polyphonic movement is positively rendered in Mann's novels, while in Faulkner's the society suffers from an attempt to impede the process that interaction between contrary people and interests would produce.

Thomas Mann's novels are almost encyclopedic in the diversity of human interests, social, political, and cultural, that they contain. These interests, often identified with particular characters, are not subjected to one particular emphasis; rather, their individuality is protected in the narrative process, and that individuality is enhanced more than compromised by interaction with representatives of differing concerns. True, Mann often gives us a single character to provide us a touchstone in the welter of conflicting interests his novels present— Hans Castorp, Goethe, Joseph, or Zeitblom, for example—but these characters secure their stature neither by submitting the variety of particulars they encounter to some single theory nor by separating among diverse considerations those that are worthy of consideration from those that are not. Rather, they have their stature by the ability to hold contrary interests in suspension and to take seriously a wide range of human experiences and preoccupations.

The effect of Mann's novels, even when they are set in India, the ancient Near East, or the Middle Ages, is to affirm that Western culture in our time, while it may seem to be threatened both by the vast number of differing human influences and interests and by the destructive conflicts that these differences have caused, can still be carried along by the polyphonic process of social interaction. Indeed, as we saw, attempting to restrict this process, to make human life less complicated, or to be selective as to what human interests shall be granted place in the process, is to subvert the forward movement and the encompassing unity of human temporality. Consequently, it is less surprising that Mann's fiction is so encyclopedic than that it is as economical as it so often is. A long list of human factors, of sets of contraries, and of conflicting forces in Western social and cultural life are included: East and West, national and international identity, technology and art, action and reflection, nature and culture—the list could go on.

We encounter a very different world in Faulkner's fiction. It is limited by a setting remote from the world of high art, urban centers, and international exchange common to Mann's work. Here, while the range is more constricted and the issues more personal and provincial, the differences and separations between kinds of people and human interests are more pronounced and retained. Men and women, those with social status and those on the fringes of society, blacks and whites, while aware of one another, inhabit worlds of their own distanced from their contraries. Other interests, such as traditional styles and technological change, rather than interact, threaten and resist one another. But while more negative and social than Mann's positive rendering of political and cultural interactions, Faulkner makes similar assumptions concerning human time. Time is actually a process produced by the interaction between particular lines of human concern and force. Time, in other words, is polyphonic.

This kind of time could be explicated with help from social and cultural theorists who have provided significant analyses of the process of sociocultural change. We could discuss the variety of temporal processes that operate within complex societies, and we could explore the reasons why sociological analyses differ from historical because of the recognition the former grant to the multiplicity of times. Social theorists, unlike historians, do not subject this multiplicity to a single, historical movement.[1] Such theorists also discern differences in social time depending upon the orientation of a society, whether external or internal. And social analyses have been extended to cultural change in such work as that of Pitirim Sorokin.[2] Work of this kind would make the point clearly that sociocultural processes, along with their political forms and expressions, constitute a particular kind of temporality; they reveal, as one theorist puts it, a temporality produced by "the unity and conflict of opposing forces."[3]

But tied as sociocultural theorists are to the empirical situations that ground their work, they do not grant us the level of abstraction that will allow us, however artificially, to understand what is at stake in this particular form of human temporality and how it can be broadly compared to others. To do so, we shall turn not to a theorist of social time but to a metaphysician whose philosophy of time is social or polyphonic, Alfred North Whitehead.

I

The usefulness of polyphony as a metaphor for understanding Whitehead's philosophy is nicely articulated by Milič Čapek. Čapek notes the similarities between ontological and musical processes. Because of their essentially temporal nature, musical structures help us to understand a philosophy such as Whitehead's, radically temporal as it is. Just as "every musical structure is by its own nature unfolding and incomplete; so is cosmic becoming, the time-space of modern physics."[4] A musical tone, for example, is produced by its relation to its antecedent as much as by its individuality and novelty.

Čapek points out particularly how revealing polyphony is when employed as a metaphor for the kind of time that Whitehead articulates. In polyphony, he says, "two or several melodically independent movements, whether harmonious or dissonant, are going on." "Thus," he goes on to say, "the polyphonic pattern is a concrete exemplification of what Whitehead called by the term, significantly borrowed also from the language of music, 'unison of becoming.'"[5] Polyphony is so apt a metaphor for Čapek and for Whitehead because both are working with the consequences for time produced by developments in modern physics, particularly relativity and quantum theory.

While no elaborate treatment of time in modern physics is required here, we should keep in mind the kind of Copernican revolution it created. For just as a geocentric universe suits common sense since we relate to the world around us from our own position as a center, so also Newtonian and other forms of absolute time are compatible with common sense. Consequently, just as it takes a particular effort of mind to remember that our position in the universe differs vastly from what it appears, indeed that the notion of "center" is problematic in the actual isotropic situation that prevails, so also time is not the inclusive whole that our clocks and common assumptions lead us to think.

The principal point to bear in mind is that Whitehead works with the modern notion that time, rather than something we share in common, rather than something that is a unifying container for events, is actually our name for an innumerable series of individual processes. And there is no privileged position from which to view this plethora of processes as subjected to one that dominates them. Such a position is merely a particular perspective. Čapek refers to time so understood as the co-becoming or contemporaneity of "causal tubes."[6]

Polyphony can help us understand this sense of time. Various melodic lines can intersect and react with one another in a musical piece without loss to their individuality. This musical metaphor not only emphasizes, then, the radically temporal nature of Whitehead's cosmology; it also points out that this temporality is constituted by an unnumbered array of particular tubular or epochal processes which are in varying states of distance and proximity, dissonance and harmony with one another.

II

The entire effort of Whitehead's philosophy is to present a coherent depiction of reality in temporal rather than in spatial, in dynamic rather than in static, terms. This attempt, of course, carries a contradiction within it, since formulation or depiction of a reality that is constantly in process will fail to convey the sense of process itself, given the inherently solidifying effects of formulation. This problem is aggravated by our tendency to think of language as static, as propositional, and as dominated by the verb "to be." Consequently, any description of reality as a process is bound to be incomplete, tentative, and largely open-ended.

One of Whitehead's basic moves, then, is to depict reality not as constituted by particles of matter but by events or actual occasions. Implied in this move is a shift from being to becoming, from substance to process, from entity as thing to entity as occurrence. Implied, as well, is a refusal to think of time in some classical or Newtonian sense as a reality in itself. Indeed, it is not fruitful to look in Whitehead's philosophy for a separate discussion of time. To treat time itself as an entity or individual instances of time as entities is an example of what he calls the fallacy of misplaced concreteness.[7] "Time," as we generally use that word, is an abstraction from process and should not be mistaken for something real. Consequently, Whitehead does not believe that time is a whole in which moments of time find their place nor that instances of time have a reality apart from any event. There is no absolute or neutral time in this post-Newtonian formulation.

Process relies primarily on the sequential or causal relation between events. An actual occasion depends upon events that antedate it, and it will have a sequential relation to events that follow from it. Lest we think, however, that this causal relationship adequately describes sequence, we should bear in mind that an actual occasion also produces novelty for Whitehead. This means that of the possible antecedents that can go into the creation of an actual occasion, some will be included and others not or some will become more important than others. Furthermore, an actual occasion has a certain sub-

jective aim, which means that there is a measure of self-
determination not only in this selection and arrangement but
in the sort of unity that the various factors going into the event
assume. This internal freedom of actual entities accounts for
the occurrence of novelty. We do not live in a closed system in
which a set number of possibilities are played out. While there
are limits as to what may occur, it is not possible entirely to
predict events. This stress of Whitehead on the self-creative
potential within actual entities accounts for the attention he
gives to individual entities and to subjective terms, such as
"feeling," "experience," and "satisfaction" when referring to
events. While we will be noting the sense of wholeness and
unity in Whitehead's work, a matter appropriate to our discussion of time in the narrative form, we should recognize
his attention, as well, to individual occasions subjectively
described.

The process by which an occasion occurs is called *concres-
cence*. This is a coming together into an experienced unity of a
number of more or less diverse factors, a unity provided by the
subjective aim present in that event. When this unity occurs,
when the aim is fulfilled, novelty has also entered into the universe. Reality is constituted of a wide assemblage of diverse
concrescences. "The actualities of the Universe are processes
of experience, each process an individual fact. The whole Universe is the advancing assemblage of these processes."[8] Not
only human life but all actualities, however minimal and apparently insentient, are involved in a complex advancement
governed both by causal necessity and by a range of freedom by
which individual processes seek to satisfy subjective aims. "It
is to be noted that every actual entity, including God, is something individual for its own sake, and thereby transcends the
rest of actuality."[9] Whatever we say later about the unity of
the process as a whole should not detract from this stress of
Whitehead on the individuality, even the independence, of epochal occasions, of the relation between causation and novelty,
of limitation and possibility in particular concrescences. Indeed, the point could be greatly expanded in describing his
work, and it could be argued that most of the difficult issues
involved in the philosophy of time—the attention to event

rather than particle as the basic actuality, the relation of past to future, and the relation of duration or continuity to change— are focused on these formulations.

While it is true that Whitehead asserts the individuality of actual entities, it is also true that no actual entity is self-sufficient. With process goes the idea of interrelation. When a moment of experience occurs, it has a relation, even if only a negative one, to what preceded and what will follow it, and this is true regardless of the amount of originality evinced in that occasion. No actual occasion can be so novel as to be without relation, even without dependence. Whitehead's idea of "prehension" secures this connectedness. An actual occasion prehends, takes into itself, factors that preceded it, and it then becomes a datum that can be prehended by later occasions.

While it may be quite clear that an actual occasion is related in some degree to what precedes and what will follow it, there is little to give us immediate assurance that actual occasions that are contemporaneous are related. By definition, contemporary events lack causal relation, for if they were causally related they would precede or follow one another rather than be contemporaneous. Contemporary events, then, constitute an array of independent occurrences; "the contemporary world is in fact divided and atomic, being a multiplicity of definite actual entities."[10] Whitehead gives depth to this sense of the independence of contemporary events by his notion of epochs, so that not only the event but the process that leads to and issues from the event is independent and, in varying degrees, internally determined.

The notion of considering entities as contemporaries introduces the very important problem of simultaneity. With the demise of Newtonian time, of an absolute time that all entities share or in which all find a place, it becomes very difficult, if not impossible, to speak of simultaneity, to speak of events as occurring "at the same time." Simultaneity assumes a common temporal substructure to events, and it grants time what for Whitehead's thought is an intolerable spatiality. There is no common time to which all events can be related or which they all have in common. The notion of contemporaneous events, although less a problem, is also difficult because it suggests a relationship between events that is not temporal. Consequently, when we consider the relation of events to other contemporary events we must be careful not to impute to Whitehead's thought some abridgement of his basically temporal formulations.

III

Implied in the question of the relation of contemporary events is that of unity, and Whitehead's key metaphor for unity is a social one. Contemporary events are socially related. "The real actual things that endure are all societies," he says,[11] and "every actual entity is in its nature essentially social."[12] This can be said not only of an actual occasion; it is true of the unity of all events: "the Universe achieves its values by reason of its coordination into societies of societies, and into societies of societies of societies."[13] Participation in societies is not only a voluntary self-limitation; it is necessary: "every entity is in its essence social and requires the society in order to exist."[14]

Actual occasions have a social relation to one another because they do not have antecedents that are solely their own. Two or more separate entities can draw on very similar antecedent occasions. Some occasions, indeed, are widely shared. This means that while two contemporary entities cannot prehend exactly the same data nor do so in exactly the same way, differing occasions can prehend shared data and be creative in similar ways. Moreover, it is even conceivable that, while contemporary events and processes have only external relations to one another, there may be some level of awareness between contemporaries and some reaction to a neighboring process or occasion, either positively in some kind of sympathetic emulation or negatively in some form of competition or exclusion.

This matter of a society of contemporaries in Whitehead is controversial because, as we saw, it goes somewhat against the grain of his thought. One of Whitehead's major representatives, Charles Hartshorne, actually departs from him by stressing the social over the individual in describing process. For example, in one of his major publications, Hartshorne chooses a title that is a deliberate variation on Whitehead's *Process and Reality*, namely, *Reality as Social Process*. The stress on social process modifies, if it does not ultimately threaten, the theory of epochal reality, the idea that process is, so to speak, tubular. The idea of internally directed, individual lines of development seems to be compromised by Hartshorne. He says that no "individual is totally without sensitivity or responsiveness to other individuals" and that no existent is what it is "without regard for other contemporary individuals."[15]

A position on this matter contrary to Hartshorne's is offered by F. Bradford Wallack, for whom society, as a metaphor for relations between entities, can be applied only to sequence. Wallack's treatment is very much determined by his estimation that Whitehead's is a metaphysics of and for modern physics, for relativity and quantum theory. "Society," for Wallack, refers principally to the peculiar quality of endurance or continuity. "A personally ordered, serial society (enduring object) is what appears to us as one enduring thing when it is in fact a succession of actual occasions."[16] The relation between actual occasions is their mutual availability in contributing together to a new occasion. "Any two occasions have a potentiality such that together they can create a new occasion of some sort, however trivial, relevant to their mutual aim and real potentiality with respect to one another."[17] Thus, he concludes, "every occasion affects others and depends upon others; it is for this reason that the entire continuum and every occasion permeate one another."[18] It is only in retrospect that occasions can be recognized as contemporary.[19]

Interpreters of Whitehead such as Wallack, while they admit the social aspects of process in his thought, despite his emphasis on individual occasions, depict social relations as the interconnections between an actual occasion and the variety of factors that have gone into its formation. That is, the society is related primarily to past time. For example, another of them says, "Each occasion is essentially social, creating itself out of the data contributed by other realized occasions, each of which is itself (has its own unique associative hierarchy), but creates that self out of the contributions of still others."[20] Wallack flatly asserts, "no present occasion is prehendable."[21] Hartshorne, however, allows more effect on and more awareness of one another among contemporary occasions. While this may threaten process by opening up present time, it seems to be required by experience and by Whitehead's emphasis on unity. For if contemporary events have some measure of internal relation to one another, however negative that relation may be, far less strain is placed on the principle of unity. Indeed, however uncertain and elusive the formulation, one must emphasize both the individuality of contemporary occasions and a degree of relation between them.

This dual formulation is also suggested by the musical metaphor Whitehead supplies. It is a metaphor almost indispensable, it seems, to a grasp of the idea of unity in his thought. Here is one of many examples of its use: "There is the deep underlying Harmony of Nature, as it were a fluid, flexible support; and on its surface the ripples of social efforts, harmonizing and clashing in their aims at ways of satisfaction."[22] Discord is emphasized when the individuality of epochal processes is central; "the value of discord arises from this importance of the forceful individuality of the details. . . . It brings into emphatic feeling their claim to existence in their own right."[23] Without discord there would be no novelty. However, harmony is an equally important category because the many compose a unity; "there is the one all-embracing fact which is the advancing history of the one Universe."[24] Whitehead seems more inclined than Hartshorne to stress discord, individuality, and novelty. A more apt musical metaphor than harmony for this purpose would have been polyphony.

The matter of unity, which Hartshorne stresses, leads quickly to belief, religious feeling, and theological speculation. Belief is fundamental to Whitehead's thought. It is a part of the subjective description of actual occasions, and it is fundamental to his concept of *prehension*, that is, the process by which an event is related both to the objective data of past epochal occasions and to the eternal objects characteristic of its teleology.[25] Prehension is, among other things, axiological, for it involves the grasping of what lies outside or beyond the individual. Such goals as truth, beauty, and peace attract the prehending subject and lure it toward a future that finds its final validation in God.

God, in Whitehead, is ultimately responsible for order in the universe and for the appearance of novelty, responsible, that is, both for individuality and unity.[26] This doctrine of God is not a beginning point in his thought but a concluding one, for the reality of God is required by the description of process. Awareness or knowledge of God is not dependent on special revelation or religious authority but on reflection concerning those matters of relationship and value of which we are aware but which we mistakenly think of as derivative and dependent. Novelty and relationships grant intuitions of the fundamental nature of reality as it finds its basis in God. Since without God there would be no process, no reality, intuitions of the deity's role in process and reality are very significant. That sense of the whole that we have, of direction, of the upward turn of events, is a sense of the activity of God in the universe. "He is the realization of the ideal conceptual harmony by reason of which there is an actual process in the total universe—an evolving world which is actual because there is order."[27] God is the lure that allows the processes of prehension, as directed toward the future, to be conditioned by a reciprocity between God and the believing, prehending subject. Temporality could not be more firmly related to belief than it is by Whitehead, and this belief finds its articulation in a doctrine of God. For an interpreter of Whitehead with theological interests, such as Hartshorne, reality is described as a monarchial society of which God is the supreme member, "able to dominate the rest" and "coordinate their activities into a world order, a single complex society."[28] In an instance of religious expression Hartshorne professes, "so our least experience, thought, or feeling is an indelible note in the divine symphony."[29]

Although he uses musical more often than literary metaphors in his work, and although unlike Eliade he is not himself a novelist or an interpreter of narratives, Whitehead provides a helpful guide to the study of narrative temporality, particularly as it appears in works such as those we have considered by Mann and Faulkner. We find ways of giving thought to the proposition that in their fiction temporal process has reality and primacy and is not dependent upon human awareness or initiatives. We are able also to understand the importance in their work of the relation between past and present events—

the limitations and possibilities provided by the past and the possibility of innovation in the present—and the need, if there is to be human fullness, to accept change, along with continuity, as a given in life. But Whitehead, most of all, gives us help in understanding the importance of the interaction upon one another of contrary and often conflicting interests and forces for the creative social process. Finally, his work allows us to see why belief—the emphasis on the trustworthiness of process and on the ability of the process to take even highly negative events such as the wars of this century into itself—is essential to allowing temporality to have its way despite its uncertainty, to reveal order and direction in spite of the multiplicity of often conflicting memories and motives in human life. In other words, Whitehead, without directly saying so, allows us to see the invaluable role of narrative in the depiction of human life as sociocultural process, to reveal the wholeness that emerges from the welter of disparate events, and to recognize the importance of belief in and for an affirmation of that process.

Melodic Time

EIGHT

Virginia Woolf

T o the subject of time in Virginia Woolf's novels, *To the
Lighthouse* affords a good introduction. While all three
kinds of time have major roles in it, melodic time, to which we
now turn, dominates its crucial third part. Social or polyphonic
time is basic to the first part; natural or rhythmic temporality
underlies the second. Furthermore, in the third section of the
novel the defining qualities of melodic time are available to us.

The opening section, "The Window," renders a movement
from discord to new harmony. The responses of Mr. and Mrs.
Ramsay to the immediate issue, sailing to the lighthouse, reveal differences between them in personality and attitude.
Both parties must be taken seriously, for the narrative point of
view does not favor one side.[1] Mrs. Ramsay proposes attractive
activities which her husband, being more practical, must question.[2] Furthermore, Mrs. Ramsay's desire to retain her maternal role is detrimental to her marriage.[3] These tensions in the
couple's relationship are eventually overcome. Here, as in other
of Virginia Woolf's novels, negative aspects of a relationship are
included within a larger, positive process. Mrs. Ramsay describes it by using a musical metaphor: "Every throb of this
pulse seemed, as he walked away, to enclose her and her husband, and to give to each that solace which two different notes,

one high, one low, struck together, seem to give each other as they combine."[4] The resolution to which they move at the end of the section is not the product of their conscious design. Their relationship is carried forward from dissonance to harmony.

Rhythmic or natural time, while it appears in the first part of the novel, is basic to the second section, "Time Passes." Time here is relentless and threatening, "Day after day," "week after week," and "night after night,"[5] the house falls into disrepair, and people die. This is not to say, however, that throughout the novel rhythmic time is only destructive. In the first part Mrs. Ramsay perceives the sound of the waves as a murmur, "'I am guarding you—I am your support,'" while they are also "like a ghostly roll of drums [which] remorselessly beat the measure of life, [and] made one think of the destruction of the island and its engulfment in the sea."[6] In this as well as in Virginia Woolf's other novels, rhythmic or natural time has a dual quality of support and threat.[7]

The last section of *To the Lighthouse* renders processes of personal development that are, to continue the musical metaphor, melodic. Lily Briscoe moves from suspension and uncertainty to a moment of peace while the Ramsays' son, James, finds release from his childhood perception of his father as an obstacle. In other words, this section depicts the process by which these two characters, in quite separate ways, free themselves from the elder Ramsays' hold and become independent. Lily must go beyond the life provided by Mrs. Ramsay's designs, and James must advance beyond the shelter of his parents to a position of personal worth. While apparently small achievements, James's success in the sail to the lighthouse and Lily's completion of a painting which she had begun during the first part of the book are crucial moments of personal individuation. The melodic time of this third section completes the time of the other two because of its position at the end and because the earlier sections present the conditions that make the internal achievements of Lily and James both difficult and necessary.

In the final section, moreover, the principal features of melodic time are made clear. First, personal time is depicted, as it is in all Woolf's fiction, as forward movement into uncertainty. Both completing the painting and sailing to the lighthouse are ventures requiring individual action, and the breakthrough, the independence and completion, is unexpected. Second, the sense of death as a threat to personal significance is both a goad and a hindrance to personal time. Lily is aware of the death of Mrs. Ramsay, along with that of several others in the ten-year interval between the first section of the novel and the third, and James is made aware of the death of sailors in the sea he is crossing. The ambiguous meaning of death for the time of her characters can be found in many of Virginia Woolf's novels. The third characteristic of melodic time to be found in this last section of *To the Lighthouse* is the intimidating but also empowering influence of the past. Both Lily and James are aware of the authority of the elder generation. Mrs. Ramsay did not approve of Lily's interests, her desire to paint, and her unmarried state. The Ramsays, she in her domestic roles and he by virtue of his academic position, are intimidating figures, and this is aggravated by the respect the young people have for them. The matter is further complicated by the distance that exists between the first section, which has a prewar setting, and the third, which follows the war. The cultural hiatus produced by war means that no simple continuity exists between the beginning and ending of the novel. The Victorian past, impressive but imprisoning, must be both valued and rejected, and this occurs in the third section through the influence that the Ramsays continue to exert and the ability of Lily and James to move out from under it and to become independent.

I

The qualities of melodic time in the last section of *To the Lighthouse* are found throughout Virginia Woolf's fiction. The first of them, movement into an uncertain future, is clearly depicted in *The Voyage Out* and *Mrs. Dalloway*.

The process suggested by the title of Virginia Woolf's first novel, while including travel and social initiation, is essentially personal. Although natural and social contexts complicate the process of individual development, the principal movement is created by Rachel Vinrace's journey toward her own future. This venture is more risky and uncertain than the physical voyage.

Because fear of the future had been instilled in Rachel by her father, her development requires release from his control. Helen Ambrose gives her the insight needed to achieve this freedom, and Rachel's journey can begin: "By this new light she saw her life for the first time a creeping hedged-in thing, driven cautiously between high walls, here turned aside, there plunged in darkness, made dull and crippled for ever—her life that was the only chance she had—the short season between two silences."[8] Rachel's move into uncertainty is contrasted not only with her father's fear of the future but also with the behavior of other characters who lack her spirit of adventure. For example, the English tourists remain in the security of the hotel rather than venture into Santa Maria at night, as Rachel and Helen do.

The courage of Rachel's journey rests on a natural or onto-logical faith. Because she is amazed "that things should exist at all,"[9] she is also engaged by the wonder of her own emerging existence. This faith is not a sentimental disregard for the haz-ards and instabilities of life; she realizes that she lives in the midst of unpredictability.[10] She journeys upriver uncertainly, but the dense, exotic setting does not diminish her willingness to enter the unknown, to forgo security, and to allow herself to be shaped by the future. She reflects on the temporal quality of life with remarkable insight:

> That was the strange thing, that one did not know where one was going, or what one wanted, and following blindly, suffer-ing so much in secret, always unprepared and amazed and knowing nothing; but one thing led to another and by de-grees something had formed itself out of nothing, and some-one reached at last this calm, this quiet, this certainty, and it was this process that people called living.[11]

Personal time is movement into the future, and that future, be-cause it is uncertain, requires courage and faith. This venture, this voyage out, is affirmed in the novel despite Rachel's death and represents one of the principal characteristics of personal time in Virginia Woolf's novels.

We find it again in *Mrs. Dalloway*, although life as venture into the future is, in this novel, neither an affair of youth nor an experience terminated by death. It occurs in middle age, and it ends in continued life. But, like Rachel Vinrace, Clarissa Dalloway must take risks and have faith to achieve her movement outward.

The morning that Clarissa enters at the beginning of the novel is marked by newness: the war is over, winter is past, Clarissa herself has recently recovered from an illness, and Peter Walsh has returned to England. But the day that lies ahead also holds uncertainties. Peter's return reminds Clarissa of her own unresolved feelings; she had rejected him in favor of Richard Dalloway so that her father, a vicar, would approve. Clarissa is also challenged because her roles as wife and mother are being questioned. Lady Bruton, who thinks that Clarissa retarded Richard's career by resisting appointments abroad, has invited him to a luncheon. And Doris Kilman, who combines a religious fanaticism with an impressive grasp of modern history, seems intent on influencing Elizabeth, the Dalloways' daughter. Finally, Clarissa must face the demands of the evening party. Unlike Mrs. Ramsay, she does not engage such responsibilities easily, for she realizes the uncertainties of bringing diverse people together. Indeed, she prefers solitude, the "privacy of the soul."[12] Aggravating these specific problems is the general loss of confidence that comes to Clarissa as an aging woman and as a person who, because of the accidental death of her sister, rejected the religion of her father in her youth.

Clarissa's movement forward into her uncertain day is contrasted to the story of Septimus Smith. The course of his experience draws attention to the larger social-historical situation, especially World War I. English society, we learn, is unable to understand and to accommodate itself to those who experienced the war. Holmes and Bradshaw, Smith's physicians, represent society's repression of this important historical event by refusing to take the gravity of his dislocation and disorientation seriously. They expect him to return to civilian life as though nothing had happened.

The story of Septimus Smith also reveals, in contrast to the larger, inclusive narrative centered around Clarissa, a personal time lacking the support of courage and faith. Smith moves toward skepticism and cynicism: "it might be possible that the world itself is without meaning,"[13] he thinks; "human beings have neither kindness, nor faith, nor charity beyond what serves to increase the pleasure of the moment."[14] While the devastation to his trust in time, wrought by the war, is not a reason to blame Smith, the contrast between the two characters is sharp.

Unlike Smith, Clarissa engages life despite problems and uncertainties. She feels connections with people she does not know, such as the woman in the dwelling across the street and even Smith himself. This sense of continuity permits her to bring people together in the hope of establishing social unity. She does not accomplish this goal coercively, like Holmes and Bradshaw, who attempt to force social integration; neither is her approach utilitarian like that of Lady Bruton, who unites people for social and political ends. Nor is Clarissa's manner of unifying mechanical or abstracted, like the chronological simultaneity exerted by Big Ben. Yet somehow, at her party, Clarissa provides an occasion for a shared wholeness.

By facing the challenges of the future, Clarissa is able to accept her past, to develop a relationship with people who threaten her, and to feel moments of rapport with her husband and daughter. Most important, her movement forward into the uncertainties of her day is rewarded with a new sense of achievement and peace.

Clarissa's voyage outward toward a sense of wholeness is supported formally by the novel; the work is framed by her story. Consequently, the experiences of Septimus Smith, with all the personal, historical, and social discontinuity, are contained within a more positive structure. By formally affirming the belief that order contains disorder, sanity insanity, and life death, the work advocates Clarissa's confidence in time and personal growth.[15]

II

Personal time as movement into the future is always, too, related to death. Temporality is threatened by the awareness of death; yet the fact of death serves to define or to actualize authentic temporality. While an important factor in the three novels considered above, the role of death in *Jacob's Room* and *The Waves* is crucial.

The first of these two works explores the relation of death to personal identity. Jacob's life was ended abruptly, and consequently people have incomplete knowledge of him.[16] Personal time, shaped by lines of continuity that place the past in a meaningful relation with the present and future, loses an identifiable value when the process is suddenly ended.[17] Like the notes of a melody severed in midphrase, the moments of Jacob's life, however fascinating, are not related to a whole, and the narrative lacks full coherence. Exaggerated by untimely death, the point is more generally true that death always puts a person's life out of the reach of others' comprehensions.

In addition to death, the novel is attentive to other factors that make personal identity both rich and difficult to grasp from without. For example, Jacob's life includes the many places where he has lived—Cornwall, Cambridge, London, and Europe—as it also embraces the cultures and times he has studied, such as the Romantic and Elizabethan periods. Wholeness in personal experience is achieved from within, and it has an ambiguous relation to external appearances.[18] There can even be a disjunction between a person's outward manner and his or her inner content.[19] Consequently, when we ask what we really know of a person, we find that our knowledge is fragmentary and insubstantial.[20] This situation is revealed by the very fact that we spend so much time trying to analyze other people; this "character-mongering"[21] implies that "a profound, impartial, and absolutely just opinion of our fellow-creatures is utterly unknown."[22]

In addition, Jacob is difficult to comprehend because of the ambiguities in internal time. The narrator is attentive to the tension between constancy and ephemerality in an individual's life. Jacob's room is both a place where he no longer is and where, simultaneously, his books, papers, and work remain. Internal time also allows widely diverse events and processes to be unified within the individual in undeclared ways, as newspapers allow disparate events to stand together in a fixed arrangement, as though "thin sheets of gelatine [are] pressed nightly over the brain and heart of the world. They take the impression of the whole."[23] Similarly a culture has an internal life that unifies mysteriously widely separated materials and events; a university, for example, allows languages and literatures from many times and places to coexist, and in the British Museum, Plato continues his dialogues "in spite of the rain; in spite of cab whistles."[24]

Jacob's untimely death, while it contributes to the elusiveness of his identity, also grants access to the nature of individual existence. The very fact that his life is unfinished reveals the external, tentative, and even disguising quality of the unity that others perceive in anyone's life. Because the many aspects of his life stand out in their independence and even incoherence, the general truth appears that the real unity of personal time is an internal affair.

Appropriately this novel, concerned with the uncertain identity of a life broken off abruptly, is told by a narrator whose identity is also puzzling. Were it not for conflicting evidence, the Reverend Jaspar Floyd would be the most logical candidate. He had lived in Scarborough, had proposed to Mrs. Flanders, and has been looking for the letter she had sent rejecting him after he had seen Jacob in Picadilly a few days earlier. He had also tutored Jacob in Latin and, retired, had time to reflect upon the nature of Jacob's life. The enigmatic narrator allows the substance of the story, identity or the unity of a life as an internal matter unavailable from without, to be supported by the tone.

The Waves also explores the role of death in personal time. The monologues that compose the book reveal the thoughts and lives of six individuals. While there are shared background and interests and at times even sexual attraction among them, the six have little in common. Louis, although later Rhoda's lover, feels alienated not only from the other five but from all of English life. Rhoda, equally alienated, distrusts other people and lacks confidence, even personal identity: "I am broken into separate pieces; I am no longer one."[25] Her contacts with members of the group fail to alter her drift toward suicide. Neville and Jinny feel similarly unconnected. Neville, a poet, finds it incredible that his gifts are not more widely recognized. Jinny, meanwhile, is reduced to a narcissistic sexuality and is roused to identity only by parties and the attention of men. Unattached to anything, she persistently issues invitations to new lovers, while aware that aging will lead to a point when these offers will go unanswered. Susan, the fifth voice, has been submerged by her roles of wife and mother, but her total identity with these roles fails to alleviate her feelings of alienation. At the end she seems tired of her life.

Bernard, the sixth member, takes a more important and complex position in the novel. He is largely responsible for holding the group together because he visits the others more than they visit one another. He also resents them less than they resent him. Most important, he is directly concerned with death, and a major change in his life has been brought about by this preoccupation. This concern distinguishes him from his friends who are unable to confront their mortality. Bernard's importance is enhanced by the fact that he addresses the reader directly; thus the other five characters have been brought together and presented by him. Their attitudes, consequently, must be interpreted in relation to his.

Bernard's interest in mortality is not gratuitous for his relation to the group. Their principal focus is the young man Percival; their first reunion as adults is occasioned by his departure for India and their second by his death. Some members of the group are deeply attached to Percival. Neville loves him and is shattered by his death; Louis thinks of him as a medieval commander; Rhoda looks to him as her protector; and Susan believes she refused his hand. These attachments at first appear unfounded, since Percival, unlike his admirers, is a symbol of British colonial swagger and is more easily associated with sporting fields than with libraries. The members of the group are far more stationary and introspective; they have needed and depended upon this symbol of physical and political strength. Its loss throws them on their own, meager self-resources. The five, with nothing to cling to, are greatly diminished.

Bernard, however, has assumed a more active role. Once as spectral as the others because of his identification with words, he addresses the reader from across the table with a bravado that contrasts with his previously passive and dependent manner.[26] He now faces death, "hair flying back like a young man's, like Percival's," "unvanquished and unyielding."[27] The reality of his own life has changed him from mere spectator or reporter of events to a participant, and his own life becomes an adventure. By taking on this adventure, he may even assume, for the group, the central and consolidating position that Percival previously held.[28]

By presenting five characters who, in contrast to Bernard, have not accepted the importance of death for their own temporality, the novel is indirectly a lyric on the dependence of living and dying on one another. Bernard's ability to face dying brings him into life, from the static passivity of a dependent observer to a temporality that is his own.

III

Personal time, while it engages an uncertain future, has a simultaneous involvement with the past. As suggested, Virginia Woolf was intensely concerned with the role of history and its effect on the present. In three of her novels, *Night and Day*, *Orlando*, and *The Years*, this dimension of time is fully explored.

In *Night and Day* much of the difficulty that Katharine Hilbery faces in the present arises from her family's evaluation of the past. Her mother, the daughter of an important poet, lives entirely in the past and has set aside one room of the house, filled with mementos and portraits of the dead, as a shrine. Mrs. Hilbery is also writing a biography of her father, a labor in which Katharine is assisting. Augmenting her devotion to the past is Mrs. Hilbery's high regard for Shakespeare. Her literary and historical interests are shared by her husband and serve to determine life in the Hilbery home.[29]

Such historical obsession would be only idiosyncratic if forceful reasons were not offered for the allurement and authority of the past. The size of ancestors puts the present "to shame"; "'I think that my grandfather must have been at least twice as large as anyone is nowadays,'" Katharine says.[30] Although her friend Ralph Denham scorns this nineteenth-century regard for "greatness," the stature of those now dead is not easily dismissed. The lives of the remembered dead are complete, and consequently they render the existence of those still living small in comparison. Past lives are also interpreted, major and minor matters having been sorted, the inconsequential forgotten, and the compromising overlooked. They have a significance, then, that current lives lack. Finally, the past can be known as the present cannot; when Katharine moves among her ancestors, she feels that she is "better acquainted with them than with her own friends, because she knew their secrets and possessed a divine foreknowledge of their destiny."[31] Viewed by the living from the midst of their own daily uncertainties and trivialities, the dead look, as Mrs. Hilbery puts it, "'like majestic ships, holding on their way, not shoving or pushing, not fretted by little things, as we are, but taking their way, like ships with white sails.'"[32]

Because of their size, ancestors threaten to lord it over their heirs. A major problem for *Night and Day* is Katharine's need to emerge from domination by the past and to turn toward her own future. The change of orientation is made more difficult by the fact that other characters hold attitudes toward the future with which Katharine cannot agree. Mary Datchet, who identifies her future with her work, attempts to manipulate time; "she felt that no work can equal in importance, or be so exciting as, the work of making other people do what you want them do do."[33] Mary's style and interests disqualify her as a loving person, and she is related to Ralph Denham through impersonal topics such as "housing of the poor, or the taxation of land values."[34] Katharine's turn toward the future is also complicated by her decision to marry Denham, a man who lacks a prestigious family and despises the nineteenth century, instead of Rodney, a traditional and literary person.

The reason for Katharine's ability to shift her orientation from the past to the future, even to look toward the future as something "splendid,"[35] is not clearly given. We may conclude, however, that her positive assessment of the future is made possible primarily because she has a large appreciation for the meaning and allure of the past. While it threatens to imprison her, the past also grants Katharine the stature to accept the present and the future. She is affected by the size of those preceding her and moves forward on the cultural inheritance they have provided.

In *Orlando*, Virginia Woolf relates personality to culture by treating a period of history as a single life and by depicting a particular life in terms of a cultural era. The novel presents a period of time that emerges as a distinctive era when it ends. The moment is emphatically and precisely noted: "the twelfth stroke of midnight, Thursday, the eleventh of October, Nineteen Hundred and Twenty-eight."[36] Its beginning point, which coincides with the inception of Orlando's poem, "The Oak Tree," in 1586, is less abrupt because Orlando is aware of continuity with his ancestors, their exploits, and the estate they constructed. However, the poem represents a turning away from his ancestors' accomplishments and toward literature. Furthermore, it represents a change in style; the poem's language is more personal and grounded in nature.[37] The moment of beginning is also characterized by a turn from religion. The shift in orientation, from the past and to the future and personal expression, constitutes a major cultural as well as individual break.

Signs of the period's ending are clear. One, of course, is the completion of "The Oak Tree." Its publication, moreover, coincides with a change in poetry from being personal expression to a more impersonal quality. A second sign is the loss of the house. While this event is strongly tied to the occasion of the novel's composition—Victoria Sackville-West's separation from her family's estate—and while it concerns the book's social polemic against the practice of female disinheritance, it also marks the end of a period, of families as representing tribal histories and cultures within general English society. Coinciding with the loss of familial coherence is the force of technology. Riding in a lift, Orlando is aware that people have become surrounded, even conveyed by, things that they do not understand. The presence of machines, motor cars, and airplanes increasingly requires reorientation.

This era, from 1586 to 1928, presented as the life of a single person, has an individual identity. In turn, Orlando, Vita Sackville-West, and, perhaps, other people living in 1928 can be thought of as representatives or embodiments of traditions. The novel, therefore, presents the impact of the past and the place of a person in a tradition as important for understanding the meaning of personal time. A personal life like Orlando's can become as capacious as the family estate in which she lives. In *Orlando*, two points are mutually reinforcing: a cultural epoch has a single although complex personality, and personal history is cultural. In 1928, however, a period ends, and this interrelation between the individual and tradition, personality and culture, and present and past may have been terminated as well.

A third novel in which the importance of the past for personal time is explored is *The Years*. When, in the last chapter, we gather with the Pargiters in the present day (midthirties), we already know much about them from the more than fifty years of family history that has been presented. Depth is granted to the present by the past through the depiction of selected moments in the characters' lives.

Years prior to the present are depicted most often by single days, some of them eventful—as those days when Mrs. Pargiter, Parnell, and Edward VII died—others not. The predominant characteristic of the time is personal; even when public events are noted, the major import is their impact on the family members. The death of Parnell, for example, reveals the difference in attitude toward him manifested by the Pargiter daughters, Eleanor and Delia, and their father, Abel. This personal dimension, coinciding with a period of social, economic, and political transitions, 1880 to the 1930s, grants a complex view of time.[38]

Within this era of radical discontinuities, the time rendered by the narrative reveals the tenacity of and the continuity granted by personal duration. This perpetuity is realized by glimpses into the continuing flow of the family's personal history. Such continuity does not, however, mean that the Pargiters remain static. A number of situations—the deaths of the parents, the political and social interests of the children, the selling of the family house, and the travels of family members—indicate change.

Some characters, particularly North Pargiter and Eleanor, possess a larger perspective granted by knowledge of history. Eleanor reveals a good historical sense, and her interests in classical and Christian cultures provide a developed view of her surroundings. Consequently, she deserves her significant role in the book's final section. Other characters are more restricted than North and Eleanor. Edward, Eleanor's brother, although a classical scholar, lives in Oxford as one whom life has passed by. Kitty, the woman he loved but was unable to wed, prefers life in the country because there she feels that "time had ceased."[39] These characters reveal that distance can provide unfruitful escape as well as perspective and depth.

The sensitivities and the stature of the Pargiter children and grandchildren, especially of Eleanor and North, are greater than those of their elders. The depiction of the father, for example, is unrelentingly negative. Self-indulgent, sinisterly deformed, and rapacious, Abel is far less amiable than his children, even than Morris and Edward. Abel's brother Digby, while less disagreeable, is also cold and punitive, a man from whom his wife shields their children. Because of the increasingly positive role of the later generations, the public history of trauma and loss is accompanied by a personal history of enlarged awareness and maturity.

Eleanor is the principal embodiment of this movement forward. Unlike Celia's socially reactionary husband, Eleanor affirms the present and the future. She has recently traveled to India; she would like to go to Tibet; and she admires contemporary styles of dress. She is also stronger and more confident than North's sister, Peggy, a physician who is anxious about social and political circumstances, who is governed by clock time, and who believes that life lacks unity. In contrast, Eleanor thinks personal life has a continuity similar to a theme in music,[40] and, since the events of the future cannot be anticipated in all their dimensions, she considers life to be a process of constant discovery.[41] She lives confined neither to a house nor to a historical period, and, while others, such as Peggy, turn skeptical with the advent of social and cultural changes, Eleanor maintains her belief in the positive effects of temporal movement.

Eleanor's attitude to time, then, provides a norm by which other characters can be judged. Rose is haunted by the past and has a hostile relation to her present circumstances. Martin, better suited to the eighteenth century than to the twentieth, is dislocated, a military man who wishes he had been an architect and who regrets the loss of family property. Sara has taken an interest in religion, turned fey, and has written North that life is hell. True, Eleanor also has regrets and disappointments, but despite them she retains her fresh outlook. Whether enjoying dinner during an air raid in the basement of Maggie's house or, at the very end, looking with interest at the couple on the street below, Eleanor has survived a critical half century of cultural change intact, supported by a past that she does not want maintained or repeated and facing the dawn with anticipation.[42] The past she inherits and her attitude toward it somehow allow her to convey cultural continuity into the future.

IV

The three characteristics of personal time at which we have been looking, along with additional ambiguities, are found in Virginia Woolf's last novel, *Between the Acts*. This final work is her most elaborate and deliberate address to the temporal character of life.

Attention is drawn to time in several ways. The narrative covers a twenty-four-hour period, with principal concern paid to the annual village pageant, presented on a Sunday afternoon in June 1939. It depicts cultural history in a series of tableaux: Chaucerian, Elizabethan, Augustan, Victorian, and contemporary. The setting for the pageant is an old English country house which, along with the surrounding countryside, has existed virtually unchanged for centuries. And those who attend the pageant, especially the neighbors and village people, are tied to the area by long family histories.

Some characters add particular temporal or historical interests. Giles Oliver, who works as a bookkeeper in London, is aware, as others are not, of foreboding events in Europe, a concern underscored by the appearance overhead of airplanes. He finds the contrast between international events and the interests of the people at home disconcerting. Lucy, his widowed aunt, has a strong interest in history; during the time of the novel she is reading about primeval England when the island was joined to the continent, large wild creatures roamed the land, and thick vegetation covered places where urban centers now stand. Isa, Giles's wife, dislikes the present and wishes for an entirely new plot for her life. Near the end of the pageant she murmurs her wish that her life would also end.[43]

Further complexities arise from the relation of various characters to certain moments in English history. These affiliations are made particularly clear during the pageant. Mrs. Swithin, a devout Christian who is most closely connected to the Chaucerian scene, stands in tension with her brother Bartholomew, who is related to the Age of Reason. Their guest, Mrs. Manresa, identifies herself with the Elizabethan period.

The pageant itself adds depth to the novel's explication of time. Since the players are the same but change clothing for the different scenes, the audience questions whether human nature, or only style, actively changes.[44] Moreover, a radical disjunction is introduced between the historical scenes and the depiction of the present day, when mirrors are turned on the audience and the line between spectator and participant is blurred. The pageant is related to time, finally, through Miss La Trobe's sense of the insubstantiality of the art form she has produced; when the scenes are completed and the people disperse, her work evaporates.

Last, music is important for the pageant and for time in the novel generally. Miss La Trobe uses a gramophone to provide music, and even the click, click of the machine unifies people by its rhythm. The narrator finds music to be a way in which people are brought together and employs it as a metaphor both for the unity within the diversity of life and for the forward movement of experience.[45]

These many aspects arise from a depiction of time as natural and social as well as personal. The diurnal round and the annual pageant suggest a natural, rhythmic component to time, while the interactions of the various characters, especially between Bartholomew and his sister and between Giles and Isa, point to a social or polyphonic element. Melodic or personal time is epitomized in the quest for spiritual and artistic fulfillment manifested particularly by Mrs. Manresa, Isa, Lucy, and Miss La Trobe.

In this novel, more than in any others, however, human time is related to art, especially to temporal forms such as music and drama. "Music wakes us. Music makes us see the hidden, join the broken," says the narrator.[46] The pageant brings people together, and it reveals the unity of the history even while it presents discrete periods. And art releases the audience into life; as the eyes of the spectators often turn from the pageant to the surrounding landscape, art, rather than providing an escape, prepares for or nurtures a relation to the larger world. That encompassing environment prevails; the wind often carries off the words; the sounds of animals distract attention; and, at the end of the pageant, the people turn to other concerns.

Between the Acts, like *To the Lighthouse*, summarizes and complicates much that is characteristic of time in Virginia Woolf's fictions. It presents time as primary and, by virtue of its rhythmic, polyphonic, and natural elements, as complex. Time is also revealed to be trustworthy, and her characters move forward even though the future is uncertain.[47] Death, while a threat to the continuity of a person's life, grants identity and a hidden individuality to existence. Personal time is greatly enriched by the past, since characters hold within themselves not only the sums of their own experiences and those of their families and even cultures but, by reading and travel, also carry forward and express distant times. Virginia Woolf's novels disclose personal existence as temporal, and, because of this temporality, as essentially mysterious.[48]

NINE

Hermann Hesse

Melodic time, the movement of an individual or culture toward self-actualization and wholeness, also dominates the novels of Hermann Hesse. Like melodies, the patterns exposed by the experiences of his characters and by the culture have a linear form in which beginning and ending anticipate and recall one another.

Hesse's task is made more difficult by the fact that modern society, as presented in his novels, devalues personal time by preferring notions of time that are impersonal, uniform, and universal. Consequently, Hesse's work, no less than that of the other writers presented here, offers access to a time that conforms more closely to the potentials and actualities of human life than do the understandings of time that are depicted as typical of Western society.

Personal time is marked by several contraries or ambiguities. The first of these is the relation of the past and future to one another. If there is to be personal time, a never-ending search must be undertaken for a sense of continuity between the obscure past and a future that is always beyond one's grasp. Present time, for Hesse's fiction, is the sense of relation discovered between a person's origins and destiny. While the two always differ from one another—the future is not a simple return to the past but a genuine advance—the future is anticipated in the past and the past is recalled or illuminated by the future.

A second set of contraries marking personal time is change and permanence. Although characters in Hesse's fiction undergo transformations that are often quite radical, even traumatic, they also are rendered as basically unchanged. Personal time is actualized when permanence and change are related.

Finally, personal time is both individual and cultural. An interdependence is exposed between the two, so that the individual and the culture both require and reveal one another. The more fully realized persons become, the more they actualize their own potential, the more they become culturally significant and representative. There ought to be no antagonism between the development of individuals and the actualizations of a culture's identity.

We shall look at these three sets of contraries in Hesse's fiction, moving, as we do, from his first to his last novel. This procedure is appropriate because each of these three characteristics of personal time, while found throughout the corpus, appears to be a principal interest in phases of his work. The relation of past to future dominates the fiction from *Peter Camenzind* through *Demian*; the relation of change to permanence is primary in *Siddhartha* and continues through *Narcissus and Goldmund*; and the contraries of the individual and cultural find principal roles in *The Journey to the East* and *The Glass Bead Game*.

I

The importance granted to origins in the determination of personal time is clearly suggested by the opening sentence of Hesse's first novel, *Peter Camenzind*: "*Im Anfang war der Mythus.*"[1] This mythic beginning concerns not the cosmos or the society but Peter's life, especially the impressions made upon him during his early years by the beautiful countryside around his home and the integrity of memorable and forceful characters, such as his Uncle Konrad. In other words, a person, without realizing it, is marked by certain values, awarenesses, and expectations that, however unarticulated they may be, exert a powerful influence upon the rest of his life. This novel testifies to the force and significance of origins in and for a person's development, especially when they are ignored.

Another influence on Peter is his future. He is drawn away from the confines of a small, southern German town by the lure of poetry, beautiful and mysterious women, and the music to which his friend Robert introduces him. But the artists and intellectuals he meets in Zurich reveal analytical attitudes that appear hypocritical to Peter. Italy provides a more congenial setting. Prepared by his origins to be responsive to nature, Peter finds the countryside, the Mediterranean Sea, and the antics of animals appealing. With St. Francis of Assisi as a model, he combines this sensitivity to nature with aesthetic aims and resolves to become a poet who would give voice to the "*urschöne Sprache*" of nature through art.[2] But he discovers that he lacks personal integrity. While he can speak about St. Francis's love, he cannot himself minister to a sick and disfigured man. Aware of his personal deficiency, Peter returns to his home to live a less ambitious or pretentious life as the owner of a local inn.

This first novel establishes a principle found in all of Hesse's work. Beginnings exert a strong, even determining influence because they affect a person's future and are clarified by it. If the myth of the beginning—the prelingual impressions of a person's early life—is denied, personal time cannot be actualized.

The task of discovering the mutually revealing relation between past and future in a person's life is made more difficult by the society in which that person is reared, particularly its educational system. Modern society discounts the importance of this process and the primacy and integrity of personal time that it implies. The educational system represses personal time and requires a child to conform to a different schedule, to subject personal life to a uniform, universal, and impersonal agenda of interests. The conflict that results between a child with a strong sense of individual worth and an educational system determined to discount the value of personal time is central to Hesse's second novel, *Under the Wheel*.

Young Hans is treated by the pastor and teachers of his

hometown and later by the faculty at Maulbronn as though there were no values or directives already operating within him. His own being is taken, instead, to be a wilderness without paths or order,[3] raw material that must submit to impersonal forms dictated by society. Hans is taught to feel guilt for the force of his personal interests and needs. He suffers further from the lack of a mother, from an insensitive father, and from separation, while at school, from natural things such as fishing and the rabbit pen in his garden.

Because his own personal interests continue to influence him, Hans experiences a conflict between them and the values and intentions of the educational system. He cannot both answer the demands of his own uniqueness or genius and the expectations of his teachers. His own problem is duplicated by a fellow student, Hermann Heilner, who rebels against the institution. Hans, unlike Heilner, tries to remain loyal both to himself and the system, but he finally fails to do justice to either side. In addition, his schooling estranges him from resources in his youth—especially a sense of mystery gathered from stories he had heard—that would be helpful for securing his own development. The estrangement and the struggle become so severe that Hans, attracted to the possibility of an unbroken peace, drowns himself. Yet, even after his death, Hans's teachers, pastor, and father do not recognize their own contribution to his suffering.[4]

Under the Wheel attacks the assumption that a general, uniform educational process supersedes a personal one. Because the society denies personal time, the unfolding relation within a life between past and future, it invades that process and destroys the individual.

This first characteristic of time in Hesse's novels, the relation of a person's past to the future, is often expressed by musical metaphors and feminine symbols. Continuity between past and future is related to music because a melodic composition actualizes a direction established in the beginning. Melody reveals a strong, reciprocal relation between past and future. Female images for personal time also reveal this relation because the woman is, for the male characters, both the mother and the alluring object of desire. While the two are not the same, they are also not unrelated. The mother and the potential lover stand as interdependent figures, as origin and goal.

Both symbols, music and the woman, are found in Hesse's *Gertrude*. The composer Kuhn, by narrating his life, testifies to the belief that his music originates from an *Urmusik* in his own experience. His personal time and his musical compositions are mutually revealing. This belief in an originating, personal music is related by Kuhn to his attachment both to his mother and to Gertrude. Although he also feels somewhat rejected by his mother, Kuhn eventually finds her to be the necessary support for his work. Gertrude, meanwhile, stands at the opposite pole, as an ideal image which draws music out of him.[5] In her nobility and suffering she represents the direction of music toward silence and perfect form.

The story Kuhn tells primarily concerns this mutually revealing relation between past and future, origin and goal. This does not mean that he experiences a smooth passage from experience to music or from woman as mother to woman as ideal. His forward movement is often negatively provoked— by an injury, rejection of his mother and cousin, and inability to dominate Gertrude—and writing music is not something he does easily. The relation between past and future must be discovered by means of a persevering quest for a future that will reveal the past and for an appropriation of the past that will disclose the future.

Some of Hesse's characters, such as the protagonist in *Rosshalde*, find discovering the relation of past to future a task too difficult or uncertain to pursue. Johann Veraguth, a painter, is entrapped by stasis. In his life he has not crossed thresholds, and we find him desperately clinging to a situation in which he is stagnating. He maintains an opposition to his wife, who, he thinks, is trying to bring their younger son under her domination. This negative position is unproductive, and Veraguth is finally released from it when the boy dies.

Stagnancy is also suggested by Veraguth's relation to his art. His method is to impose his intentions and techniques on his material. For example, the painting he completes during the period of the story merely reproduces the situation that has developed among himself, his wife, and his son. His art does not venture forward toward some way out of the impasse. It is not an art of discovery. For Hesse's characters all art, even spatial forms such as painting and sculpture, should have a temporal and futural quality. Sinclair and Goldmund, as we shall see, are involved, as artists, in a process of growth and discovery. But art for Veraguth merely helps solidify an already frozen present.

Forward movement is occasioned by Veraguth's old friend, Otto Burkhardt. Their swim together awakens memories in Veraguth of his own boyhood, and the pictures Otto shows him of India and the Far East present a world that is both strange and attractive, a world suggesting a future different from his present, confining existence. In other words, forward movement occurs when the negative consequences of a static present are exchanged for the awakening of Veraguth's past and future. Preoccupation with the present produces stagnancy and resentment because it divorces an individual from personal time, from the task of discovering a relationship between past and future. The damage done by Veraguth to himself and to others cannot be wholly undone; particularly, his sons are lost to him. The cost of choosing fixed hostilities rather than the uncertain process of growth is irrevocable. At the end, however, his reorientation to time, the new relation of past and future, begins to show positive results.[6]

This first characteristic of personal time, the gradually developing relation between the past and the future in one's life, the process by which origin and goal reveal one another, has important consequences for the plots of Hesse's novels. Many of them depict the movement of a character from youth to adulthood. That process clarifies the nature of personal time because the achievement of adulthood, the attaining of one's destiny, is anticipated already in the beginning. This relation between plot and the nature of personal time is clear in *Demian*.

The first part of the plot renders Emil's struggle for freedom from his surroundings. Initiated into the church, he realizes that its myths are partial. Seeking a more comprehensive world

of meaning, he falls into the hands of the sinister Kromer. Demian delivers him from this threat, but Emil must then free
himself from the authority of his rescuer.

The second section finds Emil on his own, free from the mas-
teries of home, enemy, and savior. During this part he moves
erratically, from debauchery to the adulation of a perfect, unat-
tainable woman. Finding his way through these alternatives en-
tails discovering a connection between his past and future. He
does so by painting. The emerging figure of a bird represents the
development of an integrated self. As Pistorius helps Emil to
recognize, human temporality becomes a reality when past and
future, what one needs and what will occur, are no longer divorced. This fact gives rise to the peculiar narrative technique in
which it is not always easy for the reader to distinguish between
what the character is actually experiencing and what he may be
imagining.

In the third part of the plot, Emil achieves an extraordinary
level of recognition and insight. First, however, he must make
his way between a society that contradicts his values and an
alternative community, presided over by the mother and potential lover Frau Eva, that conforms to his deepest needs. Emil is
tempted to accept this community as a permanent haven and to
end his quest. But the temptation is lifted by the advent of war.
The war is a symptom of the distressed society split between a
dispirited and neurotic majority and a community of a few fine
individuals. Emil sees it as an inferno that may forge a new cultural whole from these divided parts.

The first characteristic of time in Hesse's novels, then, often
gives them their particular shape. The struggle to discover the
relation between the impressions made on one's soul in infancy
and the goal toward which a life moves provides the plot of
many of his fictions. Plots of this kind stress temporality because they define a person's life in terms of past and future rather
than present. In addition, such plots distinguish personal time
from the values of a society that invades the processes of personal time, imposing interests that ignore the uniqueness of an
individual's quest for the relation between origin and destiny.

II

As in *Demian*, the plot of *Siddhartha* relates, in three clear stages, the past and the future, the movement from youth to adulthood, in a man's life.[7] In both novels, personal time arises from integration of these two poles. But a second characteristic of personal time becomes central in *Siddhartha*, the relation between permanence and change.

At the outset of the novel, Siddhartha is discontent with his father's religion because of the distance between human life and the transcendent gods to whom sacrifices are made. He breaks with his home in order to find a spiritual life that will stress human proximity to divine life. With the Samanas he practices the repression of sense, memory, and desire in order to achieve unity with the divine. After three years he seeks out the great Gotama and finds in him a person of recognizable holiness who has achieved the spiritual goal. But Siddhartha, believing that by subjecting himself to spiritual authorities and models he has lost a sense of himself, moves on again. He begins to take delight in his awareness of the particularities and mutations of the world around him.

This change in orientation introduces the second major phase. Siddhartha, rejoicing in his role as an individual in a tangible world, crosses the river and enters the sensual life of the city. There he does well, primarily because his earlier spiritual training gives him a lighthearted attitude toward his dealings with people. But eventually he becomes more like the other citizens, petty and anxious. His erotic life with the beautiful Kamala takes on the flavor of death. In his quest for tangible, temporary satisfactions, he has again lost a sense of self.

When he returns to the river, Siddhartha has behind him two conflicting worlds, one of spirit, another of flesh; one of unity, another of diversity; one of permanence, another of transitoriness. The problem is the conflict between the two. Each was unsatisfying in its exclusiveness, and in each he lost a sense of his own completeness. He turns toward the river not as the boundary between these two orientations but as a symbol of their unity. Siddhartha gives himself to a personal time symbolized by the river as a union of the permanent and the fleeting.

Although very different from *Siddhartha*, *Steppenwolf* also reveals an interest in the relation of change to permanence within an individual life. But the matter here is reversed. Siddhartha found the goal of his search in a position between two extremes; in *Steppenwolf* such a position is presented negatively, for it can also take the form of a deadening compromise which must be avoided if the relation between the fleeting and the permanent is to be recognized. The major problem that Harry Haller encounters, one that leads to a deadening form of compromise between diversity and unity or permanence and change, is his fear of extremes and his preference for a safe position in the middle.

All three kinds of material that constitute *Steppenwolf* depict this problem. The preface provided by the landlady's nephew presents Haller's attraction to and distance from the bourgeois, urban setting. Haller's record—the major section—provides a personal account of the change that occurred in him and the continuity with his former life that change created. And the treatise grants a theoretical analysis of the tendency both to deny time by accepting one social or personal form as final and to escape extremes for the comfort and security of a compromising position between them.

The cause of Haller's problem is the mistake of attributing permanence to one form of personal identity. He is unable to realize on his own the possibility of change. This error is easily made because permanence offers an appealing steadiness in the midst of complexity and uncertainty. The surrounding society reinforces this error by trying to maintain stability and authority for itself. It seeks some middle position between extremes and so excludes its lowest and its highest members, both the derelicts or prostitutes and the immortals.

Change begins to occur when aspects of Harry's potential self, repressed by the desire for a permanent, simple identity, are aroused by segments of urban society that have also been repressed—the denizens of seedy bars and drug dens—or severely compromised—as are immortals such as Mozart and Goethe whom society has tried to domesticate or relegate to a decorative position. Harry's problem begins to be solved, in other words, when the stability of both self and society are not identified with some particular form.

The issue here is the fear change creates in both the individual and society. This fear obscures the role of change in human identity. Under Hermine's guidance, Haller begins to meet people and to engage in activities that awaken repressed aspects of his self. These aroused potentials bring about change, for any form of identity is a construct that exists at the expense of neglected possibilities. These possibilities derive from both ends of the social and personal spectrum, the lofty and the crude. Both individual and society achieve stability and avoid change by excluding the base and the lofty from serious consideration. Greatness and seediness are both productive because each extends human potential beyond the limits imposed by a steady structure. Both extremes are realities that personal and social identities will have to eschew if they want to avoid change.

Permanence, however, is not confined to this false sense of personal and social finality. The novel also suggests that revealed by the constant changes to which the self is subjected stands an eternal whole in which the possibilities of life, both personal and social, are contained. This permanent whole is a spiritual reality and an object of belief.[8] It is hidden because no self or society is able to comprehend its potential at any one time, and any personal or social form is only a partial actualization of that whole. But by change, by the variation in self-identity, some sense of the whole can be gained and faith in it substantiated.[9] In *Steppenwolf*, then, an exchange is made of a permanence that denies change for an assent to change that reveals permanence.

The dialectic of change and permanence is rendered quite differently in *Narcissus and Goldmund*. The setting is medieval Europe, rather than the contemporary urban environment of Harry Haller. Orientation to the contrary poles of this dialectic in human time is divided between separate individuals who, despite their sharp differences, hold a relationship to one another of respect and trust.

The two characters in the novel stress the contraries of change and permanence in their elected life-styles. Narcissus pursues a spiritual life at the monastery while Goldmund wanders about the countryside, experiencing changes in his condition, confronting the variety of life outside the walls, and pursuing his vocation as an artist. The relation between these two orientations is enhanced by the structure of the book, which has two parts, the frame story of life at the monastery and the enfolded, picaresque center. These two sections are nicely balanced. The story of Goldmund's experiences has authority because of its adventurous qualities, the variety of events, and his development as a sculptor. But the section in which Narcissus dominates has authority both because it houses the picaresque tale and because the adventures of Goldmund are made possible by the security that the monastery grants him and from which he launches himself into the world.[10]

The dialectic between these two ways of life, the novel implies, can be maintained in a medieval setting where the interdependence of permanence and change is recognized.[11] While the world of Narcissus exists through its exclusion of many possibilities, especially sexual experience, Narcissus does not discount the power and even validity of Goldmund's immersion in sundry events. And Goldmund, while rejecting the enclosed and protected life of the monastery, does not disdain it or those who live there. Permanence and change, the thinker and the artist, spirit and flesh: these contraries, which have, in the twentieth century, become contradictories, are held within this novel in fruitful, mutually revealing structural tension.

III

The third characteristic of temporality in Hesse's fiction, the relation of the development in an individual's life to the surrounding culture of which it is a part, is central to the later novels.[12] *The Journey to the East*, the first of these texts, reveals both how individual events are included in a cultural process and why faith is important if one is to recognize the relation between one's own time and this ongoing cultural whole.

The narrator, H. H., had been a member of a group of artists and intellectuals earlier in his life, which had made him aware of the interrelation between personal and cultural movement. This group related him to individuals from many cultures and periods of history, people unified not by common subjects or methods but by a common spirit, a sense of an inclusive future. Rather than achieving completion, the group was always in process, moving toward a unity that would not be fully realized.

Distractions and traumatic events in the immediate world, such as World War I, materialism, and cynicism, however, corroded his faith in the league. H. H. unfortunately mistook his own loss of faith in its ideals and goals for the league's disappearance. The story depicts the process by which he learns that the league continued without him, and it ends with his reinduction into it.

The league is Hesse's symbol for the inevitable forward movement of culture, its capacity to project the horizon of a broader future.[13] Lack of vision, loss of faith, pride, materialism, and self-preoccupation are all deterrents to this movement. Corresponding to the time of an individual's development stands another process, the universal, transcultural development of the spirit toward levels of higher realization. Personal time requires faith in the unity between individual endeavors and the development of the culture.

The personal time of the individual and the culture is symbolized by music, especially melody. H. H. is a violinist, and one outstanding characteristic of the guide Leo is his whistling.[14] Melody grants unity by its single direction into the future. Although music has other meanings in Hesse's fiction, especially that of unity amidst the diversity of human experience, the future orientation of his work and the actualization of personal and cultural potential grant music, and especially melody, its significant symbolic role.

The relation of personal development to the cultural whole is also of great importance to *The Glass Bead Game*. This culminating work in the Hesse corpus stresses not only this third characteristic of time but the other two as well. Time in this novel is complicated by the fact that the narrator treats time that is in the future for the reader as the past. One consequence of this temporal organization is to overcome the separation between past and future; the two reveal one another as do also history and fiction.[15] Primarily, he suggests that the split between past and future may be overcome by discounting the twentieth century, a period marked by a failure to recognize their continuity.[16] Especially in the general introduction and in Joseph Knecht's letter of resignation to the Board of Educators toward the end of the novel, the twentieth century is harshly depicted as a time of violence and lack of culture, riddled by cynicism and irrationality, and oriented to superficiality and titillation. Its only value was to create a vacuum, a longing for a new kind of order, morality, and rationality and to provide, at least for Knecht, an example of what might recur if the dangerous tendencies in his own time become more severe. Knecht's resignation of his office as Master of the Glass Bead Game, an event of such significance that it accounts for the narrator's writing his biography, is occasioned by his sense that, centuries later, the mistakes and distortions characteristic of the twentieth century are reappearing. He resigns in order to call attention to these problems and to the crisis that he believes they will create.

The twentieth century is further revealed as seriously faulted by a preference for other cultures and periods, which the three lives written by Knecht reveal. In an archaic society, an early Christian world, and an Indian setting individual events are housed within larger, positive unities. The twentieth century stands isolated; it is unmatched by any other era or civilization in its lack of relation between past and future, change and permanence, and the individual and the cultural whole.

The rather mysterious ending of the narrative, which the narrator provides in the form of a widely circulated, popular legend of Knecht's death, encourages the inference that Knecht's unprecedented act successfully averted the crises he feared. The Order, while waning in his own day and falling increasingly into a mistaken sense of human life, was able, in the face of his resignation and death, to right itself. It finds new vitality by overcoming the separation from history that it had begun to institutionalize. The form of the novel reveals an interdependence between individual and cultural development and process; a general description of the Order and the interests which produce the Glass Bead Game is juxtaposed with a chronological depiction of the life of Joseph Knecht.[17] Knecht has importance because of his position in the Order, but the Order would have suffered seriously had Knecht been fully identified with it. Because he was able to withdraw from it, he could recognize its errors and value the claims and realities of history that it had excluded. The conflicts, so common to the reader's own time, between order and change, culture and the individual, are overcome in the narrative through Knecht's role as harbinger of cultural inadequacies and flaws.

Three features of the Order contribute most heavily toward the growing separation from history that alarms Knecht. The first is the tendency to treat culture as a closed, static system. Intellectual and imaginative achievements form one vast repertoire from which those playing the Glass Bead Game draw. The various games are performances based on a set of fixed possibilities. This feature of the game gives rise to the criticism, voiced by Plinio Designori, that nothing new is actually created by the games, that those engaged in them become adept at working with what already is there. Limitless and complex as the games may seem to be, they treat culture as a putative whole, as complete. The consequence is to divorce culture from history, even to make it atemporal and simultaneous.

A second aspect of the game that expunges temporality is the disinterested attitude of its adherents. One objection the Board of Educators makes to Knecht's letter of resignation is its combination of personal and professional matters. The two are not to be confused. Likewise, Fritz Tegularius chides Knecht for importing personal considerations into this poem "Transcend!," thereby clouding its fine insights into the possibility of pure music. Those who participate in the game do so with a lightness of touch, with the freedom of pure improvisation, and not to press some personal interest. The result is a removal of questions of power from the arena of cultural activity. Power is relegated to the realm of politics and society, a realm separate from the Order and marked by history. History is understood by advocates of the Order such as Tegularius to be the struggle with and for power. Disinterestedness is supported by a doctrine of vocation that reduces competition. For those suited to this kind of world and capable of employing its advantages, no anxiety is needed, since all one could want is already present. Competition is reduced by turning attention not to what a person can or has accomplished but to what new combinations the system can provide.

Finally, the Glass Bead Game discounts temporal movement by preferring metaphoric to sequential relations. The principal effect of the game is to relate disparate matters taken from separate disciplines or even from differing cultures. Linear relations are sacrificed in the process, and the sense of forward movement is diminished.

These features of the Glass Bead Game make it vulnerable to the criticisms of Plinio Designori and give rise to the debates between him and Knecht. The principal plot of the story, the relation between these two characters—their friendship, their protracted separation, and their reunion toward the end—then, serves to epitomize the tensions between culture and history; it reveals the tendency of each to exclude and disdain the other. By leaving the Order and entering ordinary life Designori becomes Knecht's opposite.

Knecht is aided in recognizing the importance of change both in the individual's life and in that of the Order by Father Jacobus.[18] He then can see what his colleagues tend to ignore, that there was a time before the existence of the Order and that there will be a time when the Order is no more. All human creations are temporal. Knecht takes this awareness of history back to the Order; there, he is able not only to detect development within it but also to judge that the Order in its present form has reached its zenith and has begun to wane. Like all creations, its existence is temporal rather than separate from and defiant toward time.[19] In his attempts to relate the Order more closely to the external, historical world, Knecht contradicts Tegularius, for whom the Order is self-contained and unchanging. While Knecht longs for the outside world, Tegularius takes refuge from what he considers to be enslavement to time and instinct.

The reunion of Knecht with Designori reveals the weariness that results from the fracture between time and culture. The two come together with concessions from both sides. Designori begins meditating again, and he begins to recognize the unity and permanence that house the fragments of his life, while Knecht acknowledges that people require change because no human creation, even one so vast and complex as Castalia, is fully and permanently satisfying.

Knecht's letter to the Board of Educators recapitulates the insights he has achieved. He criticizes the Order for disregarding history. Such disregard repeats the wrongs of the twentieth century, primarily the assumption of two, distinct worlds, the changing world of power, instinct, nature, and history on one side, the static world of human mind, language, and imagination on the other, a split exacerbated by the disdain of each world for the other.

The significance of Knecht's thoughts and actions is to offer the twentieth-century reader two options, both positive.[20] The first is that such splits as that between the individual and the culture will lead to a craving for a new beginning and the restoration of a new relationship. The second possibility is that this book, like Knecht's life, may be enough to signal the gravity of the situation. If so, the culture can evaluate the price of the present split and prevent the crisis that it would otherwise inevitably create.

While the relation in human time between the individual and culture is central to *The Glass Bead Game*, therefore, the other aspects of personal time that we have studied have important roles in it as well. The continuity between past and future is secured by the temporal setting of the novel, the treatment of the reader's future as the past. The relation of change to permanence is depicted in the conflict between the stasis of the Order and the changes in the social, political context that the Order ignores. This culminating novel, consequently, is Hesse's most complete rendering of personal or melodic time, the problems and also the possibilities for a process of self-actualization in both the individual and the culture. Personal time depends on belief in the relation between past and future, permanence and change, and the individual and the culture.

TEN

Martin Heidegger

T ime in the novels of Virginia Woolf and Hermann Hesse can, as we saw, be distinguished from that of the other fiction we have examined. Rather than rhythmic or polyphonic, it is, in a word, melodic. That is, the readers of these novels find themselves engaged by a personal, developmental process, usually individual but often cultural as well, that is directed toward the future. The individuality or identity of the person or culture is established by the process, since distinctive potentialities are brought to some stage of fruition. This process toward self-articulation or fulfillment places this kind of time less in a natural or social context than in a psychological or personal one. Furthermore, this kind of time is primarily oriented to the future, to the goal of self-actualization, more so than rhythmic and polyphonic time, which are immediately concerned with the past and the present, respectively.

The title of Virginia Woolf's first novel indicates this process quite well. *The Voyage Out* describes the development of Rachel Vinrace from a young woman sheltered by social and parental structures and directives to a person who begins to act on her own. Over and over we find in Virginia Woolf's novels characters who, often against difficult obstacles and restraints, are attempting to move forward to their own sense of personal integrity and strength. Some of them find this process to be difficult because older people around them, particularly parents, want to impose certain roles on their lives, and the younger people, simply out of high regard for their elders, doubt the worth of their own individually secured futures. James and Lily share this problem in *To the Lighthouse,* as do Katharine Hilbery in *Night and Day* and Eleanor Pargiter in *The Years.*

The temptation to accept an assigned role is great because the person involved in the process cannot be certain beforehand what kind of product will result from the process. The uncertainty of the goal has an inhibiting effect. Furthermore, the characters, as they embark on their own "voyage out," often are led to locations and to associations with people that differ from those with which they are familiar or for which they were prepared. A nice image of this uncertainty in the process of self-development is the creation of a work of art, such as Lily Briscoe's painting in *To the Lighthouse.* Simple duplication of other paintings or the imposition on a painting of a preconceived idea or purpose does not result in an original creation. But if trusted, the process leads to completion. This image of life as a process of development or discovery similar to an artist's work accounts for the many artists as characters in the fiction of both Woolf and Hesse.

Since this process is open and unpredictable it must be trusted, but trust in the future is made difficult by the prospect of death. While the end of the developmental process is uncertain, namely the kind of individual who will be actualized, death is certain. Its role is both as stimulant and as inhibitor. One cannot postpone the process of self-actualization indefinitely, yet the process may be cut off before it is completed. Death takes on, in the fiction, then, a strong and ambiguous force. *Jacob's Room, The Waves*—indeed, death is on the minds of most of Virginia Woolf's characters and is present throughout her fiction, not because of an inherent morbidity but because of its future orientation.

The role of the past in this future orientation is to provide resources for personal development. If a character is not controlled by or imprisoned within the past and is free enough from it to embark on a voyage of self-articulation, then the past can also help. Precedents, strength and stability, and a sense of place and purpose can be established by a relation to the past, and Woolf's characters are concerned to have such a relationship. Achieving it, however, is seldom easy, given the often authoritative nature of the past. Relation to the past is made even more difficult by the hiatus produced by World War I or by breaks with or resentments toward one's own past such as those felt by Clarissa Dalloway.

Finally, an individual's development and cultural processes are related to one another in Virginia Woolf's novels not only for the obvious reason just alluded to—that events, such as World War I, affect the lives of young people deeply—but also because cultures as well as persons have identities. In such books as *Orlando*, *The Years*, and *Between the Acts* the interplay between the personal qualities of cultural development and the cultural quality of individual maturation is intricately displayed.

What has been said of the fiction of Virginia Woolf can almost wholly be applied, *mutatis mutandis*, to the fiction of Hermann Hesse. His characters, many of them artists, are involved in the work not only of artistic creation but, at the same time, of self-discovery. They are, consequently, oriented to an uncertain future which holds out the promise of completion for this process. But they must press on despite many temptations and impediments that threaten or block the way, such as an educational system that lacks patience and respect for individual development; authoritative and intimidating figures such as Emil Sinclair encounters in his home in Kromer and Demian; or the imposition of a present impasse in the process and a halt to the process itself, as in Veraguth's artistic work in *Rosshalde* or Haller's relation to his social and cultural environment in *Steppenwolf*; or a lack of trust in the process, as in *The Journey to the East*.

Furthermore, death is a forceful presence in Hesse's novels as it is in Woolf's. Harry Haller has suicide before him as a promised termination that will make life tolerable, and the change in him is an exchange of this definite termination for the new indefinite one of self-fulfillment. Goldmund, in his wanderings and personal reflections, encounters the goading and the threatening reality of death repeatedly. The principal character of *Under the Wheel* is so hedged about with familial and cultural restraints that the only individuating and self-fulfilling act he can perform is his own suicide.

Despite the uncertainties of the future and the certainty of death, the characters of Hesse's novels, as they undergo developmental processes, are not quite so much as Woolf's at odds with their pasts. While it is not identical with the person's remote past, the future and its actualization in Hesse's fiction allow a simultaneous, unfolding interrelationship with the past. For example, when Harry Haller encounters people and interests foreign to him, they awaken in him repressed or hidden memories of early experiences and acquaintances. Goldmund's venture into the future of his own personal and aesthetic quest is also the gradual appropriation of the image of his mother. While the past cannot be duplicated, it also cannot be forsaken, and it provides someone free to venture into life a gradually apprehended resource for encountering the new. Both the future and the past are hidden, and the plots of Hesse's novels are frequently depictions of the growing interrelationships and mutual revelations between the two.

Finally, as in Woolf's novels, cultural development is inseparable from the individual's development. Society in *Under the Wheel* forces the two to collide. In *Steppenwolf*, Haller and the society err in repressing or domesticating those influences, both of a lofty or spiritual and of a coarse and carnal kind, which are a part of human culture but stand at its edges. By misappropriating or resisting such factors rather than being open to them, both culture and individual suffer. The cultural impact of World War I is strongly felt in the individual development of both Sinclair in *Demian* and H. H. in *The Journey to the East*. And, of course, *The Glass Bead Game* is, as we have seen, an elaborate and complex rendering of the interrelations not only between culture and history but between culture and individual development and insight.

While the metaphor of melody does not convey all features of the time rendered by these novelists, it does help us to understand some of its salient features. For one thing, melody is future-oriented. Anticipation of its ending is crucial to appreciation of it. No melody can be interminable; we speak of a melodic line. We are anticipating its ending even as we hear it. Broken off midway, a melody has failed to identify itself. Furthermore, in a melody the subsequent notes reveal the beginning, and the beginning is not fully understood until the whole of it has been completed. The beginning and ending of a melody reveal one another. Finally, we can understand that each note we hear of a melody, rather than standing by itself, is stretched between, is affected by and affects, those notes that preceded and will follow it. As one theorist puts it:

> When I am hearing the fourth note (say) of a familiar melody, the third note is slipping away and a fifth is looming up. When I am listening to the fifth note, the fourth will be fading out, and the retention of note four that I leave when I am listening to note five includes the retention of note three that I had as I was listening to note four. Thus, the awareness I have of successive fillings is made possible by a nesting of previous retentions in the present one.[1]

It is not surprising, therefore, to find the use of melody as a metaphor for personal time in Edmund Husserl's *The Phenomenology of Internal Time-Consciousness*,[2] but in our further delineation of melodic time we turn not to Husserl but to his student Martin Heidegger, who goes beyond Husserl in establishing the radically personal nature of human temporality.

I

To say that for him the question of time is first of all personal is not to accuse Heidegger of solipsism or narcissism. Grounding the question of time in personal existence results, instead, in a breaking open of self-containment. Consequently, a self-preoccupied person will shun the temporality of his or her own existence in favor of some more general theories of time. Indeed, self-containment will impart a timelessness to personal existence rather than recognize its fundamental temporality. Solipsism, narcissism, or any form of self-containment, of locating meaning in an already realized personal identity, results, for Heidegger, in a loss of personhood. Raising the question of temporality means facing the incompleteness and uncertainty of one's own existence, and it locates the meaning of that existence in something yet outstanding in and for one's life. Raising the question of temporality to the level of consciousness is, consequently, a difficult act for any person, but it is that person's defining and individuating act.[3]

Since the question of temporality is no further away from us than our own existence, we may think of it as a question readily answerable. Nothing seems closer and more available to us than our own existence. As a matter of fact, this proximity makes for grave difficulties. For this reason, according to Heidegger, the question of temporality in its radically personal nature has been avoided throughout the whole of Western culture's reflections on the nature and meaning of time. Its threatening and elusive qualities have been suppressed in theories of time from Plato and Aristotle to Bergson and Husserl. To bring up the question of time, then, is to counter the entire tradition of suppression concerning its radically personal nature, and, according to Heidegger, our stake in maintaining that tradition and in avoiding the temporality of our own existence is enormous. The most common form of such avoidance is a theory of time as a common attribute of all entities or as a general reality in which we exist or which exists within us.

The basis for the personal nature of the question of temporality is that I recognize my life as still outstanding. My existence is first of all a going out beyond what I am to what I will or can be, to what may or could happen to me. The very meaning of "existence" is standing out in this way. I do not define myself exclusively by what I have been or now am; I understand myself in terms of possibilities that have yet to be realized. This means that I understand my life not as first of all given to me but as fundamentally my own to the degree that I do something with it, have something intended for it, make something of it. To raise the question of temporality is, therefore, to raise the question of the meaning of my existence, the question of what I am doing with my life. This is not only a distinctively human act, it is a distinctively personal act. It is not only the way that I as a human being am distinctive in relation to non-human beings; it is the way in which my own existence is distinguished from that of other people's. However, raising the question is not easy, for I always, in doing so, face the difficult question of whether what I am making of my life is what I ought to be making of it and whether, if the general direction seems to be the right one, I am actualizing possibilities most fully. Raising the question of my temporality, of what I am doing with my life, then, is fraught with uncertainty and guilt; I am always tempted to inauthentic modes of existence, such as allowing others to determine for me what I should be or failing altogether to realize the distinctiveness of my own existence.

Since the inquiry concerning my existence directs attention to what I am making of or doing with my life, the aspect of time that is of first importance for personal existence is the future. Possibility, therefore, becomes crucial to my sense of personal existence. The future is "primary because it is the region toward which man projects and in which he defines his own being."[4] Possibility defines existence, consequently. Rather than static, my identity is always something yet to be fulfilled or achieved. Rather than as a completed actuality, a person's being is defined in relation to possibilities, to the future.

This futurity of personal existence grants a person a "world." This means that a person and a "world" are inseparable. Heidegger does not take "world" to be something prior to or independent of persons but as characteristic of and required by personal existence. "World" is constituted by the primordial, unified, and meaningful undergirding of a person's relation to entities and, even more, to possibilities; "the structure of that to which *Dasein* assigns itself is what makes up the *worldhood* of the world."[5] World is the grounding by which a person is already related to a possibility before that possibility is actualized. This grants "world" an inherently temporal nature as well. I can have a relationship with entities and I can actualize possibilities because I move toward them in an unarticulated relationship with or understanding of them. I am always projecting ahead of me a possible relationship with something new. Understanding, which gives rise to meaning, is future-oriented in that it reveals how I can always go out beyond the range of my actual relationships in terms of a horizon of already anticipated and partially incorporated relationships. The basic epistemological situation, according to Heidegger, rather than marked by a gap between a perceiving subject and a field of discrete objects, is first of all to be described by a common ground in which subject and object are already in some kind of undeclared relationship. This common ground grants understanding, and it accounts for the unity that marks my existence as "world."

While the future is the primary tense for Heidegger, the past cannot be ignored. If a person is able to be stretched toward the future, with all the uncertainty that that implies, that person is also able to have a past. What it means to have a past is to take into one's sense of personal existence all of the contingencies and peculiarities of birth and nurture. I cannot, of course, choose my parents or how I am to be reared; yet these matters are very important for my existence and the life I am able to make for myself. To make something of my life is to deal as well with these unalterable facts, with all the potentials, limitations, and arbitrariness that they convey, with what Heidegger calls the "thrownness" of my existence. The strangeness of my existence, the fact, for example, that if conditions had been different I would not have been born or I could have been raised in some other kind of way, grants my past a certain strangeness that I must own as my own if my existence is to be personal. And, of course, what I can and should make of my life is greatly determined by the facts of my "thrownness." As a consequence, the future of possibilities to which by anticipation and understanding I am related, this world ahead of me, is related, in more ways than I may realize, to my past.

One sign of the influence of the past upon me is the impact of moods on the way I relate myself to entities and possibilities in my world. Moods come upon us in unexplained ways. We find ourselves to be in a mood. Although they seem to be caused by factors in present or future time, such as the actions of other people or the anticipation of threatening or exciting events, moods actually derive from the past. They have to do, for example, with early experiences that affect the way we respond to the actions of other people or anticipate coming events. Moods are an indication of how the past influences present and future time in ways we do not control or even expect.

Being a person, then, requires a gradual appropriation of the past as well as an anticipation of a future. The process of appropriating one's particular birth and heritage, of taking the "thrownness" of one's existence into oneself, Heidegger calls "repetition."

II

When I take my existence as clarified by possibilities toward which I project myself and as a thrownness that, despite its limiting and arbitrary qualities, I can appropriate as I move into the future, then I can also have an authentic present. The order of priorities in time is important for Heidegger—from future to past to present—because this order differs from that usually created by thought about time. Public time and notions about time that we generally accept and uncritically promulgate begin with present time. This is because public time is an elaborately constructed means by which many people can say "now" simultaneously. Consequently, when public time is taken as primary, time becomes understood as an infinite sequence of undifferentiated and inherently meaningless "now" points. A serious problem, a hopeless distortion, occurs, therefore, when public time, with its stress on "now," becomes the norm for interrogating the nature of human temporality.

Heidegger does not consider public time to be dispensable or evil. But we should remember that public time "belongs to everybody—and that means to nobody."[6] As societies become more complex, more accurate ways of making time distinctions and of saying "now" are required. Because we live in complex social situations, such devices and conventions form important parts of our daily lives. We all need to refer often to watches and clocks to be sure that our activities are appropriate for the concerns of a larger whole. We need to get to work and meet appointments "on time." But we ought not to think of time as a series of points at which a group of people can agree that "now" is the time when work or a meeting should

begin. Time is not a string of meaningless points to which significance is attributed. While people may become preoccupied
with this kind of time and substitute it for an awareness of
their own personal temporality, we should remember that time
is not something first of all neutral and general.

Heidegger discusses authentic present time in an intriguing
way of meditating on the German equivalent to our phrases
"it's time" or "there is time"—"*es gibt Zeit.*"[7] This phrase, lit-
erally, "it gives time," suggests first of all that we recognize
time as something given to us. Time is not something we possess without first being granted it. Time is basically awaited
and received. We have such notions of time embedded in "the
time is ripe" or "now's the time." A certain recognition of a
temporal situation that we do not ourselves create is preserved
in such phrases. Furthermore, such phrases suggest that our
sense of time in the present is a matter of grasping or actualizing a certain relationship. We notice time—"it's time"—when
it has become an issue, when it is important. We claim or recognize its significance. This awareness reveals an underlying
relationship. We articulate a significance already there. Present
time, then, is time as it comes to attention.

Future time, the time of anticipation and possibility, and
past time, the time of conditions and memories, have to do
with present time because things future, while not yet existing, can be matters of concern in the present, and things past,
while no longer existing, concern me as well in the present.
Present time, then, the time of attention, produces a gathering
of time. However, while the past and the future can be gathered
into and related by the present they are never exhausted by it.
The past contains much that it refuses to yield to the present,
and the future withholds much from us and will not yield
what it holds until due time. "What does the future hold for
me?" is a question that both intrigues and frustrates us. Consequently, there is a dynamic relation of these three aspects of
time to one another. The past both yields to the present and
conceals itself from it, and the future both withholds from the
present and grants something to it. Furthermore, what the past
yields and the future grants are related to and affect one another. What we expect from the future is greatly affected by

our past, and what we remember and can appropriate from our past is largely activated by anticipation and possibilities provided by the future. In other words, present time provides us a sense of the unity of our temporality. Yet, for Heidegger, this unity of time should not be confused with present time. Present time is only one aspect of time, albeit it is that aspect in which the unity of time is perceived. That unity is a kind of fourth dimension of time. Furthermore, the fact that this added dimension is revealed in present time does not grant present time a privileged status. Indeed, that status is always reserved for future time.

III

We must return to future time in order to discuss an outstanding matter which is, according to one critic, the "key" to Heidegger's philosophy of time: death.[8] As we saw, an act that distinguishes me both as a human being and as a particular person is the act of projecting my identity toward future possibilities: "there is always something *still outstanding*, which, as a potentiality-for-being for *Dasein* itself, has not yet become 'actual.'"[9] These possibilities may be many and varied—a kind of work, marriage and family, a vocation. But one possibility stands as unavoidable and unelected—my death. I am aware that it can occur at any time. If to live is to appropriate my future, to be a person means always, as well, to be a person who at any time can die.

Since my temporality and my being able to die at any time are inseparable, death can be a terribly effective inhibitor to recognizing the temporality of my existence. I can easily, as a result, flee it and take on an identity not my own. But death can also free me to accept my life as my own, to claim the freedom that my own existence gives me. Since no one can do my dying for me, then no one can or should do my living for me. If my dying is my own, then my living can become my own as well. Furthermore, dying and its integral relation to my temporality grant my life a sense of wholeness even while in course. My life becomes a whole when it ends, but I can have this sense of wholeness while it is still in process by an acknowledgment of my mortality. This freedom toward dying grants "an authentic potentiality-for-Being-a-whole."[10] As John Macquarrie puts it: "we have seen that one of the characteristics of a fallen or deteriorated existence is that its possibilities are scattered and incoherent. But to anticipate death and to recognize the boundary of one's existence is to achieve an overarching unity that gathers up the possibilities of existence."[11]

Not only does an awareness of my dying allow me to recognize my life as my own and my life as a whole, it also grants me a sense of what it means to exist or to be alive. When I recognize the certain possibility of death, I can recognize the strangeness of existence and life. "Only because Nothing is revealed in the very basis of our *Da-sein* is it possible for the utter strangeness of what-is to dawn on us. Only when the strangeness of what-is forces itself upon us does it awaken and invite our wonder. Only because of wonder, that is to say, the revelation of Nothing, does the 'Why?' spring to our lips."[12]

As James Demske makes clear, the turning point in Heidegger's thought, the distinction between the earlier and later Heidegger, concerns this interrelation between death as a constitutive element of human existence and Being which is both revealed and concealed by beings. Not only is the strangeness, the peculiarity of my existence, revealed to me by recognition that dying is the ultimate and most certain possibility for me, something also can be revealed to me about Being. This gives personal existence and Being a mutually revealing relationship. Perhaps this ambiguity can be compared to John Calvin's uncertainty, in the opening of his *Institutes of the Christian Religion*, as to whether he should begin with a discussion of humanity or of God, since he cannot speak of one without also speaking of the other. While it would be a mistake to substitute Heidegger's authentic existence and Being for humanity and God in theology,[13] the state of interdependence between the two poles of *Dasein* and Being and Heidegger's ambivalence about which topic should be used to reveal the other are analogous. In any event, a person, by a recognition and appropriation of mortality defers to that from which his or her existence is derived and reveals, thereby, the primacy of that source. Death, therefore, takes on a particularly significant status for Heidegger as the means by which we become aware not only of our own existence but of its derivative nature, of its having been given, as arising from Being. Death is "the place of being's greatest illumination, the locus of the concealing-revealing event of truth, the most highly concentrated gathering of the mystery of being itself."[14]

There are other ways in which Being is revealed, however. "The language of a people, like their art, is a key to their collective understanding of the world and of themselves, and thus of the way being appears to them."[15] For Heidegger, the poet is particularly able to avoid the concealment of Being that is affected by everyday language and to uncover uses of language that speak freshly, that can be the very voice of Being.[16] The work of the poet is to bring a people to that sense of language not as flattened or wasted by use but able to address a culture and to reveal how Being is revealing itself historically.

We need not rehearse the characteristics of time in the fiction of Woolf and Hesse in order to recognize points of similarity between it and time as described by Heidegger. The uncertainty of the future, the role of the past, the sense of the unity of time, and the awareness of death: these marks of personal time are, as we saw, easily gleaned from the fiction and fully articulated in Heidegger's thought.

Time as here presented is personal; it is the gradual unfolding of a person's own life in and through its temporality. This means that the most appropriate context for articulating this kind of time is a psychological or personal one. It is time as uniquely clarified by an individual life and as known primarily internally.

However, personal time is not only individual. For Woolf and Hesse as well as for Heidegger, the culture and history of a people also constitute the gradual unfolding of a particular identity. For Heidegger a culture or language, as well as an individual, has a certain identity, reveals a particular mode of existence, and is the occasion for Being's self-disclosure.

Finally, Heidegger has given in his own way, as have Eliade and Whitehead in theirs, a particular reason for taking seriously the revelation of human temporality that novelists are able to give us. For his creative task is to move behind our generalized and undistinguished mode of existence to a more authentic awareness of temporality in its threatening but also revealing force and meaning. It is not only, then, his philosophy of time that makes him an appropriate counterpoint to the time of Woolf's and Hesse's fiction but also his estimation of the role of the artist in the revelation of human temporality in language that makes him so. He joins the other two, therefore, in presenting a philosophy that at many points is made accessible to the literary critic or theorist. He, along with Eliade and Whitehead, gives us reasons for thinking that the study of time in fictional narrative may bring us more directly and completely to a sense of the nature and meaning of time than could otherwise be possible.

Conclusion

ELEVEN

The Image of Time and the Question of Belief

The conclusion to which this examination leads is that nine writers, different and distant from one another in many ways, agree that time, as it appears or is experienced in human life, has three characteristics: it is primary, complex, and trustworthy. As these characteristics were brought to the surface, questions concerning their relation to belief appeared, often indirectly and incompletely, with them. It remains now to gather these questions and to treat them more directly. *Primacy* leads to the question of belief concerning the status of time in narrative and human experience, and it draws our attention to present time, to ongoing human lives, whether individual or communal. *Complexity* raises the question of the relation of the three forms of human time—rhythmic, polyphonic, and melodic—to beliefs inherited from our cultural past. *Trustworthiness* turns attention toward the future. It carries the question of belief concerning the applicability of these nine writers to the future our own time appears to portend. Rather than occasions for dogmatic answers, these questions provide an opportunity at most to indicate that the questions themselves are worthy of further study and thought.

I

Although we need not repeat all that has already been said about the primacy of time in the work of these writers, we should recall this characteristic briefly before pursuing the question of belief to which it leads. We can use the occasion to point out differing emphases among the writers.

In Hemingway's fiction the primacy of time is revealed when characters and narrators find themselves in situations contrary to their expectations, when their lives are determined by events they cannot control, such as weather, war, and love, when their experiences follow the pattern of a temporal cycle that they do not themselves originate, and when they undergo changes, even transformations, that they need but are powerless to provide for themselves. In Mann's fiction, similarly, the primacy of time is revealed by forces that determine the situations and experiences of characters and that characters neither initiate nor control, such as war, aging, illness, prophecy, and the inheritance of family attributes. In addition, the lives of individuals are determined by the way in which attitudes, interests, and kinds of people are drawn to and interact with their contraries, producing an array of complex relationships. And in Virginia Woolf's novels characters are similarly affected by events they do not control or understand—urbanization, war, and aging, for example—and they must venture, despite losses and threats, the internal adjustments and developments that lead to maturation, freedom, and insight.

In Lawrence's fiction, along with strongly positive instances of the primacy of time in human experience, we are given striking examples of human lives mistakenly lived out in defiance of this characteristic. People like Gerald Crich and Clifford Chatterley, for example, try to control time and subject it to their own intentions and directions. Their role is greatly extended by the fact that they appear to typify a culture that in general, for Lawrence, has cut itself from its temporal nature. Characters in his fiction, then, who are able to let processes have their way with them are exceptional, and many are alienated from their immediate cultural environments. Such negative images concerning the primacy of time are even more pervasive in Faulkner's fiction. He depicts a society that suffers the effects of attempts to arrest temporal change both by disassociating social meaning from temporal movements and by preventing people who differ from one another from interacting. And Hesse's fiction, while it also presents many characters who are granted personal health and integrity by a process that unites their futures to their remote pasts, presents the general cultural situation as one in which the primacy of time is denied. He does this, for example, in the image of an educational system that denies and represses the internal development of the individual child in *Under the Wheel*, of urban life, especially in *Steppenwolf*, and of the fixing of culture as a synchronic whole in *The Glass Bead Game*.

The three thinkers included here have their own ways of stressing the primacy of time in human societies and personal experience. For Eliade, individuals and societies must be analyzed primarily in terms of their temporal orientations, and he unfavorably compares modern Western to archaic societies in this way. The recurring movement from depletion to renewal or fragmentation to reconstitution has been generally lost in our own time with consequences that are seriously damaging, and moderns should value the temporal orientation that marks traditional societies as well as that which characterizes participation in art forms such as narrative. In Whitehead's work, time is so primary that he avoids separate discussions of it, as though such discussions would make time appear as less fundamental and inclusive than it is. Reality for him is process, and there is neither refuge from nor exception to it. Finally, for Heidegger human existence is what it is primarily because of and through its temporal nature. It is only by being temporal that a person can experience integrity and authenticity.

To approach the question of primacy we must begin with the narrative theory that was presented in the introductory chapter and then suggest a relation between the narrative form and basic constituents of an ongoing life. Narrative was described as discourse that stands out as a form by bringing into prominence and unity images of four kinds: atmosphere, character, plot, and tone. They concern the nature and potentials within discourse of boundary, subject, action, and attitude. Since

these are pervasive features of discourse, no sharp line sepa-
rates narrative discourse from discourse in general. Yet, narrative is immediately recognizable as a particular kind of discourse because it brings to attention these four aspects as
clusters of human interest and concern.

The reason that these four kinds of images are major foci
of human concern is that each has within it questions both
urgent for human existence and not susceptible to certainty.
That is, they are questions that must be answered even though
the answers do not yield to verification or to universal agreement. Atmosphere raises the question of the boundaries of the
human world, what is or is not to be expected, what is or is not
possible. People differ in their expectations, and a person's experience is as much affected by expectation as expectation is
molded in response to experience. What can be expected, the
possible, is a matter of belief. The same situation exists in regard to character. Is human nature mean or worthy, on the as-
cent or the decline, fixed or transformable? While answers to
such questions are fundamental to relationships with other
people, we do not have certainty concerning them. Tone raises
axiological questions: What is worthy of discourse? What position to the material should be taken by a teller? And what values do the implied author and implied reader share? No less
than these, plot, which brings to focus the nature and potentials of time, leads to questions that are answered by beliefs.

The nature and potential of time and time's relation to human identity and well-being were so fully developed in the fiction we studied because plot was a dominant element in it.
The dominance of plot allowed time to appear as a reality that
outstrips human understanding and control. Conclusions to be
drawn concerning the nature and potential of time in the fiction, therefore, have the status of beliefs. Like the other elements of narrative, plot raises questions that, while requiring
answers, do not yield to certainty. By requiring answers but
preventing certainty, the status of time in narrative makes belief unavoidable. The four elements of narrative are all matters
of concern because they correspond to the structure undergirding a person's or people's ongoing life. If one, so to speak, takes

the lid off an ongoing life, four kinds of assumptions will be exposed. A person or a people assumes that some things can and some things cannot be expected or are possible, that humans are basically mean or worthy, communal or individual, fixed or transformable, that phenomena have variously to be valued and related to, and that existence and identity are in some way affected by time. The ontological (atmosphere), ethical (character), axiological (tone), and teleological (plot) questions are always answered, and the answers to them implied by any ongoing life are beliefs. To put the matter the other way, no life can be ongoing if answers to questions of these four kinds have not been assumed.

The relation of narrative art to experience, then, is the relation of articulated images to implied and often unconscious beliefs. Narrative art, by virtue of its form, matches the belief structure implied by an ongoing life. The beliefs of these four kinds that can be inferred from a particular narrative may either reinforce or challenge the beliefs of its readers or hearers, but the potential for significant engagement between the beliefs of the narrative determined by its form and the belief structure of the reader is crucial to the relation of narrative to human life.

The three thinkers included here indicate an alliance between narrative's ability to reveal the primacy of time in human experience and the arguments for that primacy based on observations, speculation, or analysis. More than that, the common testimony of narrative art and intellectual work of diverse kinds concerning time serves to demonstrate the common dependence of both imagination and mind on assumptions concerning a reality that, because of its primacy, cannot be articulated apart from belief.

Without denying the urgency and significance of the primacy of time, however, we must bear in mind, if we do justice to the total potential of the narrative form, that primacy is not an exclusive potential of plot. All the elements of narrative carry the potential for primacy even when that potential is not fully actualized. Nor are the three thinkers other than partial in their emphasis on the primacy of time in human experience and reflection. When attention shifts to a differing set of images or human concern, the primacy of time will be more or less eclipsed. While all four centers of interest are fundamental and indispensable, doing justice to the primacy of one will likely mean subordinating the others to the overriding emphasis.

II

The second major characteristic of time, its complexity, leads us to the question of belief in our common past, rather than to the role of belief in our ongoing lives. How is it that nine writers, some of them narrative artists, some of them philosophers of differing kinds, and all of them distinctive in their styles, methods, and interests, unintentionally conspire to present time as a complex system? Before pursuing this question we should recall this composite image of time, although the need for repetition here is less than it is with the other characteristics since complexity provided the structure for separating the nine writers into three groups.

In the works of Hemingway, Lawrence, and Eliade, the pattern of events has a rhythmic quality. There is a stress on return, on events as constituting a cycle of alienation and reincorporation, fragmentation and reconstitution, depletion and renewal, or disorientation and rerooting. The most common emphasis in this pattern is on the natural context for human life, even though the distinction between human life and nature is maintained. Human time and natural time are closely allied by means of a common rhythmic base.

In Mann, Faulkner, and Whitehead, a polyphonic pattern appears. Time, whether assented to by characters or not, is a process of interaction among diverse, often sharply differing kinds of people and human interests. The setting of this kind of time is social, and the overall image is of time as an assemblage of individual developmental lines clarified and enriched by interaction with one another, interaction that can be dissonant as well as harmonious.

Finally, Woolf, Hesse, and Heidegger give us time with patterns that are melodic, that is, in which events are related along lines of personal development, of an individual's or of a culture's emerging identity. The settings of such time are internal and, in the case of individuals, psychological.

Rather than needing to choose among these three forms of time, it is possible to take them together and to describe human time as characterized by three aspects or orientations. The differences arise among the three groups as one aspect dominates the others. Indeed, as we saw, all three aspects were present in the work of several of the writers, even while one aspect dominated the others. The conclusion, in other words, is that narratives and human beings differ in their temporality according to which of the three aspects is most important. And it appears that at any one time, in any one narrative, or in any one life, one aspect must be more important than the others.

The complexity of time, which these writers have unintentionally revealed, poses a quite different question concerning belief than does the primacy of time because it draws attention to our common past and our relation of it. Put simply it is this: What source or container gives rise to and houses these three kinds of time? Is there a system that carries them all and accounts for both the differences and the continuity between them? I think that there is and that when we pursue the question we will find that it leads to a system of beliefs.

I proposed in a previous book that the depiction of character in modern fiction was influenced by a system of beliefs with a wholeness, integrity, and autonomy of its own and a very ambiguous relation to systems of belief assumed and promulgated by religious institutions. I further suggested that not only narrative character but also the anthropologies of religious philosophers and certain theologians were indebted to, even determined by, such a system. In order to nominate this system of beliefs I used the term "wisdom." Finally, I went so far as to suggest that this wisdom, while derived from classical and folk cultures as well, finds a major source in biblical wisdom. I went on, then, to describe the nature of wisdom and distinguished it from two other kinds of belief systems, priestly and prophetic.

Along with many other characteristics that could be mentioned, three aspects of biblical wisdom can be noted. The first is its orientation to the natural context and dimensions of human life. "The sun also rises," Hemingway reminds us, and when we turn to Ecclesiastes, and to Job, Proverbs, and the other wisdom texts as well, we see how often we are called on to recognize our involvement in and relation to natural phenomena. For wisdom, such recognition is healing to and supportive of human life, and attempts to abstract ourselves above these natural associations and dependencies distort human existence hopelessly. Injunctions to go "back to nature" are, in wisdom literature, calls for insights, restoration, and correction that are not otherwise available. Ancient sages, consequently, would have little trouble understanding and appreciating the kind of temporality depicted and advocated in the works of Hemingway, Lawrence, and Eliade.

Just as important for wisdom is trust in the process of interaction among various interests within human life and even between or among cultures. Thomas Mann grants access to the complex life of Joseph, and he reveals, indirectly, why the Joseph narrative is increasingly taken by biblical scholars as important to the traditions of wisdom in ancient Israel. Its positive rendering of cultural interchange makes it important. Joseph goes into Egypt and participates fully in its life. The result is not a loss of his identity or a slighting of the integrity of his origins, not a denial of either culture but a gain for both, an enrichment of life's possibilities neither could have created alone. Indeed, the wisdom of ancient Israel thrived in the royal courts, particularly that of Solomon, which were deeply involved in cultural interchange, and wisdom trusted that process. Wisdom was both the enabling context for cultural interaction and the result of that process.

The future held up as a goal in Proverbs by Wisdom herself offers the kind of transcendent and spiritual wholeness and completeness toward which melodic time is oriented. The way to wisdom is never completed in a human life, but one always moves ahead. There can be constant participation in the goal of wisdom even though there cannot be arrival and complete possession.

These three orientations, toward nature, cultural complexity, and spiritual completion, while indicating important differences, do not militate against one another but are aspects of a full human life. The sapiential tradition includes all three, and wisdom as a system continually calls for fullness in each of these separable directions. Human time becomes a complex of all three.

The purpose of these remarks is not to subject modern fictions and philosophies of time to biblical wisdom. It serves only to indicate that it may be appropriate to use the label complex "wisdom" for the system of beliefs that accounts for the unintended image of time in narrative art and in theoretical formulations.

These three aspects of wisdom, along with some of its other characteristics—its stress on personal growth, the value it places on experience, and its tendency to emphasize specific religious authority and identity less than universal human attributes and divine revelation in the majesty and intricacies of the created order—make it a good candidate for the role described. Wisdom is an appropriate name, it seems, for a system of belief large enough to give rise to the threefold nature of time as it appears in the works we have studied. And it is a system inclusive enough to house both literary art and philosophical formulation. Finally, wisdom is universal enough to qualify as the kind of belief system that can be articulated in a pluralistic and largely secular culture.

To establish the historical moment when wisdom emerges as a belief system on equal footing with the priestly and the prophetic would take us beyond the bounds of this study, even if the potential fully to establish that point were firmly in hand. Let us simply designate Erasmus and Rabelais figures as crucial to the articulation of a sapiential system as Luther and Calvin are to a prophetic. At one time both systems emerged to challenge the hegemony of the priestly. The distinctive orientations of modern culture—to the natural order, to human diversity, and to utopias—can be more directly related to a sapiential system of belief than to either a prophetic or a priestly. It is from such a system, as well, I suggest, that our complex image of time arises.

III

The third characteristic of time, its trustworthiness, is more obviously related to belief and may, therefore, require less comment than the other two. In the fiction it arises as an affirmation rooted in the unavoidable coherence that narrative grants to time, however minimal that coherence may be. Even when events are depicted as arbitrary or as contrary to human needs and desires, the very fact that they are housed between a beginning and an ending, even if the termini are merely the first and last words of the narrative, grants to the time of the narrative an irrepressibly positive quality.

Rather than repressing as much as possible the coherence-granting qualities of narrative time, the fictions we have studied have augmented them. Indeed, narrative art appears here as an affirmative response to highly negative events and attitudes incorporated within it. We can conclude from these fictions that faith in the trustworthiness of time is to be advocated in the face of highly disconcerting events and that loss of such faith seriously diminishes humanity. We are led to conclude from the fiction that no event, grievously negative as it may be (the death of a loved one, serious injury and dislocation, the betrayal of trust, the dislocations created by rapid urbanization, or the destruction caused by war), is so hostile to narrative coherence that it cannot be incorporated. Even when the negative event is left outside the narrative, as occurs in some of Hemingway's major work, for example, the event carries the positive trace of impelling characters from darkness into the well-lit time of the narrative itself.

In Lawrence's novels people who put their trust in processes that they do not control or understand are rewarded by an expanded life, by union with another human being, and by the reconstitution of society. The trustworthiness of time is severely taxed and tested in Mann's novels because of the destructive consequences of events in this century. War, which could seem too negative an event to be included within the boundaries that grant coherence to time, becomes, along with other stressful occurrences within the period, a part of the forward-moving and all-incorporating temporal coherence. Exceptional as they are in Faulkner's fiction, moments when people trust the recognition and interaction that can occur between those who differ in sex, race, or social location flicker like beacons of hope on the generally dark landscape of distrust in social time. The principal characters of Virginia Woolf's novels, diminished by losses and faced with uncertainties, seem carried forward to new confidence, freedom, insight and unity with others when they trust processes while unable to predict or control their outcome. And in Hesse's fiction, loss of faith in the creative movement either of culture or of one's own life causes loss and disorientation while trust in those processes leads to integrity and creativity.

Trustworthiness of time in the work of the three thinkers is so important that it accounts for the fact that each of them has fathered a school of interpretation of religious thought and experience. Their combined contributions to the appreciation, understanding, and reformulation of religious behavior and theological interests are immense, due largely to their reflections on time in human experience, treating it as a reality in human life requiring faith or as itself a form of faith.

For Eliade traditional societies trust the creative and recreative direction of time because cycles return them, they believe, to the time of the gods, to a time that stands as an inexhaustible reservoir for renewal. Moderns are alienated from such a source, and if their own time is to have any meaning it must once again be aligned with one. This realignment occurs, in however unconscious and minimal a way, whenever we enter the time of an art form such as narrative.

Trust in process undergirds Whitehead's theory of prehension and accounts for his interest in religion and in God. A sense of the unity of reality, of the relation between contemporaries, and of the forward, creative movement of reality are validated, finally, by a God who is inseparable from, although not exhausted by, that process itself. For Whitehead, reality as a process does not exhibit unity by chance. Rather, there is an actual world because there is order, and reliance on this order is an act of faith. The recognition of time as trustworthy and of participation in process as creative and unifying grants trust a religious quality in his work.

Finally, for Heidegger I can affirm the wholeness and meaning of my life not in spite of but through its temporal nature. Time, from which temporality arises, and Being, from which I as a being arise, are revealed in and by temporality and death. Living and dying reveal the trustworthiness of Being and time. Rather than by fleeing time and death, I become a person to the extent I am identified with the time of my origins and personal destiny.

The question to which all of this gives rise is whether these writers, by virtue of their affirmations concerning the trustworthiness of time, confine their relevance to the first half of this century. Is it not precisely at this point that a gap appears between their time and our own? We live in a period marked by the Holocaust and leading, it appears, with increasing speed toward the likelihood of nuclear annihilation. With a future horizon clouded by such horror, can we treat the affirmations we have listed as anything more than curiosities from a less threatened and more optimistic time?

While no final answer to such questions can be given, two observations seem fundamental. The first is that discourse in our own time must differ from that of their time because it must reach out to the unthinkable. Discourse is and will be truly repressive or abstracted if the disconcerting realities and possibilities that mark our time are ignored. Discourse will not be of our own time if it does not reach out to include what is most disconcerting and threatening to it.

The other point is that our discourse, however much it may differ from that of a former generation by being stretched to include the unthinkable, will also be continuous with it. Both narrative discourse and discourse in general have the characteristics now that they had then, and narrative and discourse are inseparable from our very nature as human beings. Whatever the threats to coherence may be, discourse will continue to reach out and incorporate the new.

These two points, concerning discontinuity and continuity, must both be affirmed. We can take the unthinkable into our discourse not to defuse and domesticate it by our language but to extend the limits of discourse and of our humanity. The threats to our future, with whatever else they portend, also challenge us to recognize in the limits of our discourse possibilities for a more inclusive coherence.

APPENDIX

"Polyphony" in the Poetics of Mikhail Bakhtin

With the recent publication in English of Mikhail Bakhtin's major work, the term "polyphony," which is central to his understanding of the novel, will become more familiar and commonly used among American critics than it is now. Since the term figures largely in the second section of my book, I would like to offer a fuller discussion than could be given there concerning its relation to Bakhtin's theory. While there are points of overlap, the differences between the two uses should be made clear.

"Polyphony," along with such terms as "heteroglossia" and "dialogical language," defines the novel in Bakhtin's work. It is his way of distinguishing the language of the novel from that of the epic or of poetry. He ties the rise of the novel to axiological changes crucial to the origins and nature of modern culture.

While prepared for by many centuries of novelistic impulses prior to the modern period, the novel, beginning with Rabelais' *Pantagruel* and *Gargantua*, appears in the modern world as its characteristic and enabling literary form.[1] Its displacement of both the epic and of poetry from their central position constitutes a Galilean revolution.[2] The Ptolemaic literary world preceding the rise of the novel had two major, defining characteristics. One was an attitude of reverence and subservience of the narrator and reader toward the material, a distinction in value between the time of the narrative and the time of its telling. Epic depended on and reinforced that normative distance.[3] The novel alters this situation radically. In it the time of the narrative and the time of the teller are on the same axiological plane. In other words, the novel deals with and affirms the validity of present time, even when it deals with the past.[4]

A second characteristic of the epic and poetry is that they are monological. By this Bakhtin means that there is not in these forms a plurality of languages. Even if there are sundry discourses, dialogues of sorts, they are subjected to a single, dominating language. Epic and poetry are forms reflecting and reinforcing a situation in which one group or one worldview holds privilege over others. In such a situation, other languages and views, if they are depicted, are treated as objects integrated into a whole provided by the privileged language. The novel, in contrast, presents or allows for a variety of languages, all of which have an integrity and validity of their own, points of view contending with and complementing one another in a whole which no one of them provides.[5]

When Bakhtin uses the term "language" to describe these changes and contrasts he does not only mean national languages. He also means the languages of groups within a society and the languages of individuals. Language is discourse that reveals a particular relation to, perspective on, and interest in the world. He resists the abstraction of language from that grounding in particular uses and shapings. Language divorced from that grounding is lifeless, in important ways even meaningless.[6] The novel, then, is a polyglot of differing, embodied worldviews that intersect and affect one another.

Bakhtin makes an extraordinary claim for the importance of Dostoevsky: that his work brings the nature or potential of the novel into actuality for the first time. Dostoevsky's art effects an Einsteinian revolution in the history of literature.[7] While the modern period succeeded in providing a marketplace for contending worldviews, the rationalism of the period, epitomized in the Enlightenment, coupled with capitalism, tended to abstract ideas from voices and particular, rooted points of view and to treat ideas as leading to or revealing *idea* as abstract and uniform.[8] Dostoevsky, however, allowed points of view and ideas to be fully embodied in particular voices within his works.[9] By doing so, he created the "polyphonic novel," the novel as it can and should be. In his novels we find, according to Bakhtin, autonomous voices on an equal plane not subjected to the voice of the narrator. This radical decentering releases a dynamic process created by the interaction of conflicting ideologies, beliefs, and opinions. Such an achievement is not the end of the novel but its beginning, for now its nature and function have been revealed and released. The polyphonic novel is not one kind of novel; it is the novel as it should be, for it stimulates and reflects the tension that always exists between the centripetal and the centrifugal forces in language, between factors that create diversity and those that create unity.[10]

Bakhtin thereby ties the novel closely to the nature of language or of discourse as he understands it actually to be. In this sense he is a realist.[11] The novel and its development are closely tied to the rise of the modern period and to crucial changes within it: the subversion of authority and its monological forms, the interactions among various languages and cultures, the granting of equal footing to contending ideologies, and, finally, the rooting of all perspectives in particular forms of life and experience. In this situation the novel is not merely a passive reflection of such developments and changes; it stimulates and models them. It and the modern period cannot be thought of apart from one another, and other genres, if they are to continue, must be influenced by the novel.

Far from relating "polyphony" to one of the elements of narrative, as I have done, Bakhtin uses the term much more broadly. While he speaks of all four of the elements of narrative, he takes the novel to be not a unity of images of atmosphere, character, plot, and tone but an image of language. The novel is the image of language as a system of diverse languages, as social heteroglossia.[12] Epic is an image of elevated language, the language of a privileged time, while poetry is the image of monological language. Since he defines the novel in this way, he subjects the elements of narrative to the larger, defining quality of the novel as an image of linguistic polyphony. When he talks of the mystery and autonomy of characters, then, he does so to describe not character but, rather, the particularity of perspective that marks an individual language within a novel.[13] When he speaks of plot, he does so only to account for the situations created in the novel that allow voices to interact.[14] He treats tone in his discussion of the equal plane that the narrator shares with the characters.[15] And when he refers to atmosphere, he does so to describe the borders or boundaries of particular languages as they are clarified by the encounters of differing languages with one another.[16]

Despite the significant differences between "polyphony" in the work of Bakhtin and its use here, there are two points of agreement: the emphasis on present time, which Bakhtin also takes to be central to polyphony,[17] and his frequent use of sociological metaphors to describe the polyphonic situation.[18] Both points figure largely, as well, in my section on polyphonic time. These two aspects of his use of "polyphony" grant Bakhtin's work an affinity to the novels of Mann and Faulkner. And anyone acquainted with the work of Whitehead can, while reading Bakhtin, easily translate many of his observations into Whiteheadian categories.

These points of similarity, however, should not conceal the major differences. The first concerns the nature of narrative time, the second the nature of narrative itself.

Although "polyphony" is not, for Bakhtin, descriptive of plot, it does have a predominantly temporal quality in his theory. He describes it frequently as a process, open-ended and never complete, created by the intersection and conflicts between differing worldviews. But Bakhtin denies the validity, even the reality, of the other two kinds of time. He is particularly negative concerning rhythmic, or what he calls cyclical, time. He thinks of it as denying the validity of present time and the independence of language from nature.[19] And melodic time, one can infer, for Bakhtin, is inseparable from a monological situation, which he deplores.

Two things can be said in response. First, I assume that narrative or theories of human time will be dominated by one of the three elements of the time system. It is not surprising, then, that in Bakhtin's work one of the three—in his case the polyphonic element—should deform and subject the others to itself. But it is not as though he has eliminated the other elements from his work, however much he may distrust them. The place of rhythmic time is revealed in Bakhtin's work by his fascination for beginnings. He goes upstream, in his discussion of the novel, to trace its origins in the rivulets of parody, satire, and the carnival spirit in ancient times.[20] Furthermore, in his study of Rabelais, whose novels he takes to be crucial texts in the exchange of a static, hierarchical view of the world for a temporal and inclusive one, he designates rhythmic time as basic to the novels and to the traditions of satire, laughter, and carnival upon which Rabelais draws. "This is the drama of laughter," he writes, "presenting at the same time the death of the old and the birth of the new world."[21] And, as to melodic time, he treats the novel as a genre that is constantly developing, that is constantly actualizing its inner potential. It is not that Dostoevsky created the polyphonic novel but rather that the novel's potential to become polyphonic is first released in and through his work. Now the novel continues to move toward its actualization. Furthermore, it is strange that Bakhtin can be so aware of the peculiar and defining qualities of the modern period and ignore both its preoccupation with returning to the simplicity or natural groundings of beginnings and its orientation toward the future self-actualization of individuals, groups, and mankind. No objection need be raised about his exclusive interest in polyphonic time, but the tendency to limit narrative and human time to one of its elements should be checked.

As to the nature of narrative, it can be said first of all that Bakhtin is less eager to describe narrative than to describe the novel. There need not be any challenge raised here to his eloquent depiction of the rise of the novel as coinciding with the loss and subversion of closed and authoritative social structures. The question is whether it is enough to define the novel as an image of language or as a system of languages. The problem begins to emerge when Bakhtin attributes the characteristics of polyphony to prose in general.[22] The question of the novel as a particular *kind* of prose discourse, that is, as narrative, cannot be repressed. The novel in particular and narrative generally are immediately recognizable as certain kinds of discourse. While we have no difficulty recognizing narrative discourse when we encounter it, the reason it is immediately recognizable is not obvious at all. My offered answer is that narrative stands out as a particular kind of discourse because it offers a unified set of four kinds of images, kinds designated by the terms atmosphere, character, tone, and plot. While Bakhtin treats all of these elements, he wants polyphonic language to be definitive of the novel. The problem is that he has taken a characteristic of the novel, one with important historical ties and axiological implications, and made it definitive of the novel as narrative.

Notes

1. Plot and the Image of Time

1. Frank Kermode, *The Sense of an Ending: Studies in the Theory of Fiction.*
2. Readers convinced that Hemingway was too much the nonintellectual to worry about such things should consult two recent studies: Brian Way, "Hemingway the Intellectual: A Version of Modernism," and Gerry Brenner, *Concealments in Hemingway's Works.*
3. Rather than place brackets around specific decades, I would identify modernist literature as that in which World War I has a central position or on which it has had a major impact. The writing treated in this study covers the first half of the twentieth century. For a discussion of the marks of modernism see Stephen Spender, *The Struggle of the Modern;* David Daiches, *The Novel and the Modern World;* Joseph Wood Krutch, *"Modernism" in Modern Drama: A Definition and an Estimate;* Edmund Wilson, *Axel's Castle: A Study in the Imaginative Literature of 1890–1930;* Richard Ellmann and Charles Feidelson, Jr., eds., *The Modern Tradition: Backgrounds of Modern Literature;* and Irving Howe, ed., *The Idea of the Modern in Literature and the Arts.*
4. John Fletcher and Malcolm Bradbury, "The Introverted Novel," p. 401.
5. For a discussion of narrative as a system constituted of four elements, for definitions of each element, and for examples of fictions in which each dominates, see my *Narrative Elements and Religious Meaning* and the introduction to my *Moral Fiber: Character and Belief in Recent American Fiction.*

6. See Günther Müller, *Morphologische Poetik: Gesammelte Aufsätze*, especially "Die Bedeutung der Zeit in der Erzählkunst" and "Erzählzeit und erzählte Zeit," pp. 247–87, and Gérard Genette, *Narrative Discourse: An Essay in Method*, p. 35.
7. See Victor Erlich, *Russian Formalism: History-Doctrine*, pp. 209–11.
8. Jonathan Culler, "Fabula and Sjuzhet in the Analysis of Narrative," *Poetics Today*, p. 28.
9. See Seymour Chatman, *Story and Discourse: Narrative Structure in Fiction and Film*; Meir Sternberg, "What is Exposition? An Essay in Temporal Delimitation," pp. 25–70; and David Higdon, *Time and English Fiction*.
10. Robert Scholes and Robert Kellogg, *The Nature of Narrative*, p. 239.
11. For an excellent analysis of the philosophical error of projecting a nonnarrated sequence of events as prior to narrative, see Barbara Herrnstein Smith, "Narrative Versions, Narrative Theories," p. 219.
12. For a more conventional instance of this error see William J. Harvey, *Character and the Novel*.
13. Vladimir Propp, *Morphology of the Folktale*.
14. See, for example, Roland Barthes, *Image-Music-Text*, pp. 81–84, 127–28.
15. A. J. Greimas, *Structural Semantics: An Attempt at a Method*, pp. 121, 171–72, 206–7.
16. See Tzvetan Todorov, *The Poetics of Prose*, pp. 223–24, and Fredric Jameson, *The Political Unconscious: Narrative as a Socially Symbolic Act*, p. 121.
17. See Joseph Frank, "Spatial Form in Modern Literature," in his *The Widening Gyre: Crisis and Mastery in Modern Literature*, pp. 3–63, and his "Spatial Form: An Answer to Critics." See also Eric S. Rabkin, "Spatial Form and Plot"; William Holtz, "Spatial Form in Modern Literature: A Reconsideration"; Frank Kermode, "A Reply to Joseph Frank"; and Sharon Spencer, *Space, Time, and Structure in the Modern Novel*.
18. See, for example, Elder Olson, *Tragedy and the Theory of Drama*.
19. Eleanor Hutchins, "An Approach through Time," p. 61.
20. Michael Hollington, "Svevo, Joyce and Modernist Time," p. 437.
21. John Vernon, in *The Garden and the Map: Schizophrenia in Twentieth-Century Literature and Culture*, argues that the major consequence of the epistemology assumed by fiction in the nineteenth century was a freezing of time and a resulting reduction of human life. See also J. Hillis Miller, *The Form of Victorian Fiction*, pp. 62–85, for a discussion of the godlike pretensions of the omniscient narrator and their consequences for narrative time.
22. Daiches, *The Novel and the Modern World*, p. 7.
23. Hans Meyerhoff, *Time in Literature*, pp. 107–15.

24. See Jerome Hamilton Buckley, *The Triumph of Time: A Study of the Victorian Concept of Time, History, Progress and Decadence*, p. 13; Matei Calinescu, *Faces of Modernism: Avant-Garde, Decadence, Kitsch*; Malcolm Bradbury, "The Cities of Modernism," pp. 98–99; and Monroe Spears, *Dionysus and the City: Modernism in Twentieth-Century Poetry*, p. 29.

25. E. M. Forster, *Aspects of the Novel*, p. 86.

26. Kermode, *The Sense of an Ending*.

27. Ricoeur, *Time and Narrative*, pp. 31–52.

28. Ibid., p. 67.

29. Ibid., p. 72.

30. Northrop Frye, *Anatomy of Criticism: Four Essays*, pp. 158–239.

31. Joseph Campbell, *The Hero with a Thousand Faces*, p. 17.

32. Kermode, *The Sense of an Ending*, p. 45.

33. Hans Vaihinger, *The Philosophy of "As If": A System of the Theoretical, Practical, and Religious Fictions of Mankind*.

34. Ibid., p. 2.

35. I am aware of two other critics who propose that differing kinds of time are discernible in modern narrative: John Henry Raleigh, *Time, Place, and Idea: Essays on the Novel*, and David Higdon, *Time and English Fiction*. While my own account of the reasons for and consequences of the diversity of time in modernist narratives differs from theirs, these works draw attention to temporal complexity. By using the term "pattern" I attempt to avoid the conflicting understanding of time revealed by Wyndham Lewis in his objections to Bergson. Lewis, resisting the imprecisions of time conceived as flux or stream, insists on time's being a sum of discrete units. "Pattern" suggests the continuity that the metaphors of flow emphasize, but it also suggests an order that stream or flow leaves out. See Wyndham Lewis, *Time and Western Man*.

36. While the hypothesis of a narrative time system constituted of three elements, one of which will dominate the other two, is my own and was developed from the work of these writers, I have found, during and after formulating this hypothesis, other references to human time using musical metaphors. "Melody" is used by Bergson and, even more, by Husserl, and it is appropriate to their interest in the processes of consciousness. See especially Edmund Husserl, *The Phenomenology of Internal Time-Consciousness*. "Melody" is also combined with "rhythm," in discussions of human time in M. Merleau-Ponty's *Phenomenology of Perception*, Thorlief Boman's *Hebrew Thought Compared with Greek*, and John S. Dunne's *Time and Myth*. "Polyphony," as the appendix to this book makes clear, is central to Mikhail Bakhtin's theory of the novel.

37. Kern, *The Culture of Time and Space*, pp. 11–15.

2. ERNEST HEMINGWAY

1. Philip Young, *Ernest Hemingway: A Reconsideration;* Carlos Baker, *Hemingway: The Writer as Artist;* Jackson J. Benson, *Hemingway: The Writer's Art of Self-Defense;* and Scott Donaldson, *By Force of Will: The Life and Art of Ernest Hemingway.*
2. Baker, *Hemingway: The Writer as Artist,* pp. 289, 290.
3. Ibid., p. 325.
4. Ibid., p. 309.
5. Chaman Nahal, *The Narrative Pattern in Ernest Hemingway's Fiction.* Also see Wirt Williams, *The Tragic Art of Ernest Hemingway* for a study of melody and harmony as important musical elements in addition to rhythm in Hemingway's fiction.
6. Sheldon Norman Grebstein, *Hemingway's Craft,* p. 23.
7. Earl Rovit, *Ernest Hemingway,* pp. 129, 131.
8. Ibid., p. 109. This skeptical reading of the relation of meaning to movement in human time is shared by Arthur Waldhorn, who writes in *A Reader's Guide to Ernest Hemingway,* "The code asks of a man that he try to impose meaning where none seems possible, that he try in every gesture he makes to impress his will on the raw material of life" (p. 27).
9. Ernest Hemingway, *In Our Time,* p. 65.
10. Baker, *Hemingway: The Writer as Artist,* p. 72.
11. Ernest Hemingway, *A Farewell to Arms,* p. 327.
12. Donaldson, *By Force of Will,* p. 160.
13. I cannot accept, therefore, Gerry Brenner's conclusion that "the thesis of *A Farewell to Arms* is that no institution, belief, system, value, or commitment can arm one against life's utter irrationality" (*Concealments in Hemingway's Works,* p. 28). Brenner's alternatives create the problem. It is generally true that no amount of anticipation or expectation seems adequate as a resource for meeting the demands that the confrontations of experience create. Henry brings little by way of resources; others who bring more will still not be able to overwhelm experience by a repertoire of beliefs, values, or commitment, and certainly no institution or system is a likely or appropriate counterpart to experience. But because events are unexpected and disconcerting, we need not conclude that in the novels they lack meaning.
14. Ernest Hemingway, *For Whom the Bell Tolls,* p. 209.
15. Ibid., p. 73.
16. John Griffith, "Rectitude in Hemingway's Fiction: How Rite Makes Right," pp. 159–73.
17. Hemingway, *For Whom the Bell Tolls,* p. 456.
18. Ibid., p. 466.

19. Political commitment as an adequate basis for meaningful dying is further undercut, of course, by the caricature of some communist leaders, especially André Marty, by Jordan's relation to Kaskin and Karkov, and by his insistence that he is an antifascist and not a communist.

20. Ernest Hemingway, *The Old Man and the Sea*, p. 68.

21. Arthur Waldhorn writes, "In an unpublished letter addressed to Philip Young, he indicated that his model was actually a young man whose penis had been shot away but whose testicles and spermatic cord remained intact" (*A Reader's Guide to Ernest Hemingway*, p. 238).

22. Ernest Hemingway, *The Sun Also Rises*, p. 11.

23. Ibid., p. 121.

24. Ibid., p. 209.

25. Ibid., p. 232.

26. Ibid., p. 237. The role of water changes in the novel in ways appropriate to the three parts.

27. Dante is mentioned on a dozen occasions. The references to Dante in this novel and in *Islands in the Stream* are discussed in Williams, *The Tragic Art of Ernest Hemingway*, pp. 165–67, 201, although with quite different results. Dante's *Divine Comedy* is also central to Gerry Brenner's analysis of the novel in his *Concealments in Hemingway's Work*, pp. 151–65. He sees the relation to Dante in the mixture of actual and fictional characters, the rivers and bridges of Venice, Cantwell's assigning people to hell, his confession and contrition, and the resemblance of Renata to Beatrice. I am unaware of any notice of the role of Dante in *The Sun Also Rises*. The point is important because it undercuts the kind of point Brenner wants to make about literary experimentation in the *later* work of Hemingway.

3. D. H. LAWRENCE

1. D. H. Lawrence, "The Novel," in *Phoenix II: Uncollected, Unpublished and Other Prose Works of D. H. Lawrence*, p. 419.

2. Graham Hough calls this life force "*mana.*" See *The Dark Sun: A Study of D. H. Lawrence*, p. 32.

3. Julian Moynaham speaks of "incremental repetition" and "incantatory rhythm" in Lawrence's fiction (*The Deed of Life: The Novels and Tales of D. H. Lawrence*, p. 53). Stephen J. Miko writes of "the extraordinary regularity of its rhythms, which strikingly reinforce the idea of cyclical repetition" (*Toward "Women in Love": The Emergence of a Lawrentian Aesthetic*, p. 115).

4. Peter Balbert, *D. H. Lawrence and the Psychology of Rhythm: The Meaning of Form in "The Rainbow,"* p. 11.

5. Aidan Burns, *Nature and Culture in D. H. Lawrence*, p. 28.
6. D. H. Lawrence, *The Rainbow*, p. 190.
7. D. H. Lawrence, "A Propos of *Lady Chatterley's Lover*," *Phoenix II*, p. 511.
8. Lawrence, *The Rainbow*, p. 345.
9. D. H. Lawrence, "The Crown," *Phoenix II*, p. 414. Also see Daniel Albright, *Personality and Impersonality: Lawrence, Woolf, and Mann*, p. 29.
10. D. H. Lawrence, *The Lost Girl*, p. 322.
11. "For Lawrence, . . . east and north were ordinarily quarters of death or dying cultures. Hope lay south, and in due time, west" (L. D. Clark, *The Minoan Distance: The Symbolism of Travel in D. H. Lawrence*, p. 45).
12. "To Lawrence the war was from the beginning a 'colossal idiocy,' a 'disintegrating autumnal process,' sheer 'decomposition,' portending the crumbling of 'the whole of England, of the Christian era.' It indicated the brutal triumph of a 'decadent life' when 'all is destruction and dying and corruption,' when 'a collapsing civilization' is finally revealed in 'so much hate and destruction and disintegration'" (George A. Panichas, *Adventures in Consciousness: The Meaning of D. H. Lawrence's Religious Quest*, p. 64).
13. Lawrence, "The Crown," *Phoenix II*, p. 404.
14. For example, Stephen J. Miko asserts that there is in Lawrence's novels an increasingly sharp distinction between civilization and the best interests of his characters until "civilization's forms are no longer capable of receiving life" (*Toward "Women in Love,"* p. 24).
15. He writes, "The true heart of the world is a book, there are sufficient among your acquaintances to make a complete world, but you must learn from books how to know them" (Letter to Mary Chambers Holbrook, 2 December 1908, in D. H. Lawrence, *Collected Letters*, 1:38. In this comment, "book" means narrative.
16. The center in Lawrence's novels is often related to origin and rebirth. Daniel Albright says, "The world of origin is intimate, impending, scarcely concealed within the corpus of the everyday" (*Personality and Impersonality*, p. 48).
17. In his "Study of Thomas Hardy" Lawrence relates departure and return to complementary sexual roles. He says, for example, that "When the two are working in combination, as they must in life, there is, as it were, a dual motion, centrifugal for the male, fleeing abroad, away from the centre, outward to infinite vibration, and centripetal for the female, fleeing in to the eternal centre of rest" (*Phoenix: The Posthumous Papers of D. H. Lawrence*, p. 457). In *Lady Chatterley's Lover* variations and complications are played on this theme.
18. D. H. Lawrence, *The White Peacock*, p. 115.

19. Mark Spilka identifies these loves as "oedipal, spiritual, and 'unbalanced-possessive'" (*The Love Ethic of D. H. Lawrence*, p. 82).

20. "The Old Testament pulse-beat in the style is in keeping with the Book-of-Genesis episodes in the story" (Harry T. Moore, *The Life and Works of D. H. Lawrence*, p. 144).

21. Lawrence, *The Rainbow*, p. 2.

22. Eugene Goodheart says that "Lawrence's imagination was oriented toward the future, that its characteristic impulse was to discover new forms of life immanent, though not actual, in the world, and that his principal discovery was the bodily or physical life that he believed man had once possessed in his pre-civilized past and must now fully recover if future *civilized* life is to be possible" (*The Utopian Vision of D. H. Lawrence*, p. 1).

23. Lawrence, *The Rainbow*, p. 494.

24. D. H. Lawrence, *Women in Love*, p. vii.

25. Ibid., p. 121.

26. Lawrence, "A Propos of *Lady Chatterley's Lover*," *Phoenix II*, p. 509.

27. F. R. Leavis, *D. H. Lawrence: Novelist*, p. 111.

28. Miko, *Toward "Women in Love,"* p. 112.

29. See Mary Esther Harding, *Woman's Mysteries Ancient and Modern*, pp. 93ff.

30. Lawrence, *Women in Love*, p. 429.

31. D. H. Lawrence, *Lady Chatterley's Lover*, p. 41.

32. Ibid., p. 41.

33. Ibid., p. 36.

34. Ibid., p. 229.

35. Ibid., p. 260.

36. Ibid., p. 282. "Forked flame" suggests the form assumed by the Holy Spirit in the Pentecost story. The religious symbols employed and the theological meaning given to that power that requires faith and ensures a future are quite fully developed in the two essays, "Study of Thomas Hardy" and "The Crown." "There must be a certain faith. And that means an ultimate reliance on that which is beyond our will, and not contained in our ego" (Lawrence, "The Crown," *Phoenix II*, p. 400). In "Study of Thomas Hardy," when Lawrence speaks of the sexual experience as a "heave over and out of Time" (*Phoenix*, p. 442), he dissociates the experience from the past, the "Has-Been," and from the present, the "This is." In other words, the experience of the release from time is related to a sense of future.

37. Goodheart says, for example, "The repudiation of the follower-leader ideal and the new reemphasis on a 'receptivity of tenderness' represent the final phase of Lawrence's career" (*The Utopian Vision of D. H. Lawrence*, p. 146). Frank Kermode follows Goodheart at this point (*D. H. Lawrence*, p. 132).

38. D. H. Lawrence, *Kangaroo*, p. 229.

39. Ibid., p. 252.
40. Ibid., p. 18.
41. Ibid., p. 156.
42. Ibid., p. 301.
43. D. H. Lawrence, *The Trespasser*, p. 21.
44. Ibid., p. 12.
45. Ibid., p. 2.
46. Ibid., p. 38. The relation of experiencing rhythm to faith is reinforced at several points in Lawrence's writing, such as in his essay "On Being Religious": "If he is sincere, it means he refers himself back to some indefinable pulse of life in him, which gives him his direction and his substance" (*Phoenix*, p. 724).
47. See, for example, Lawrence, *The Trespasser*, pp. 107, 157, 160.
48. Ibid., p. 79.
49. Ibid., p. 56.
50. See Kermode, *D. H. Lawrence*, p. 9; Miko, *Toward "Women in Love,"* p. 290; and Burns, *Nature and Culture in D. H. Lawrence*.
51. *The Trespasser*, p. 86.
52. Ibid., p. 160.
53. D. H. Lawrence, *Aaron's Rod*, p. 250.
54. Ibid., p. 132.
55. For commentary on this pattern of death and rebirth, see ibid., pp. 148, 208.
56. Ibid., p. 161.
57. Kermode, *D. H. Lawrence*, p. 92. See also Burns, *Nature and Culture in D. H. Lawrence*, pp. 9–11.
58. Lawrence, *The White Peacock*, p. 354.
59. Lawrence, *The Rainbow*, p. 118.
60. Lawrence, *Lady Chatterley's Lover*, p. 94.

4. MIRCEA ELIADE

1. Walther Dürr, "Rhythm in Music: A Formal Scaffolding of Time," p. 182.
2. J. L. Cloudsley-Thompson, "Time Sense of Animals," p. 296.
3. Mircea Eliade, *Cosmos and History: The Myth of the Eternal Return*, p. vii.
4. Mircea Eliade, *Patterns in Comparative Religion*, p. 154.
5. Ibid., p. 154.
6. Ibid., p. 180.
7. Ibid., p. 184.
8. Ibid., pp. 210–11.
9. Ibid., p. 271.
10. Ibid., p. 389.

11. Mircea Eliade, *Mephistopheles and the Androgyne*, p. 158.
12. Mircea Eliade, *Birth and Rebirth: The Religious Meanings of Initiation in Human Culture*, p. 47.
13. Eliade, *Mephistopheles and the Androgyne*, p. 122.
14. Ibid., p. 202.
15. Mircea Eliade, *Images and Symbols: Studies in Religious Symbolism*, p. 70.
16. Mircea Eliade, *Myths, Dreams and Mysteries: The Encounter between Contemporary Faiths and Archaic Realities*, p. 186.
17. Mircea Eliade, *Yoga: Immortality and Freedom*, p. 185.
18. Eliade, *Birth and Rebirth*, p. 6.
19. Eliade, *Cosmos and History*, p. 88.
20. Mircea Eliade, *Myth and Reality*, p. 141.
21. Eliade, *Birth and Rebirth*, p. xv.
22. Eliade, *Images and Symbols*, p. 57.
23. Ibid., p. 62.
24. Eliade, *Myths, Dreams and Mysteries*, p. 51.
25. Ibid., pp. 241−42.
26. See "The Terror of History," chap. 4 of Eliade, *Cosmos and History*.
27. Mircea Eliade, "Cultural Fashions and History of Religions," p. 16.
28. Eliade, *Images and Symbols*, p. 33.
29. Ibid., p. 36.
30. Mircea Eliade, "The Sacred and the Modern Artist," p. 23.
31. Ibid., pp. 23−24.
32. Eliade, *Birth and Rebirth*, pp. 134−35.
33. Eliade, *Myth and Reality*, p. 192.
34. Eliade, *Cosmos and History*, p. 52.

5. THOMAS MANN

1. Fritz Kaufmann, *Thomas Mann: The World as Will and Representation*, p. xii.
2. See Mikhail Bakhtin, *Problems of Dostoevsky's Poetics*, esp. chap. 1, "Dostoevsky's Polyphonic Novel and Its Treatment in Critical Literature." Bakhtin's use of the term "polyphony" to describe the work of Dostoevsky has important implications for the study of narrative plot, especially when he describes the emphasis of polyphonic discourse on present time and its sociological character. However, he means by it far more than, even something quite different from, what is meant by the term here. Since the term is both unusual and important for discussing the nature of narrative, Bakhtin's particular investment in it for an understanding of the novel will be discussed in the Appendix.
3. The importance of time for this novel is widely recognized. For ex-

ample, Henry Hatfield writes, "From another point of view, *The Magic Mountain* may be seen as a 'time novel' (*Zeitroman*), in three senses. It can be seen as a portrait of pre-war European society during the period 1907–1914. Further, in certain sections—which are not digressions by any means—the novel directly discusses the circular nature of time, subjective versus objective time, and the polar relation between time and eternity. Finally, one can venture the supposition that the effects brought about by time in this novel render time an active force, almost a character" (*From the Magic Mountain: Mann's Later Masterpieces*, p. 39).

4. For a fuller list of contrasts between the culture of level ground and that of the Berghof, see Richard Thieberger, *Der Begriff der Zeit bei Thomas Mann*, p. 60.

5. Thomas Mann, *The Magic Mountain*, p. 200.

6. For a discussion of the counterpoint between the time of the biographer and that of his subject, as well as between other contrasting/ revealing temporal juxtapositions in the novel, see Harald Vogel, *Die Zeit bei Thomas Mann*, esp. pp. 248 ff.

7. "Thomas Mann became increasingly taken with the idea that the life of a prince, with its insubstantial formality, lack of practical use, and unhappy isolation, was very like the life of a writer" (T. J. Reed, *Thomas Mann: The Uses of Tradition*, pp. 95–96).

8. For more examples of such conflicts, see Thieberger, *Der Begriff der Zeit bei Thomas Mann*, pp. 18 ff.

9. "That Professor Zeitblom begins his narrative on the same day that I myself put the first lines on paper is characteristic of the entire book, of the curious brand of reality that clings to it, which seen from one aspect is total artifice" (Thomas Mann, *The Story of a Novel: The Genesis of Doctor Faustus*, p. 31).

10. Patricia Drechsel Tobin, *Time and the Novel: The Genealogical Imperative*, pp. 46–81.

11. "Fate and character, therefore, are indissolubly one. Thus the novel, in all its unsparing pessimism and sceptical irony, conveys a sense of meaningful order existing not only in and through the aesthetic organization of the written work but in the world itself" (Erich Heller, *The Ironic German: A Study of Thomas Mann*, p. 32).

12. Felix Krull comments on the strength of this lure of the unlike. See Thomas Mann, *Confessions of Felix Krull, Confidence Man*, p. 276.

13. "Thomas Mann experienced his own self and the world as a multifaceted set of polarities, as tension between opposites. Resolutions of these antagonistic forces and polar opposites into a harmony more or less achieved, more or less stable, was a basic drive in Thomas Mann" (André von Gronicka, *Thomas Mann: Profile and Perspectives*, p. 134). I shall be arguing in the final section of this essay, however,

that the unity by which the diverse and conflicting elements of life are contained is not of the writer's own contriving.

14. Eric Kahler seems to have something like this in mind when he refers to the tension in Mann's work between "representation and revolution." "He was always both conservative and radical, thoroughly proper and deeply demonic, even diabolical at times—how else could he have understood the devil so well?" (*The Orbit of Thomas Mann*, p. 76).

15. Thomas Mann, *Buddenbrooks*, p. 35.

16. Ibid., p. 454. Here Tom acknowledges the threat to him posed by Christian's values.

17. Thomas Mann, *The Beloved Returns*, p. 84.

18. Ibid., p. 331.

19. Thomas Mann, *The Transposed Heads: A Legend of India*, p. 8.

20. "[Zeitblom] and Leverkühn are, as it were, two halves of the same sphere, which might be called the German spirit or mind" (Hatfield, *From the Magic Mountain*, p. 117).

21. Mann, *The Story of a Novel*, p. 29.

22. Interest in polyphony does not appear for the first time in this novel. Already in *Buddenbrooks* (p. 391), Hanno's music teacher stresses polyphony over melody.

23. Thomas Mann, *Doctor Faustus: The Life of the German Composer Adrian Leverkühn*, p. 28.

24. "The music was only foreground and representation, only a paradigm for something more general, only a means to express the situation of art in general, of culture, even of man and the intellect itself in our so critical era"; "I felt clearly that my book itself would have to become the thing it dealt with: namely, a musical composition" (Mann, *The Story of a Novel*, pp. 41–42, 64).

25. "Mann compresses five centuries of horizontal time into one short human life, and in so doing he transforms the horizontal into the vertical, succession into simultaneity; Adrian thus functions as a chord" (Gunilla Bergsten, *Thomas Mann's Doctor Faustus: The Sources and Structure of the Novel*, p. 136).

26. "The musical world penetrates the human world and extends it to reveal its deepest sources" (T. E. Apter, *Thomas Mann: The Devil's Advocate*, p. 150).

27. Mann, *Doctor Faustus*, p. 321; see also p. 374.

28. "Underlying all Mann's work is a tension between withdrawal and involvement, recognizably the same in changing contexts" (Reed, *Thomas Mann: The Uses of Tradition*, p. 408).

29. Mann, *Buddenbrooks*, p. 370.

30. While I stress the dominant role of polyphonic time in Mann's novels, I do not deny the importance of other moments of the human time

system for his work. Rhythmic time, augmented by Mann's indebtedness to Nietzsche, has been stressed by several of his interpreters—see, especially, Heller, *The Ironic German*, pp. 239–46. Furthermore, melodic time, the time of development or the actualization of the potential of an entity or person, is of great importance due to the *Bildungsroman* tradition in which much of Mann's fiction stands.

31. Mann, *The Magic Mountain*, p. 284.
32. Herman J. Weigand, *The Magic Mountain: A Study of Thomas Mann's "Der Zauberberg,"* p. 157.
33. Martin Swales, *Thomas Mann: A Study*, p. 57.
34. See Anto Krajina, *Die Zeitauffassung bei Thomas Mann gesehen im Lichte der Goetheschen Phänomenallehre*, for a defense of the proposition that for Mann the narrative form is a universal language housing the various discourses of peoples and of groups and individuals within a society (pp. 88–94).
35. "Not only is the individual life viewed as a story, but the world itself is considered to be a narrated phenomenon, with a main plot and much secondary and peripheral activity" (Elaine Murdaugh, *Salvation in the Secular: The Moral Law in Thomas Mann's "Joseph und seine Brüder,"* p. 28).
36. Thomas Mann, *The Theme of the Joseph Novels*, pp. 4, 5. See also Hatfield, *From the Magic Mountain*, p. 78, and Kaufmann, *Thomas Mann*, pp. 19–20.
37. See Heller, *The Ironic German*, p. 138; Mann, *The Story of a Novel*, p. 64; and Murdaugh, *Salvation in the Secular*, pp. 57, 58.
38. Mann, *Joseph and His Brothers*, p. 1119.
39. Mann, *The Theme of the Joseph Novels*, p. 19.
40. Mann, *Doctor Faustus*, p. 103.

6. WILLIAM FAULKNER

1. Maurice Edgar Coindreau, *The Time of William Faulkner: A French View of Modern American Fiction—Essays by Maurice Edgar Coindreau*, pp. 103–4.
2. Robert Penn Warren, ed., *Faulkner: A Collection of Critical Essays*, pp. 82–83.
3. Jean-Paul Sartre, "On *The Sound and the Fury*: Time in the Work of Faulkner," ibid., p. 93.
4. Robert Penn Warren, "Faulkner: The South, the Negro, and Time," ibid., pp. 251–72; Cleanth Brooks, *William Faulkner: Toward Yoknapatawpha and Beyond*, esp. pp. 251–83.
5. Melvin Backman, *Faulkner: The Major Years*, p. 14. For a discussion of Mikhail Bakhtin's use of this term, particularly its relation to sociological interests, see the Appendix.

6. William Faulkner, *Sartoris*, p. 7.

7. Backman, *Faulkner*, p. 103.

8. Cleanth Brooks, *William Faulkner: The Yoknapatawpha Country*, p. 68. See also Sally Rigsbee Page, *Faulkner's Women: Characterization and Meaning*.

9. Faulkner, *Sartoris*, p. 358.

10. William Faulkner, *The Hamlet*, p. 8.

11. William Faulkner, *The Wild Palms*, pp. 11, 53.

12. William Faulkner, *Flags in the Dust*, p. 176.

13. Hugh M. Ruppersburg asserts that this novel represents a departure in Faulkner's rendering of the relation between the individual and society, that beginning here "the individual derives his identity from his participation in society, even if that society is hostile to him" (*Voice and Eye in Faulkner's Fiction*, p. 152). I would say that this situation is endemic to the Faulknerian world and has a central position in this novel.

14. David Minter repeatedly ties the inadequacies of parents and the resulting difficulties for their children in Faulkner's novels to Faulkner's difficulties with his own parents: the weaknesses and failings of his father and the strength and control of his mother (*William Faulkner: His Life and Work*, p. 17).

15. Faulkner, *Sartoris*, p. 347.

16. In *William Faulkner: Art in Theological Tension*, John W. Hunt argues that Dilsey and the black characters in Faulkner's fiction "embody the positive theme that experience can exhibit a saving and meaningful essence" (p. 99). But the role of Dilsey and other blacks is more ambiguous and symptomatic of problems in the culture than Hunt allows. However, Hunt's study is informed by a theological interest in the relation of Faulkner's narratives to process thought and is consequently important here, given my attempt in the conclusion to relate Whitehead's understanding of time to the kind of time that is fundamental to the fiction of Faulkner and Mann.

17. Michael Millgate, *The Achievement of William Faulkner*, p. 223.

18. William Faulkner, *Soldiers' Pay*, p. 326.

19. Faulkner, *Sartoris*, p. 347.

20. William Faulkner, *Go Down, Moses, and Other Stories*, p. 348.

21. William Faulkner, *Intruder in the Dust*, p. 151.

22. "I was just eleven, remember. There are things, circumstances, conditions in the world which should not be there but are, and you can't escape them and indeed, you would not escape them even if you had the choice, since they too are a part of Motion, of participating in life, being alive" (*The Reivers*, p. 155).

23. Michael Millgate, "Faulkner and History," p. 28.

24. As one critic points out, Faulkner's stated debt to Bergson's philoso-

phy may rest on precisely this point. "Bergson thought a truthful novel must create some sense of the incessant motion of reality" (Donald M. Kartiganer, *The Fragile Thread: The Meaning of Form in Faulkner's Novels*, p. 163).

25. Frederick J. Hoffman, *William Faulkner*, p. 26.
26. Olga Vickery, *The Novels of William Faulkner: A Critical Interpretation*, p. 229.

7. ALFRED NORTH WHITEHEAD

1. See Georges Gurvitch, "Social Structure and the Multiplicity of Times," pp. 171–85.
2. Pitirim Sorokin, *Social and Cultural Dynamics: A Study of Change in Major Systems of Art, Truth, Ethics, Law and Social Relationships.*
3. Robert H. Lauer, *Temporal Man: The Meaning and Uses of Social Time*, p. 42.
4. Milič Čapek, *The Philosophical Impact of Contemporary Physics*, p. 372.
5. Ibid., p. 377.
6. Ibid., p. 378.
7. Alfred North Whitehead, *Science and the Modern World*, p. 75.
8. Alfred North Whitehead, *Adventures of Ideas*, p. 199.
9. Alfred North Whitehead, *Process and Reality*, p. 106.
10. Ibid., p. 77.
11. Whitehead, *Adventures of Ideas*, p. 205.
12. Whitehead, *Process and Reality*, p. 234.
13. Whitehead, *Adventures of Ideas*, p. 207.
14. Alfred North Whitehead, *Religion in the Making*, p. 94.
15. Charles Hartshorne, *Reality as Social Process: Studies in Metaphysics and Religion*, p. 134.
16. F. Bradford Wallack, *The Epochal Nature of Process in Whitehead's Metaphysics*, p. 88.
17. Ibid., p. 283.
18. Ibid., p. 291.
19. Ibid., p. 303.
20. Elizabeth M. Kraus, *The Metaphysics of Experience: A Companion to Whitehead's "Process and Reality,"* p. 39.
21. Wallack, *The Epochal Nature of Process in Whitehead's Metaphysics*, p. 152.
22. Whitehead, *Adventures of Ideas*, p. 285.
23. Ibid., p. 282.
24. Ibid., pp. 153–54.
25. Victor Lowe, *Understanding Whitehead*, p. 28.
26. Whitehead, *Process and Reality*, p. 228.

27. Ibid., p. 405.
28. Hartshorne, *Reality as Social Process*, p. 135.
29. Ibid., p. 143.

8. VIRGINIA WOOLF

1. Although he seems somewhat to favor Mr. Ramsay in the dispute, Mitchell Leaska authoritatively establishes that the point of view favors neither side. See his *Virginia Woolf's Lighthouse: A Study in Critical Method*: "In brief, life is presented as it seems to the fictional people who are living it" (p. 43).
2. "By showing that the masculine approach to trust is valid, just as the feminine is valid, the way is prepared for the balancing of the two in the final section of the novel" (Nancy Topping Bazin, *Virginia Woolf and the Androgynous Vision*, p. 138).
3. Virginia Woolf, *To the Lighthouse*, p. 90. She does not want to release James, the last of her eight children.
4. Ibid., p. 61.
5. Ibid., pp. 194, 195, 200.
6. Ibid., pp. 27–28
7. "In this view nature subsumes individual lives but in some sense also carries them on" (James Naremore, *The World Without a Self: Virginia Woolf and the Novel*, pp. 143–44).
8. Virginia Woolf, *The Voyage Out*, p. 82.
9. Ibid., p. 125.
10. Ibid., p. 145.
11. Ibid., p. 314.
12. Virginia Woolf, *Mrs. Dalloway*, p. 192.
13. Ibid., p. 133.
14. Ibid., p. 135.
15. "Whatever the suffering involved, all the novels from *Mrs. Dalloway* on manage to end on a final note of affirmation: a party given, a lighthouse reached, a pageant produced. Such accomplishments, however trivial they might appear, suggest the basic commitment to living made by her fiction" (Michael Rosenthal, *Virginia Woolf*, p. 43).
16. Virginia Woolf, of course, had in mind more than the early termination of a single character's life. "Jacob is . . . representative of a whole group of human beings who, like her brother Thoby, disappeared before life had had a chance to mark them indelibly with a peculiar identity" (Josephine O'Brien Schaefer, *The Three-Fold Nature of Reality in the Novels of Virginia Woolf*, pp. 70–71).
17. Avrom Fleishman, *Virginia Woolf: A Critical Reading*, p. 54.
18. Virginia Woolf, *Jacob's Room*, p. 55.
19. Ibid., p. 105.

20. Ibid., pp. 118–19.
21. Ibid., p. 262.
22. Ibid., p. 118.
23. Ibid., p. 164.
24. Ibid., p. 184.
25. Virginia Woolf, The Waves, p. 106.
26. Ibid., p. 275.
27. Ibid., p. 297.
28. "As he rides out to meet death, like Percival, with his spear poised and his hair flying, Bernard achieves fulfillment by exultantly accepting his own mortality" (Rosenthal, Virginia Woolf, p. 167).
29. "Katharine moves in an atmosphere of intellectual refinement which makes every afternoon tea a literary conversazione and every casual remark about the day's routine duties a piece of literary criticism" (David Daiches, Virginia Woolf, p. 19).
30. Virginia Woolf, Night and Day, p. 13.
31. Ibid., p. 101.
32. Ibid., p. 104.
33. Ibid., p. 151.
34. Ibid., p. 74.
35. Ibid., p. 459.
36. Virginia Woolf, Orlando, p. 329.
37. "The fundamental security of Orlando is an adherence to the order of nature; and, to make the symbol inescapably obvious, Orlando carries his/her poem 'The Oak Tree' at heart through all vicissitudes, sexual, social, and temporal" (Jean Alexander, The Venture of Form in the Novels of Virginia Woolf, p. 134).
38. "Nearly all the people in the novel are powerfully affected by the conflict between social institutions and some deeper human nature; and the corollary to such a proposition is that true happiness can be attained only when civilization is brought into harmony with bios, or with what Lawrence, in another context, called the "deepest self" (James Naremore, "Nature and History in The Years, p. 249).
39. Virginia Woolf, The Years, p. 278.
40. Ibid., p. 369. Also see Alexander, The Venture of Form in the Novels of Virginia Woolf, pp. 189–91, for a discussion of the importance of music for this novel.
41. Woolf, The Years, p. 383.
42. Without minimizing the often negative relation between personal and social time in this novel, I do not agree with critics who consider it to be a highly pessimistic work. Bernard Blackstone writes, for example, "London, and London in its darkest and direst guise, is the setting: the theme is the power of society to thwart and to crush" (Virginia Woolf: A Commentary, p. 205).

43. Virginia Woolf, *Between the Acts*, p. 131.
44. "The intellectual centre of each age changes; the lovers . . . change; but the fact that there is a centre, that there is love or sex, that there is hate, that there are the masses—these do not change" (Higdon, *Time and English Fiction*, p. 126).
45. Woolf, *Between the Acts*, p. 137.
46. Ibid., p. 89.
47. In his book *Between Language and Silence: The Novels of Virginia Woolf*, Howard Harper demonstrates that Virginia Woolf incorporated her sense of temporality and its future orientation toward uncertainty in the very process of her writing as a venture in discovery.
48. "Between the woof of time the preserver and the warp of time the destroyer is woven—the self" (Maria DiBattista, *Virginia Woolf's Major Novels: The Fables of Anon*, p. 33).

9. HERMANN HESSE

1. Hermann Hesse, *Peter Camenzind, Gesammelte Dichtungen*, p. 219.
2. Ibid., p. 309.
3. Hermann Hesse, *Unterm Rad, Gesammelte Dichtungen*, p. 418.
4. See Mark Boulby, *Hermann Hesse: His Mind and Art*, p. 67, for a discussion of the role that Hesse's Pietistic heritage and paternalistic home played in this image of youthful suffering.
5. Hermann Hesse, *Gertrude, Gesammelte Dichtungen*, p. 12.
6. Several of Hesse's characters, as in *Under the Wheel* and *Demian*, find themselves in an intolerable confinement. This spatial image can be exchanged for a temporal one, in which the confined place is a present time that cuts one off from the past and future.
7. Mark Boulby relates it to the genre of the saintly *vita* (*Hermann Hesse: His Mind and Art*, p. 152).
8. "Faith, earlier novels teach, is the acceptance of fate, the sometimes sidelong recognition of a secret order in chaos" (ibid., p. 163).
9. By affirming the value of both jazz and classical music, *Steppenwolf* relates the resources for personal change to music. For a fuller discussion of the relation of music to human potentials, see George Wallis Field, *Hermann Hesse*, p. 169.
10. Ernest Rose, in *Faith from the Abyss: Hermann Hesse's Way from Romanticism to Modernity*, sees a reinterpretation of the father image in this novel and those that follow (p. 102).
11. Theodore Ziolkowski, *The Novels of Hermann Hesse: A Study in Theme and Structure*, p. 250.
12. Ibid., p. 25.
13. "A primary time-related characteristic shared by all of these novels

is their renunciation of stasis, which evidences itself in the concept of dynamic, sequential occurrence as the chief impulse of both the plots and, particularly, of their open endings. As the product, so to speak, of this sequentiality the future stands in a sense as a goal in itself—a goal in no place clearly defined, and yet as palpable as any high spirited ideal can be" (Roger C. Norton, *Hermann Hesse's Futuristic Idealism: "The Glass Bead Game" and Its Predecessors*, p. 69).

14. Ralph Freedman points out Hesse's recurring interest in melody as a metaphor for his narrative intentions. See *Hermann Hesse: Pilgrim of Crisis*, pp. 145, 243.

15. Hermann Hesse, *The Glass Bead Game*, p. 48.

16. "We are *now* what we were and what we can be. We are only prevented from seeing this by our belief in *time*, our belief that somehow the past, the present, and the future are separate" (Edwin F. Casebeer, *Hermann Hesse*, p. 51).

17. Roger C. Norton comments on the range of personal differences among the members of Castalia (*Hermann Hesse's Futuristic Idealism*, p. 90).

18. Joseph Mileck describes some implications of the relation between Father Jacobus and Jacob Burckhardt: "Later in life, Burckhardt's view of history confirmed Hesse's emerging belief in the temporality and relativity of human institutions, in the permanence of the human spirit, and in order and meaning beyond the apparent chaos of reality; it also helped open his eyes to civilization's interaction of politics, religion, and culture, to the ultimate insufficiency of such areligious and apolitical purely cultural institutions as Castalia, and to the necessary interplay of *vita contemplativa* and *vita activa* in human affairs" (*Hermann Hesse: Biography and Bibliography*, 1:19).

19. Hesse, *The Glass Bead Game*, p. 267.

20. "Hesse stresses in his final novel the theme of reconciliation with the past at the same time as he looks hopefully toward the future" (Norton, *Hermann Hesse's Futuristic Idealism*, pp. 132–33).

10. MARTIN HEIDEGGER

1. H. L. Dreyfus, "Human Temporality," p. 155.

2. Edmund Husserl, *The Phenomenology of Internal Time-Consciousness*, pp. 23, 33, and *passim*.

3. Martin Heidegger, *Being and Time*, p. 32.

4. William Barrett, *Irrational Man: A Study in Existential Philosophy*, chap. 9, "Heidegger," p. 203.

5. Heidegger, *Being and Time*, p. 119.

6. Ibid., p. 477.
7. Heidegger, *On Time and Being*, pp. 1–24.
8. James M. Demske, *Being, Man, and Death: A Key to Heidegger.*
9. Heidegger, *Being and Time*, p. 279.
10. Ibid., p. 311.
11. John Macquarrie, *Martin Heidegger*, p. 31.
12. Martin Heidegger, "What is Metaphysics," in *Existence and Being*, p. 378.
13. See James L. Perotti, *Heidegger on the Divine: The Thinker, the Poet, and God.*
14. Demske, *Being, Man, and Death*, p. 175.
15. Ibid., p. 122.
16. See Martin Heidegger, *Poetry, Language, Thought*, esp. pp. 189–229.

Appendix

1. Mikhail M. Bakhtin, *The Dialogic Imagination: Four Essays*, pp. 4, 12. The crucial position of Rabelais in the change of one model of human existence for another is the subject of Bakhtin's *Rabelais and His World.*
2. Ibid., pp. 327, 366.
3. Ibid., pp. 13, 15–16.
4. Ibid., pp. 11, 14, 20, 27, 30, 40, and Mikhail Bakhtin, *Problems of Dostoevsky's Poetics*, p. 29.
5. *Dialogic Imagination*, pp. 67, 292, 367; *Problems of Dostoevsky's Poetics*, p. 26.
6. *Dialogic Imagination*, p. 354.
7. *Problems of Dostoevsky's Poetics*, pp. 272, 298.
8. Ibid., pp. 61, 82.
9. Ibid., pp. 17, 88, 93–96.
10. Ibid., pp. 6, 16; *Dialogic Imagination*, p. 67.
11. *Dialogic Imagination*, p. 253.
12. Ibid., pp. 47, 263.
13. Ibid., p. 396; *Problems of Dostoevsky's Poetics*, pp. 47, 68, 78.
14. *Dialogic Imagination*, p. 365; *Problems of Dostoevsky's Poetics*, pp. 252, 277.
15. *Dialogic Imagination*, pp. 27–40; *Problems of Dostoevsky's Poetics*, p. 29.
16. *Dialogic Imagination*, pp. 327, 370; *Problems of Dostoevsky's Poetics*, pp. 287–90.
17. *Dialogic Imagination*, pp. 11, 14, 20, 27, 30, 40.
18. Ibid., pp. 129, 300; *Problems of Dostoevsky's Poetics*, pp. 32, 276.
19. *Dialogic Imagination*, p. 128.

20. Ibid., pp. 20, 58; *Problems of Dostoevsky's Poetics*, pp. 160, 176.
21. *Rabelais and His World*, p. 149. See also pp. 50, 75, 91, 195, 217, and 327. Bakhtin attempts, I think unsuccessfully, to subject rhythmic time in Rabelais, what he calls the "cyclical time of natural and biological life," to the future-oriented time of social, historical development (p. 25).
22. *Dialogic Imagination*, p. 331; *Problems of Dostoevsky's Poetics*, p. 200.

Works Cited

Albright, Daniel. *Personality and Impersonality: Lawrence, Woolf, and Mann.* Chicago: University of Chicago Press, 1978.

Alexander, Jean. *The Venture of Form in the Novels of Virginia Woolf.* Port Washington, N.Y.: Kennikat Press, 1974.

Apter, T. E. *Thomas Mann: The Devil's Advocate.* New York: New York University Press, 1979.

Astro, Richard, and Jackson J. Benson, eds. *Hemingway in Our Time.* Corvallis: Oregon State University Press, 1974.

Backman, Melvin. *Faulkner: The Major Years.* Bloomington: Indiana University Press, 1966.

Baker, Carlos. *Hemingway: The Writer as Artist.* Princeton, N.J.: Princeton University Press, 1963.

Bakhtin, Mikhail. *The Dialogic Imagination: Four Essays.* Translated by Caryl Emerson and Michael Holquist. Edited by Michael Holquist. Austin: University of Texas Press, 1981.

————. *Problems of Dostoevsky's Poetics.* Translated by Caryl Emerson. Introduction by Wayne C. Booth. Minneapolis: University of Minnesota Press, 1984.

————. *Rabelais and His World.* Translated by Helene Iswolsky. Cambridge, Mass.: MIT Press, 1968.

Balbert, Peter. *D. H. Lawrence and the Psychology of Rhythm: The Meaning of Form in "The Rainbow."* The Hague: Mouton, 1974.

Barrett, William. *Irrational Man: A Study in Existential Philosophy.* Garden City, N.Y.: Doubleday and Company, Inc., 1958.

Barthes, Roland. *Image-Music-Text*. Translated by Stephen Heath. Glasgow: William Collins Sons and Company, 1977.

Bazin, Nancy Topping. *Virginia Woolf and the Androgynous Vision*. New Brunswick, N.J.: Rutgers University Press, 1973.

Benson, Jackson J. *Hemingway: The Writer's Art of Self-Defense*. Minneapolis: University of Minnesota Press, 1969.

Bergsten, Gunilla. *Thomas Mann's "Doctor Faustus": The Sources and Structure of the Novel*. Translated by Krishna Winston. Chicago: University of Chicago Press, 1969.

Blackstone, Bernard. *Virginia Woolf: A Commentary*. New York: Harcourt, Brace, 1949.

Boman, Thorlief. *Hebrew Thought Compared with Greek*. Translated by Jules L. Moreau. London: SCM Press, Ltd., 1960.

Boulby, Mark. *Hermann Hesse: His Mind and Art*. Ithaca, N.Y.: Cornell University Press, 1967.

Bradbury, Malcolm. "The Cities of Modernism." In *Modernism: 1890–1930*, edited by Malcolm Bradbury and James McFarlane. Atlantic Highlands, N.J.: Humanities Press, 1978.

———, and James McFarlane, eds. *Modernism: 1890–1930*. Atlantic Highlands, N.J.: Humanities Press, 1978.

Brenner, Gerry. *Concealments in Hemingway's Works*. Columbus: Ohio State University Press, 1983.

Brooks, Cleanth. *William Faulkner: The Yoknapatawpha Country*. New Haven, Conn.: Yale University Press, 1963.

———. *William Faulkner: Toward Yoknapatawpha and Beyond*. New Haven, Conn.: Yale University Press, 1978.

Buckley, Jerome Hamilton. *The Triumph of Time: A Study of the Victorian Concepts of Time, History, Progress and Decadence*. Cambridge, Mass.: Harvard University Press, 1966.

Burns, Aidan. *Nature and Culture in D. H. Lawrence*. Totowa, N.J.: Barnes & Noble, 1980.

Calinescu, Matei. *Faces of Modernity: Avant-Garde, Decadence, Kitsch*. Bloomington: Indiana University Press, 1977.

Campbell, Joseph. *The Hero with a Thousand Faces*. New York: Meridian Books, 1956.

Čapek, Milič. *The Philosophical Impact of Contemporary Physics*. New York: D. van Nostrand Company, Inc., 1961.

Casebeer, Edwin F. *Hermann Hesse*. New York: Thomas Y. Crowell Company, 1972.

Chatman, Seymour. *Story and Discourse: Narrative Structure in Fiction and Film*. Ithaca, N.Y.: Cornell University Press, 1978.

Clark, L. D. *The Minoan Distance: The Symbolism of Travel in D. H. Lawrence*. Tucson: University of Arizona Press, 1980.

Cloudsley-Thompson, J. L. "Time Sense of Animals." In *The Voices of Time*, edited by J. T. Fraser. New York: George Braziller, 1966.

Coindreau, Maurice Edgar. *The Time of William Faulkner: A French View of Modern American Fiction—Essays by Maurice Edgar Coindreau*. Edited and translated by George McMillan Reeves. Foreword by Michel Gresset. Columbia: University of South Carolina Press, 1971.

Culler, Jonathan. "*Fabula* and *Sjuzhet* in the Analysis of Narrative." *Poetics Today* 1 (Spring 1980): 27–37.

Daiches, David. *The Novel and the Modern World*. Revised ed. Chicago: University of Chicago Press, 1960.

———. *Virginia Woolf*. New York: New Directions, 1963.

Demske, James M. *Being, Man, and Death: A Key to Heidegger*. Lexington: University Press of Kentucky, 1970.

DiBattista, Maria. *Virginia Woolf's Major Novels: The Fables of Anon*. New Haven, Conn.: Yale University Press, 1980.

Donaldson, Scott. *By Force of Will: The Life and Art of Ernest Hemingway*. New York: The Viking Press, 1977.

Dreyfus, H. L. "Human Temporality." In *The Study of Time II*, edited by J. T. Fraser and N. Laurence. New York and Berlin: Springer Verlag, 1975.

Dunne, John S. *Time and Myth: A Meditation on Storytelling as an Exploration of Life and Death*. Garden City, N.Y.: Doubleday and Company, Inc., 1973.

Dürr, Walther. "Rhythm in Music: A Formal Scaffolding of Time." In *The Voices of Time: A Cooperative Survey of Man's View of Time as Expressed by the Sciences and by the Humanities*, edited by J. T. Fraser. New York: George Braziller, 1966.

Eliade, Mircea. *Birth and Rebirth: The Religious Meanings of Initiation in Human Culture*. Translated by Willard R. Trask. New York: Harper and Brothers, Publishers, 1958.

———. *Cosmos and History: The Myth of the Eternal Return*. Translated by Willard R. Trask. New York: Harper & Row, 1959.

———. "Cultural Fashions and History of Religions." In *Papers of the Center for Advanced Studies*, no. 8. Middletown, Conn.: Wesleyan University, 1967.

———. *Images and Symbols: Studies in Religious Symbolism*. New York: Sheed and Ward, 1961.

———. *Mephistopheles and the Androgyne*. Translated by J. M. Cohen. New York: Sheed and Ward, 1965.

———. *Myth and Reality*. Translated by Willard R. Trask. New York: Harper & Row, 1963.

———. *Myths, Dreams, and Mysteries: The Encounter between Con-*

temporary Faiths and Archaic Realities. Translated by Philip Mairet. New York: Harper & Row, 1957.

———. *Patterns in Comparative Religion.* Translated by Rosemary Sheed. New York: New American Library, 1974.

———. "The Sacred and the Modern Artist." *Criterion* 4 (Spring 1965): 22–24.

———. *Yoga: Immortality and Freedom.* New York: Pantheon Books, Inc., 1958.

Ellmann, Richard, and Charles Feidelson, Jr., eds. *The Modern Tradition: Backgrounds of Modern Literature.* New York: Oxford University Press, 1965.

Erlich, Victor. *Russian Formalism: History-Doctrine.* The Hague: Mouton and Co., 1955.

Faulkner, William. *Absalom, Absalom!* New York: Random House, 1951.

———. *As I Lay Dying.* New York: Random House, Inc., 1930.

———. *Flags in the Dust.* New York: Random House, 1973.

———. *Go Down, Moses, and Other Stories.* New York: Random House, 1942.

———. *The Hamlet.* New York: Random House, 1940.

———. *Intruder in the Dust.* New York: Random House, 1948.

———. *Light in August.* New York: Random House, 1950.

———. *Mosquitoes.* New York: Liveright Publishing Co., 1927.

———. *The Reivers.* New York: Random House, 1948.

———. *Sartoris.* New York: Grosset and Dunlap, 1929.

———. *Soldiers' Pay.* London: Chatto and Windus, 1930.

———. *The Sound and the Fury.* New York: Random House, 1946.

———. *The Wild Palms.* New York: Random House, 1939.

Field, George Wallis. *Hermann Hesse.* New York: Twayne Publishers, Inc., 1970.

Fleishman, Avrom. *Virginia Woolf: A Critical Reading.* Baltimore: Johns Hopkins Press, 1975.

Fletcher, John, and Malcolm Bradbury. "The Introverted Novel." In *Modernism: 1890–1930,* edited by Malcolm Bradbury and James McFarlane. Atlantic Highlands, N.J.: Humanities Press, 1978.

Forster, E. M. *Aspects of the Novel.* New York: Harcourt, Brace and Company, 1954.

Frank, Joseph. "Spatial Form: An Answer to Critics." *Critical Inquiry* 4 (Winter 1977): 231–53.

———. *The Widening Gyre: Crisis and Mastery in Modern Literature.* New Brunswick, N.J.: Rutgers University Press, 1963.

Fraser, J. T., ed. *The Voices of Time: A Cooperative Survey of Man's View of Time as Expressed by the Sciences and by the Humanities.* New York: George Braziller, 1966.

Freedman, Ralph. *Hermann Hesse: Pilgrim of Crisis*. New York: Pantheon Books, 1978.

———, ed. *Virginia Woolf: Revaluation and Continuity*. Berkeley and Los Angeles: University of California Press, 1980.

Frye, Northrop. *Anatomy of Criticism: Four Essays*. New York: Atheneum, 1966.

Genette, Gérard. *Narrative Discourse: An Essay in Method*. Translated by Jane E. Lewin. Foreword by Jonathan Culler. Ithaca, N.Y.: Cornell University Press, 1980.

Goodheart, Eugene. *The Utopian Vision of D. H. Lawrence*. Chicago: University of Chicago Press, 1963.

Grebstein, Sheldon Norman. *Hemingway's Craft*. Carbondale: Southern Illinois University Press, 1973.

Greimas, A. J. *Structural Semantics: An Attempt at a Method*. Translated by Daniele McDowell, et al. Introduction by Ronald Schleifern. Lincoln: University of Nebraska Press, 1983.

Griffith, John. "Rectitude in Hemingway's Fiction: How Rite Makes Right." In *Hemingway in Our Time*, edited by Richard Astro and Jackson J. Benson. Corvallis: Oregon State University Press, 1974.

Gurvitch, Georges. "Social Structure and the Multiplicity of Times." In *Sociological Theory, Values, and Sociocultural Change*, edited by Edward A. Tiryakian. New York: Harper & Row, 1963.

Halperin, John, ed. *The Theory of the Novel: New Essays*. New York: Oxford University Press, 1974.

Harding, Mary Esther. *Woman's Mysteries, Ancient and Modern*. New York: Pantheon Books, 1955.

Harper, Howard. *Between Language and Silence: The Novels of Virginia Woolf*. Baton Rouge: Louisiana State University Press, 1982.

Harrington, Evans, and Ann J. Abadie, eds. *The South and Faulkner's Yoknapatawpha: The Actual and the Apocryphal*. Jackson: University Press of Mississippi, 1977.

Hartshorne, Charles. *Reality as Social Process: Studies in Metaphysics and Religion*. Glencoe, Ill.: The Free Press, 1953.

Harvey, William J. *Character and the Novel*. Ithaca, N.Y.: Cornell University Press, 1965.

Hatfield, Henry. *From the Magic Mountain: Mann's Later Masterpieces*. Ithaca, N.Y.: Cornell University Press, 1979.

Heidegger, Martin. *Being and Time*. Translated by John Macquarrie and Edward Robinson. London: SCM Press, 1962.

———. *Existence and Being*. Translated by R. F. C. Hull and Alan Crick. Introduction by Werner Brock. Chicago: Henry Regnery Company, 1949.

———. *On Time and Being*. Translated by Joan Stambaugh. New York: Harper and Row, 1972.

————. *Poetry, Language, Thought*. Translated by Albert Hofstadter. New York: Harper and Row, 1971.

Heller, Erich. *The Ironic German: A Study of Thomas Mann*. Boston: Little, Brown and Company, 1958.

Hemingway, Ernest. *Across the River and into the Trees*. New York: Charles Scribner's Sons, 1950.

————. *A Farewell to Arms*. New York: Charles Scribner's Sons, 1925.

————. *For Whom the Bell Tolls*. New York: Charles Scribner's Sons, 1940.

————. *In Our Time*. New York: Charles Scribner's Sons, 1925.

————. *Islands in the Stream*. New York: Charles Scribner's Sons, 1970.

————. *The Old Man and the Sea*. New York: Charles Scribner's Sons, 1952.

————. *The Sun Also Rises*. New York: Charles Scribner's Sons, 1926.

Hesse, Hermann. *Demian: The Story of Emil Sinclair's Youth*. Translated by Michael Roloff and Michael Lebeck. Introduction by Thomas Mann. New York: Bantam Books, 1966.

————. *Gertrude, Gesammelte Dichtungen*, Zweiter Band. Frankfurt am Main: Suhrkamp Verlag, 1952.

————. *The Glass Bead Game*. Translated by Richard Winston and Clara Winston. New York: Holt, Rinehart and Winston, Inc., 1969.

————. *The Journey to the East*. Translated by Hilda Rosner. New York: Farrar, Straus and Giroux, 1969.

————. *Narcissus and Goldmund*. Translated by Ursule Molinaro. New York: Farrar, Straus and Giroux, 1968.

————. *Peter Camenzind, Gesammelte Dichtungen*. Frankfurt am Main: Suhrkamp Verlag, 1952.

————. *Rosshalde*. Translated by Ralph Manheim. New York: Farrar, Straus and Giroux, 1970.

————. *Siddhartha*. Translated by Hilda Rosner. New York: New Directions Publishing Corp., 1951.

————. *Steppenwolf*. Translated by Basil Creighton, Joseph Mileck, and Horst Frenz. Introduction by Joseph Mileck. New York: Holt, Rinehart and Winston, Inc., 1963.

————. *Unterm Rad, Gesammelte Dichtungen*. Frankfurt am Main: Suhrkamp Verlag, 1952.

Higdon, David Leon. *Time and English Fiction*. London: The Macmillan Press, Ltd., 1977.

Hoffman, Frederick J. *William Faulkner*. 2d ed. New York: Twayne Publishers, Inc., 1966.

Hollington, Michael. "Svevo, Joyce and Modernist Time." In *Modernism: 1890–1930*, edited by Malcolm Bradbury and James McFarlane. Atlantic Highlands, N.J.: Humanities Press, 1978.

Holtz, William. "Spatial Form in Modern Literature: A Reconsideration." *Critical Inquiry* 4 (Winter 1977): 271–84.

Hough, Graham. *The Dark Sun: A Study of D. H. Lawrence.* London: Gerald Duckworth and Co., Ltd., 1956, 1968.

Howe, Irving, ed. *The Idea of the Modern in Literature and the Arts.* New York: Horizon Press, 1968.

Hunt, John W. *William Faulkner: Art in Theological Tension.* Syracuse, N.Y.: Syracuse University Press, 1965.

Husserl, Edmund. *The Phenomenology of Internal Time-Consciousness.* Edited by Martin Heidegger. Translated by James S. Churchill. Introduction by Calvin O. Schrag. Bloomington: Indiana University Press, 1969.

Hutchins, Eleanor. "An Approach through Time." In *Towards a Poetics of Fiction,* edited by Mark Spilka. Bloomington: Indiana University Press, 1977.

Jameson, Fredric. *The Political Unconscious: Narrative as a Socially Symbolic Act.* Ithaca, N.Y.: Cornell University Press, 1981.

Kahler, Eric. *The Orbit of Thomas Mann.* Princeton, N.J.: Princeton University Press, 1969.

Kartiganer, Donald M. *The Fragile Thread: The Meaning of Form in Faulkner's Novels.* Amherst: University of Massachusetts Press, 1979.

Kaufmann, Fritz. *Thomas Mann: The World as Will and Representation.* Boston: Beacon Press, 1957.

Kermode, Frank. *D. H. Lawrence.* New York: The Viking Press, 1973.

————. "A Reply to Joseph Frank." *Critical Inquiry* 4 (Spring 1978): 579–89.

————. *The Sense of an Ending: Studies in the Theory of Fiction.* New York: Oxford University Press, 1967.

Kern, Stephen. *The Culture of Time and Space.* Cambridge, Mass.: Harvard University Press, 1983.

Kort, Wesley A. *Moral Fiber: Character and Belief in Recent American Fiction.* Philadelphia: Fortress Press, 1982.

————. *Narrative Elements and Religious Meaning.* Philadelphia: Fortress Press, 1975.

Krajina, Anto. *Die Zeitauffassung bei Thomas Mann gesehen im Lichte der Goetheschen Phänomenallehre.* Bern: Peter Lang, 1978.

Kraus, Elizabeth M. *The Metaphysics of Experience: A Companion to Whitehead's "Process and Reality."* New York: Fordham University Press, 1979.

Krutch, Joseph Wood. *"Modernism" in Modern Drama: A Definition and an Estimate.* Ithaca, N.Y.: Cornell University Press, 1953.

Lauer, Robert H. *Temporal Man: The Meaning and Uses of Social Time.* New York: Praeger Publishers, 1981.

Lawrence, D. H. *Aaron's Rod.* New York: The Viking Press, 1950.

————. *Collected Letters.* Edited by Harry T. Moore. 2 vols. New York: The Viking Press, 1962.

————. *Kangaroo*. New York: The Viking Press, 1960.

————. *Lady Chatterley's Lover*. New York: The New American Library of World Literature, Inc., 1959.

————. *The Lost Girl*. London: William Heinemann, Ltd., 1955.

————. *Phoenix: The Posthumous Papers of D. H. Lawrence*. Edited by Edward D. McDonald. London: William Heinemann, Ltd., 1936.

————. *Phoenix II: Uncollected, Unpublished and Other Prose Works of D. H. Lawrence*. Edited by Harry T. Moore. London: William Heinemann, Ltd., 1968.

————. *The Plumed Serpent*. New York: Alfred A. Knopf, 1951.

————. *The Rainbow*. New York: The Viking Press, 1969.

————. *The Trespasser*. London: William Heinemann, Ltd., 1955.

————. *The White Peacock*. Preface by Harry T. Moore. Carbondale: Southern Illinois University Press, 1965.

————. *Women in Love*. New York: The Viking Press, 1969.

Leaska, Mitchell. *Virginia Woolf's Lighthouse: A Study in Critical Method*. New York: Columbia University Press, 1970.

Leavis, F. R. *D. H. Lawrence: Novelist*. London: Chatto and Windus, 1955.

Lee, A. Robert, ed. *Ernest Hemingway: New Critical Essays*. London: Vision Press, 1983.

Lewis, Wyndham. *Time and Western Man*. New York: Harcourt, Brace and Company, 1928.

Lowe, Victor. *Understanding Whitehead*. Baltimore: Johns Hopkins Press, 1966.

Macquarrie, John. *Martin Heidegger*. London: Lutterworth Press, 1968.

Mann, Thomas. *The Beloved Returns*. Translated by H. T. Lowe-Porter. New York: Alfred A. Knopf, 1940.

————. *The Black Swan*. Translated by Willard R. Trask. New York: Alfred A. Knopf, 1954.

————. *Buddenbrooks*. Translated by H. T. Lowe-Porter. New York: Vintage Books, 1961.

————. *Confessions of Felix Krull, Confidence Man*. Translated by Denver Lindley. New York: Alfred A. Knopf, 1955.

————. *Doctor Faustus: The Life of the German Composer Adrian Leverkühn*. Translated by H. T. Lowe-Porter. New York: Vintage Books, 1948.

————. *The Holy Sinner*. Translated by H. T. Lowe-Porter. New York: Alfred A. Knopf, 1951.

————. *Joseph and His Brothers*. Translated by H. T. Lowe-Porter. Harmondsworth: Penguin Books, 1978.

————. *The Magic Mountain*. Translated by H. T. Lowe-Porter. New York: Vintage Books, 1969.

————. *Royal Highness: A Novel of German Court Life*. Translated by A. Cecil Curtis. New York: Alfred A. Knopf, 1926.

————. *The Story of a Novel: The Genesis of Doctor Faustus*. Translated by Richard Winston and Clara Winston. New York: Alfred A. Knopf, 1961.

————. *The Tables of the Law*. Translated by H. T. Lowe-Porter. New York: A. A. Knopf, 1945.

————. *The Theme of the Joseph Novels*. Washington: The Library of Congress, 1942.

————. *The Transposed Heads: A Legend of India*. Translated by H. T. Lowe-Porter. New York: Alfred A. Knopf, 1941.

Merleau-Ponty, M. *Phenomenology of Perception*. Translated by Colin Smith. London: Routledge & Kegan Paul, Ltd., 1962.

Meyerhoff, Hans. *Time in Literature*. Berkeley and Los Angeles: University of California Press, 1955.

Miko, Stephen J. *Toward "Women in Love": The Emergence of a Lawrentian Aesthetic*. New Haven, Conn.: Yale University Press, 1971.

Mileck, Joseph. *Hermann Hesse: Biography and Bibliography*. 2 vols. Berkeley and Los Angeles: University of California Press, 1977.

Miller, J. Hillis. *The Form of Victorian Fiction*. Notre Dame, Ind.: University of Notre Dame Press, 1968.

Millgate, Michael. *The Achievement of William Faulkner*. New York: Random House, 1966.

————. "Faulkner and History." In *The South and Faulkner's Yoknapatawpha*, edited by Evans Harrington and Ann J. Abadie. Jackson: University Press of Mississippi, 1977.

Minter, David. *William Faulkner: His Life and Work*. Baltimore: Johns Hopkins University Press, 1980.

Moore, Harry T. *The Life and Works of D. H. Lawrence*. New York: Twayne Publishers, 1951.

Moynaham, Julian. *The Deed of Life: The Novels and Tales of D. H. Lawrence*. Princeton, N.J.: Princeton University Press, 1963.

Müller, Günther. *Morphologische Poetik: Gesammelte Aufsätze*. Tübingen: Max Niemeyer Verlag, 1974.

Murdaugh, Elaine. *Salvation in the Secular: The Moral Law in Thomas Mann's "Joseph und seine Brüder."* Bern: Herbert Lang, 1976.

Nahal, Chaman. *The Narrative Pattern in Ernest Hemingway's Fiction*. Rutherford, N.J.: Fairleigh Dickinson University Press, 1971.

Naremore, James. "Nature and History in *The Years*." In *Virginia Woolf: Revaluation and Continuity*, edited by Ralph Freedman. Berkeley and Los Angeles: University of California Press, 1980.

————. *The World Without a Self: Virginia Woolf and the Novel*. New Haven, Conn.: Yale University Press, 1973.

Norton, Roger C. *Hermann Hesse's Futuristic Idealism: "The Glass Bead Game" and Its Predecessors*. Bern: Herbert Lang, 1973.

Olson, Elder. *Tragedy and the Theory of Drama*. Detroit, Mich.: Wayne State University Press, 1961.

Page, Sally Rigsbee. *Faulkner's Women: Characterization and Meaning.* DeLand, Fla.: Everett Edwards, 1972.

Panichas, George A. *Adventures in Consciousness: The Meaning of D. H. Lawrence's Religious Quest.* The Hague: Mouton and Co., 1964.

Perotti, James L. *Heidegger on the Divine: The Thinker, the Poet, and God.* Athens: Ohio University Press, 1974.

Propp, Vladimir. *Morphology of the Folktale.* Edited with introduction by Svatava Pirkova-Jakobson. Translated by Laurence Scott. Bloomington: Indiana University Press, 1958.

Rabkin, Eric S. "Spatial Form and Plot." *Critical Inquiry* 4 (Winter 1977): 253–71.

Raleigh, John Henry. *Time, Place, and Idea: Essays on the Novel.* Carbondale: Southern Illinois University Press, 1968.

Reed, Terence J. *Thomas Mann: The Uses of Tradition.* Oxford: At the Clarendon Press, 1974.

Ricoeur, Paul. *Time and Narrative.* Vol. 1, translated by Kathleen McLaughlin and David Pellauer. Chicago: University of Chicago Press, 1984.

Rose, Ernest. *Faith from the Abyss: Hermann Hesse's Way from Romanticism to Modernity.* New York: New York University Press, 1965.

Rosenthal, Michael. *Virginia Woolf.* New York: Columbia University Press, 1979.

Rovit, Earl. *Ernest Hemingway.* New York: Twayne Publishers, 1963.

Ruppersburg, Hugh M. *Voice and Eye in Faulkner's Fiction.* Athens: University of Georgia Press, 1983.

Sartre, Jean-Paul. "On *The Sound and the Fury*: Time in the Work of Faulkner." In *Faulkner: A Collection of Critical Essays,* edited by Robert Penn Warren. Englewood Cliffs, N.J.: Prentice Hall, Inc., 1966.

Schaefer, Josephine O'Brien. *The Three-Fold Nature of Reality in the Novels of Virginia Woolf.* The Hague: Mouton and Co., 1965.

Scholes, Robert, and Robert Kellogg. *The Nature of Narrative.* New York: Oxford University Press, 1966.

Smith, Barbara Herrnstein. "Narrative Versions, Narrative Theories." *Critical Inquiry* 7 (Autumn 1980): 213–36.

Sorokin, Pitirim. *Social and Cultural Dynamics: A Study of Change in Major Systems of Art, Truth, Ethics, Law, and Social Relationships.* Boston: Porter Sargent Publishers, 1957.

Spears, Monroe. *Dionysus and the City: Modernism in Twentieth-Century Poetry.* New York: Oxford University Press, 1970.

Spencer, Sharon. *Space, Time, and Structure in the Modern Novel.* New York: New York University Press, 1971.

Spender, Stephen. *The Struggle of the Modern.* London: Hamish Hamilton, 1963.

Spilka, Mark. *The Love Ethic of D. H. Lawrence.* Bloomington: Indiana University Press, 1957.

———, ed. *Towards a Poetics of Fiction.* Bloomington: Indiana University Press, 1977.

Sternberg, Meir. "What Is Exposition? An Essay in Temporal Delimitation." In *The Theory of the Novel: New Essays,* edited by John Halperin. New York: Oxford University Press, 1974.

Swales, Martin. *Thomas Mann: A Study.* London: Heineman, 1980.

Thieberger, Richard. *Der Begriff der Zeit bei Thomas Mann.* Baden-Baden: Verlag für Kunst und Wissenschaft, 1952.

Tiryakian, Edward A., ed. *Sociological Theory, Values, and Sociocultural Change.* New York: Harper & Row, 1963.

Tobin, Patricia Drechsel. *Time and the Novel: The Genealogical Imperative.* Princeton, N.J.: Princeton University Press, 1978.

Todorov, Tzvetan. *The Poetics of Prose.* Translated by Richard Howard. Foreword by Jonathan Culler. Ithaca, N.Y.: Cornell University Press, 1977.

Vaihinger, Hans. *The Philosophy of "As If": A System of the Theoretical, Practical, and Religious Fictions of Mankind.* Translated by C. K. Ogden. New York: Harcourt, Brace and Company, Inc., 1924.

Vickery, Olga. *The Novels of William Faulkner: A Critical Interpretation.* Baton Rouge: Louisiana State University Press, 1959.

Vernon, John. *The Garden and the Map: Schizophrenia in Twentieth-Century Literature and Culture.* Urbana: University of Illinois Press, 1973.

Vogel, Harald. *Die Zeit bei Thomas Mann: Untersuchungen zu der Romanen "Der Zauberberg," "Joseph und seine Brüder," und "Doktor Faustus."* Diss., Westfälischen Wilhelms-Universität zu Münster, 1970.

von Gronicka, André. *Thomas Mann: Profile and Perspectives.* New York: Random House, 1970.

Waldhorn, Arthur. *A Reader's Guide to Ernest Hemingway.* New York: Farrar, Straus and Giroux, 1972.

Wallack, F. Bradford. *The Epochal Nature of Process in Whitehead's Metaphysics.* Albany: State University of New York Press, 1980.

Warren, Robert Penn, ed. *Faulkner: A Collection of Critical Essays.* Englewood Cliffs, N.J.: Prentice Hall, Inc., 1966.

———. "Faulkner: The South, the Negro, and Time." In *Faulkner: A Collection of Critical Essays,* edited by Robert Penn Warren. Englewood Cliffs, N.J.: Prentice Hall, Inc., 1966.

Way, Brian. "Hemingway the Intellectual: A Version of Modernism." In *Ernest Hemingway: New Critical Essays,* edited by A. Robert Lee. London: Vision Press, 1983.

Weigand, Herman J. *The Magic Mountain: A Study of Thomas Mann's*

"*Der Zauberberg.*" Chapel Hill: University of North Carolina Press, 1965.

Whitehead, Alfred North. *Adventures of Ideas.* New York: New American Library, 1958.

———. *Process and Reality.* New York: The Free Press, 1969.

———. *Religion in the Making.* New York: World Publishing, 1960.

———. *Science and the Modern World.* New York: The Macmillan Company, 1944.

Williams, Wirt. *The Tragic Art of Ernest Hemingway.* Baton Rouge: Louisiana State University Press, 1981.

Wilson, Edmund. *Axel's Castle: A Study in the Imaginative Literature of 1890–1930.* New York: Charles Scribner and Sons, 1936.

Woolf, Virginia. *Between the Acts.* London: Granada Publishing, 1978.

———. *Jacob's Room.* New York: Harcourt, Brace and Company, 1923.

———. *Mrs. Dalloway.* New York: Harcourt, Brace and World, Inc., 1953.

———. *Night and Day.* London: Granada Publishing, 1978.

———. *Orlando: A Biography.* New York: Harcourt Brace Jovanovich, Inc., 1956.

———. *To the Lighthouse.* New York: Harcourt, Brace and World, Inc., 1955.

———. *The Voyage Out.* New York: Blue Ribbon Books, Inc., 1920.

———. *The Waves.* New York: Harcourt, Brace and Company, 1931.

———. *The Years.* New York: Harcourt, Brace and World, Inc., 1965.

Young, Philip. *Ernest Hemingway: A Reconsideration.* University Park: Pennsylvania State University Press, 1966.

Ziolkowski, Theodore. *The Novels of Hermann Hesse: A Study in Theme and Structure.* Princeton, N.J.: Princeton University Press, 1965.

Index